B.E. Birr

PageMaker 5 For Windows For Dummies

Toolbox Shortcuts

Tool:	Press This:
+ Line tool	Shift+F2
+ Perpendicular Line tool	Shift+F3
+ Text tool	Shift+F4
✳ Rotate tool	Shift+F5
+ Rectangle tool	Shift+F6
+ Ellipse tool	Shift+F7
⌗ Crop tool	Shift+F8
Toggle between Arrow tool and the last tool used	F9 or Ctrl+spacebar

Type Style

To Do This:	Press This:
Plain	Ctrl+Shift+spacebar
Bold	Ctrl+Shift+B
Italic	Ctrl+Shift+I
Underline	Ctrl+Shift+U
Strikethru	Ctrl+Shift+S
Reverse	Ctrl+Shift+V
Superscript	Ctrl+Shift+\
Subscript	Ctrl+\
All caps	Ctrl+Shift+K

Getting Around

To Do This:	Press This:
Zoom to 100%	Ctrl+1
Zoom to 200%	Ctrl+2
Zoom to 400%	Ctrl+4
Fit in window	Ctrl+W
Show entire pasteboard	Ctrl+Shift+W
Toggle between 100% and fit in window	Right-click
Toggle between 200% and 100%	Shift+ right-click
Zoom to next larger zoom size	Ctrl+ spacebar+click
Zoom to next smaller zoom size	Ctrl+Alt+ spacebar+click
Magnify beyond 400%	Ctrl+spacebar+ drag around area
Scroll with hand cursor	Alt+drag
Go to previous page (or two-page spread)	F11
Go to next page (or two-page spread)	F12

D1543873

For more information about IDG Books, call
1-800-762-2974 or 415-312-0650

... For Dummies: #1 Computer Book Series for Beginners

PageMaker 5 For Windows For Dummies

Cheat Sheet

Type Size and Leading

To Do This:	Press This:
Increase to next larger type size	Ctrl+>
Decrease to next smaller type size	Ctrl+<
Increase type size 1 point	Ctrl+Shift+>
Decrease type size 1 point	Ctrl+Shift+<
Change to Auto leading	Ctrl+Shift+A
Return to 100% width	Ctrl+Shift+X

Kerning

To Do This:	Press This:
Kern text together 1/25 em space	Ctrl+Backspace or Ctrl+minus (on keypad)
Kern text apart 1/25 em space	Ctrl+Shift+Backspace or Ctrl+plus (on keypad)
Kern text together 1/100 em space	Ctrl+Shift+minus (on keypad)
Kern text apart 1/100 em space	Ctrl+Shift+plus (on keypad)
Clear all kerning	Ctrl+Shift+0 (zero)
Remove tracking	Ctrl+Shift+Q

Alignment (justification)

To Do This:	Press This:
Flush left	Ctrl+Shift+L
Flush right	Ctrl+Shift+R
Center	Ctrl+Shift+C
Justify	Ctrl+Shift+J
Force justify	Ctrl+Shift+F

Special Characters

To Do This:	Press This:
Open curly quote	Ctrl+Shift+[or Alt+0147 (on keypad)
Close curly quote	Ctrl+Shift+] or Alt+0148 (on keypad)
Apostrophe	Ctrl+] or Alt+0146 (on keypad)
Bullet	Ctrl+Shift+8 or Alt+0149 (on keypad)
Nonbreaking space	Ctrl+Shift+H
Thin space	Ctrl+Shift+T
En space	Ctrl+Shift+N
Em space	Ctrl+Shift+M
Discretionary hyphen	Ctrl+hyphen
Nonbreaking hyphen	Ctrl+Shift+hyphen
En dash	Ctrl+=
Em dash	Ctrl+Shift+=
Nonbreaking slash	Ctrl+Shift+/
Line break	Shift+Enter
Copyright symbol	Ctrl+Shift+O or Alt+0169 (on keypad)
Trademark symbol	Alt+0153 (on keypad)
Registered symbol	Ctrl+Shift+G or Alt+0174 (on keypad)
¼ fraction	Alt+0188 (on keypad)
½ fraction	Alt+0189 (on keypad)
¾ fraction	Alt+0190 (on keypad)
Automatic page number	Ctrl+Shift+3

References for the Rest of Us

COMPUTER BOOK SERIES FROM IDG

Are you intimidated and confused by computers? Do you find that traditional manuals are overloaded with technical details you'll never use? Do your friends and family always call you to fix simple problems on their PCs? Then the *...For Dummies*™ computer book series from IDG is for you.

...For Dummies books are written for those frustrated computer users who know they aren't really dumb but find that PC hardware, software, and indeed the unique vocabulary of computing make them feel helpless. *...For Dummies* books use a lighthearted approach, a down-to-earth style, and even cartoons and humorous icons to diffuse computer novices' fears and build their confidence. Lighthearted but not lightweight, these books are a perfect survival guide to anyone forced to use a computer.

> *"I like my copy so much I told friends; now they bought copies."*
>
> **Irene C., Orwell, Ohio**

> *"Quick, concise, nontechnical, and humorous."*
>
> **Jay A., Elburn, IL**

> *"Thanks, I needed this book. Now I can sleep at night."*
>
> **Robin F., British Columbia, Canada**

Already, hundreds of thousands of satisfied readers agree. They have made *...For Dummies* books the #1 introductory level computer book series and have written asking for more. So if you're looking for the most fun and easy way to learn about computers, look to *...For Dummies* books to give you a helping hand.

IDG BOOKS

PAGEMAKER 5
FOR WINDOWS
FOR
DUMMIES™

PAGEMAKER 5
FOR WINDOWS
FOR
DUMMIES™

by Deke McClelland and
Galen Gruman

IDG
BOOKS

IDG Books Worldwide, Inc.
An International Data Group Company

San Mateo, California ♦ Indianapolis, Indiana ♦ Boston, Massachusetts

PageMaker 5 For Windows For Dummies™

Published by
IDG Books Worldwide, Inc.
An International Data Group Company
155 Bovet Road, Suite 310
San Mateo, CA 94402

Library of Congress Catalog Card No.: 94-77186

ISBN: 1-56884-160-4

Printed in the United States of America

10 9 8 7 6 5 4 3 2 1

1A/QY/QV/ZU

Distributed in the United States by IDG Books Worldwide, Inc.

Distributed in Canada by Macmillan of Canada, a Division of Canada Publishing Corporation; by Computer and Technical Books in Miami, Florida, for South America and the Caribbean; by Longman Singapore in Singapore, Malaysia, Thailand, and Korea; by Toppan Co. Ltd. in Japan; by Asia Computerworld in Hong Kong; by Woodslane Pty. Ltd. in Australia and New Zealand; and by Transword Publishers Ltd. in the U.K. and Europe.

For general information on IDG Books in the U.S., including information on discounts and premiums, contact IDG Books 800-434-3422 or 415-312-0650.

For information on where to purchase IDG Books outside the U.S., contact Christina Turner at 415-312-0633.

For information on translations, contact Marc Jeffrey Mikulich, Foreign Rights Manager, at IDG Books Worldwide; FAX NUMBER 415-286-2747.

For sales inquiries and special prices for bulk quantities, write to the address above or call IDG Books Worldwide at 415-312-0650.

For information on using IDG Books in the classroom, or for ordering examination copies, contact Jim Kelly at 800-434-2086.

 is a registered trademark of IDG Books Worldwide, Inc.

About the Authors

Deke McClelland

A contributing editor to *Macworld* magazine, Deke McClelland also writes for *PC World* and *Publish*. He has authored more than 25 books on desktop publishing. He started his career as artistic director at the first service bureau in the U.S.

McClelland received the Ben Franklin Award for the Best Computer Book in 1989 and won the prestigious Computer Press Award in 1990 and again in 1992. He is also the author of the best-selling *Macworld Photoshop 2.5 Bible, CorelDRAW! 5 For Dummies,* and *Macworld FreeHand 4 Bible.*

Galen Gruman

A senior associate features editor at *Macworld* and a frequent reviewer of desktop publishing software for *InfoWorld*, Galen Gruman was an early adopter of desktop publishing in professional magazine production.

Galen's honors include being a finalist in the Computer Press Awards for best computer-oriented news story in a general-interest publication (1986) and a winner for best in-depth technical feature in the American Society of Business Press Editors Awards (1993), which he shared with Lon Poole and Arne Hurty of *Macworld*. He has been president of the Computer Press Association since 1992.

Galen is also author of *PageMaker 5 For Mac For Dummies* and coauthor, with Barbara Assadi, of the critically praised *QuarkXPress 3.1 for Windows Designer Handbook* and *Macworld QuarkXPress 3.2/3.3 Bible.*

ABOUT IDG BOOKS WORLDWIDE

Welcome to the world of IDG Books Worldwide.

IDG Books Worldwide, Inc., is a subsidiary of International Data Group, the world's largest publisher of business and computer-related information and the leading global provider of information services on information technology. IDG was founded more than 25 years ago and now employs more than 5,700 people worldwide. IDG publishes more than 200 computer publications in 63 countries (see listing below). Forty million people read one or more IDG publications each month.

Launched in 1990, IDG Books is today the fastest-growing publisher of computer and business books in the United States. We are proud to have received 3 awards from the Computer Press Association in recognition of editorial excellence, and our best-selling ...For Dummies series has more than 7 million copies in print with translations in more than 20 languages. IDG Books, through a recent joint venture with IDG's Hi-Tech Beijing, became the first U.S. publisher to publish a computer book in the People's Republic of China. In record time, IDG Books has become the first choice for millions of readers around the world who want to learn how to better manage their businesses.

Our mission is simple: Every IDG book is designed to bring extra value and skill-building instructions to the reader. Our books are written by experts who understand and care about our readers. The knowledge base of our editorial staff comes from years of experience in publishing, education, and journalism — experience which we use to produce books for the '90s. In short, we care about books, so we attract the best people. We devote special attention to details such as audience, interior design, use of icons, and illustrations. And because we use an efficient process of authoring, editing, and desktop publishing our books electronically, we can spend more time ensuring superior content and spend less time on the technicalities of making books.

You can count on our commitment to deliver high-quality books at competitive prices on topics customers want to read about. At IDG, we value quality, and we have been delivering quality for more than 25 years. You'll find no better book on a subject than an IDG book.

John J. Kilcullen

John Kilcullen
President and CEO
IDG Books Worldwide, Inc.

VIII
WINNER
*Eighth Annual
Computer Press
Awards 1992*

IX
WINNER
*Ninth Annual
Computer Press
Awards 1993*

IDG BOOKS

IDG Books Worldwide, Inc., is a subsidiary of International Data Group. The officers are Patrick J. McGovern, Founder and Board Chairman; Walter Boyd, President. International Data Group's publications include: **ARGENTINA'S** Computerworld Argentina, Infoworld Argentina; **AUSTRALIA'S** Computerworld Australia, Australian PC World, Australian Macworld, Network World, Mobile Business Australia, Reseller, IDG Sources; **AUSTRIA'S** Computerwelt Oesterreich, PC Test; **BRAZIL'S** Computerworld, Gamepro, Game Power, Mundo IBM, Mundo Unix, PC World, Super Game; **BELGIUM'S** Data News (CW) **BULGARIA'S** Computerworld Bulgaria, Ediworld, PC & Mac World Bulgaria, Network World Bulgaria; **CANADA'S** CIO Canada, Computerworld Canada, Graduate Computerworld, InfoCanada, Network World Canada; **CHILE'S** Computerworld Chile, Informatica; **COLOMBIA'S** Computerworld Colombia, PC World; **CZECH REPUBLIC'S** Computerworld, Elektronika, PC World; **DENMARK'S** Communications World, Computerworld Danmark, Macintosh Produktkatalog, Macworld Danmark, PC World Danmark, PC World Produktguide, Tech World, Windows World; **ECUADOR'S** PC World Ecuador; **EGYPT'S** Computerworld (CW) Middle East, PC World Middle East; **FINLAND'S** MikroPC, Tietoviikko, Tietoverkko; **FRANCE'S** Distributique, GOLDEN MAC, InfoPC, Languages & Systems, Le Guide du Monde Informatique, Le Monde Informatique, Telecoms & Reseaux; **GERMANY'S** Computerwoche, Computerwoche Focus, Computerwoche Extra, Computerwoche Karriere, Information Management, Macwelt, Netzwelt, PC Welt, PC Woche, Publish, Unit; **GREECE'S** Infoworld, PC Games; **HUNGARY'S** Computerworld SZT, PC World; **HONG KONG'S** Computerworld Hong Kong, PC World Hong Kong; **INDIA'S** Computers & Communications; **IRELAND'S** ComputerScope; **ISRAEL'S** Computerworld Israel, PC World Israel; **ITALY'S** Computerworld Italia, Lotus Magazine, Macworld Italia, Networking Italia, PC Shopping, PC World Italia; **JAPAN'S** Computerworld Today, Information Systems World, Macworld Japan, Nikkei Personal Computing, SunWorld Japan, Windows World; **KENYA'S** East African Computer News; **KOREA'S** Computerworld Korea, Macworld Korea, PC World Korea; **MEXICO'S** Compu Edicion, Compu Manufactura, Computacion/Punto de Venta, Computerworld Mexico, MacWorld, Mundo Unix, PC World, Windows; **THE NETHERLANDS'** Computer! Totaal, Computable (CW), LAN Magazine, MacWorld, Totaal "Windows"; **NEW ZEALAND'S** Computer Listings, Computerworld New Zealand, New Zealand PC World, Network World; **NIGERIA'S** PC World Africa; **NORWAY'S** Computerworld Norge, C/World, Lotusworld Norge, Macworld Norge, Networld, PC World Ekspress, PC World Norge, PC World's Produktguide, Publish& Multimedia World, Student Data, Unix World, Windowsworld; IDG Direct Response; **PAKISTAN'S** PC World Pakistan; **PANAMA'S** PC World Panama; **PERU'S** Computerworld Peru, PC World; **PEOPLE'S REPUBLIC OF CHINA'S** China Computerworld, China Infoworld, Electronics Today/Multimedia World, Electronics International, Electronic Product World, China Network World, PC and Communications Magazine, PC World China, Software World Magazine, Telecom Product World; IDG HIGH TECH BEIJING'S New Product World; IDG SHENZHEN'S Computer News Digest; **PHILIPPINES'** Computerworld Philippines, PC Digest (PCW); **POLAND'S** Computerworld Poland, PC World/Komputer; **PORTUGAL'S** Cerebro/PC World, Correio Informatico/Computerworld, Informatica & Comunicacoes Catalogo, MacIn, Nacional de Produtos; **ROMANIA'S** Computerworld, PC World; **RUSSIA'S** Computerworld-Moscow, Mir - PC, Sety; **SINGAPORE'S** Computerworld Southeast Asia, PC World Singapore; **SLOVENIA'S** Monitor Magazine; **SOUTH AFRICA'S** Computer Mail (CIO), Computing S.A., Network World S.A., Software World; **SPAIN'S** Advanced Systems, Amiga World, Computerworld Espana, Communicaciones World, Macworld Espana, NeXTWORLD, Super Juegos Magazine (GamePro), PC World Espana, Publish; **SWEDEN'S** Attack, ComputerSweden, Corporate Computing, Natverk & Kommunikation, Macworld, Mikrodatorn, PC World, Publishing & Design (CAP), Datalngenjoren, Maxi Data, Windows World; **SWITZERLAND'S** Computerworld Schweiz, Macworld Schweiz, PC Tip; **TAIWAN'S** Computerworld Taiwan, PC World Taiwan; **THAILAND'S** Thai Computerworld; **TURKEY'S** Computerworld Monitor, Macworld Turkiye, PC World Turkiye; **UKRAINE'S** Computerworld; **UNITED KINGDOM'S** Computing /Computerworld, Connexion/Network World, Lotus Magazine, Macworld, Open Computing/Sunworld; **UNITED STATES'** Advanced Systems, AmigaWorld, Cable in the Classroom, CD Review, CIO, Computerworld, Digital Video, DOS Resource Guide, Electronic Entertainment Magazine, Federal Computer Week, Federal Integrator, GamePro, IDG Books, Infoworld, Infoworld Direct, Laser Event, Macworld, Multimedia World, Network World, PC Letter, PC World, PlayRight, Power PC World, Publish, SWATPro, Video Event; **VENEZUELA'S** Computerworld Venezuela, PC World; **VIETNAM'S** PC World Vietnam

Acknowledgments

The authors would like to acknowledge all the great folks at IDG Books World-wide whose hard work and talent helped make this book a reality.

(The publisher would like to give special thanks to Patrick J. McGovern, without whom this book would not have been possible.)

Credits

Publisher
David Solomon

Managing Editor
Mary Bednarek

Acquisitions Editors
Megg Bonar
Janna Custer

Production Director
Beth Jenkins

Senior Editors
Tracy L. Barr
Sandra Blackthorn
Diane Graves Steele

Production Coordinator
Cindy L. Phipps

Project Editor
Julie King

Copy Editor
Pamela Mourouzis

Editorial Assistant
Elizabeth Reynolds

Technical Reviewer
Tim Cole

Production Quality Control
Steve Peake

Production Staff
Linda M. Boyer
Chris Collins
J. Tyler Connor
Kent Gish
Sherry Gomoll
Patricia R. Reynolds
Gina Scott
Robert Simon

Cover Design
Kavish + Kavish

Proofreader
Michele Worthington

Indexer
Sherry Massey

Book Design
University Graphics

Contents at a Glance

Cartoons at a Glance
By Rich Tennant

page 9

page 136

page 293

page 45

page 153

page 243

page 322

page 85

page 209

page 323

Table of Contents

Introduction

Desktop publishing began with PageMaker on the Apple Macintosh computer. In fact, many argue that PageMaker and desktop publishing were the single most important force in the Mac's early success. The program had such an impact that Apple pressured Aldus not to develop PageMaker on the Microsoft Windows platform. Apple offered Aldus space in its advertisements, corporate endorsements, and all sorts of other glittering prizes. But as Aldus assured Apple not to worry, it secretly worked on what would soon become one of the best-selling Windows products ever.

Such treachery! Such intrigue! Such a lucky break for hundreds of thousands of Windows users that publish with PageMaker today.

Despite having loads of competition over the years, PageMaker has managed to remain the number-one desktop publishing program, thanks to a surprisingly straightforward design. It works exactly like traditional paste-up pages and layout tools, except without the wax and X-acto knives. Over the years, PageMaker has grown to be a lot more than an electronic galley-waxer, though. It provides the tools you need to make your words attractive, to integrate images and photos with your prose, and to put together a whole document — whether it's a one-page ad, a 16-page employee newsletter, a 30-page annual report, a 100-page technical manual, or a 350-page book. In fact, the very book you're reading was created using PageMaker.

Why a Book . . . For Dummies?

Gee, all those types of documents and just one little program. Well, not so little — in fact, PageMaker is stuffed with features, tools, and those Additions add-ons that create even more menu choices. You won't need most of the tools on any one given project, and you'll probably be able to live your life not using a third of them. So how do you know which tools you need for a particular kind of document and which you can leave to that whiz-bang artist down the hall who produces 3-D posters? The answers to all your questions — well, a couple of them anyway — as well as a few questions you never thought to ask are revealed in the pages that follow.

This book shows you how to create the kinds of documents that most people need to produce. The real fancy stuff is best left to those who do that kind of work all day, and they can read someone else's book. This book is for you: the person who has more to do than just use PageMaker.

About This Book

You can approach this book from several perspectives, depending on how you learn:

- ✔ If you're a reader — as in, you *like* to read, which you must if you're reading the introduction — you can follow the book from cover to cover, building up your expertise as you progress.

- ✔ If you're looking for a reference to how something works, and you can't find it in the PageMaker manual, look here. IDG Books has kindly provided a thorough index to all the wonderful tips and techniques in this book.

- ✔ If you have already used PageMaker but want a quick refresher on a seldom-used feature, information on this latest version, or a quick take on a feature you've never had to use, flip through the book looking at the tidbits. And don't forget to check out the contents pages.

- ✔ If you're looking for water-cooler talk to impress your friends and neighbors, check out Part VII, which is full of trivia and factoids about PageMaker. You may even be able to take advantage of a few of these golden nuggets when you get back to your desk.

No matter which way you read the book, enjoy it. (That's an order!) Desktop publishing is a creative experience. It's often fun, but it's just as frequently frenetic and even frustrating. When it's not so fun, take a break, read a chapter, learn a neat trick, and then go back to your project better equipped and a little more relaxed.

How to Use This Book

To make sure that you understand what we're talking about, this book uses several conventions to indicate what you're supposed to type, which menus you're supposed to use, and which keys you're supposed to press.

If we describe a message you see on-screen or something you type, it looks like this:

```
Insert Disk 2 into the internal drive
```

Or it may look like this:

Type **Bill** and then press the Enter key.

Menu commands are listed like this:

File⇨Print

This instruction means that you click on the File menu name and then click on the Print command in the menu.

Keyboard shortcuts are listed like this:

Ctrl+Shift+D

This instruction means that you should press the Ctrl key, the Shift key, and the D key simultaneously. An easy way to do this is to hold the Ctrl and Shift keys, press D, and then release all the keys. (In the PageMaker menus, this keyboard shortcut — for File⇨Links — is listed as Sh^D, where ^ stands for the Ctrl key.

For your reading pleasure, we've underlined command and menus names just as they appear in PageMaker. Underlines indicate the Alt+key equivalent. For example, to choose File⇨Save As — which has no Ctrl key shortcut — press Alt+F to display the File menu and then press the A key. (After the menu is displayed, you don't have to press Alt again to choose the Save As command.)

Although the information in this book is presented in basic, simple terms that the most novice of PageMaker novices can understand, it does assume that you're at least somewhat familiar with the basics of using Windows and Windows programs. If you're totally new to Windows as well as to PageMaker, you may want to pick up a copy of Andy Rathbone's *Windows For Dummies*, also published by IDG Books, and keep it nearby as a reference.

How This Book Is Organized

We've divided *PageMaker 5 For Windows For Dummies* into seven parts, not counting this introduction, to make it easy for you to find the material you need right away. Each part has anywhere from two to six chapters, so you don't have to worry about making a lifelong commitment to find something out.

Part I: How to Start (Before I Even Launch PageMaker)

The best place to start publishing is *outside* of PageMaker. Sometimes, your word processor is all you need, and sometimes PageMaker is the right tool for the job. Before committing to using one or the other, read this part to see how to decide which is best. You should also think a moment about the type styles you'll use — even though you may have access to hundreds of type fonts, that doesn't mean you should use them all at once! Look in this part for a gentle introduction into the art of typography. And then, when you're primed to use PageMaker, this part explains what you need to do to prepare your text and graphics files for use in PageMaker.

Part II: There's a Blank Page: Now What?

When you actually start up PageMaker, you're confronted by a blank screen. Here's where the fun starts: You begin creating your document. This part explains how to automate some common tasks (after all, computers are supposed to make your work easier), and how to use some publishing basics — like bulleted lists, fancy type tricks, and text wraps — to make a cool page. And when you're done with one page, you'll probably create more, and soon have a whole bunch of pages, perhaps arranged in chapters, and perhaps using text from your word processor. This part ends by showing you how to manage those chapters and source files.

Part III: That's Nice, But I Want It to Be Different

No one puts together a document perfectly the first time — expect to fiddle and change your documents until they look just right. This part shows you how to fiddle *effectively* and *efficiently* (yes, we realize that these words aren't usually associated with *fiddle*, but it's true). And for efficiency experts, this part shows how to reuse the results of all that fiddling so that the next time you do something similar, you don't need to fiddle as much. (No matter what anyone tells you, you'll always have to do some fiddling; otherwise, it wouldn't be real publishing.)

Part IV: Documents for the Suit-and-Tie Set

All kidding aside, one of PageMaker's greatest strengths is in putting together corporate documents. You know: proposals, manuals, annual reports, price sheets, and phone lists. This strength is often overlooked because it's so easy to get caught up in cool graphic effects or a gazillion colors, but it's a core reason to use PageMaker. This part shows you some techniques for creating attractive but appropriate business documents.

Part V: Cool Designs They Never Knew You Could Do

Of course, it would be a terrible waste to have PageMaker and not indulge in some of its more artistic tricks. After reading this part, you won't waste those tricks. Instead, you'll be using them in all sorts of places, from party invitations to newsletters. And if you have a color printer, this part shows you how to do electronic finger-painting.

Part VI: You Mean There's More?

At this point, you're almost ready to dive into one of those *Bible* or *Everything You Ever Wanted to Know* books about PageMaker. Almost. Before you do, you should know a few more things about PageMaker, such as how to take the plunge and send your PageMaker documents to an outside service bureau — or a colleague in the next office — for further work. After reading this part, you'll have graduated from PageMaker 101 and be ready to handle almost any typical document. Of course, if you want to forge ahead and buy a 700-page book to learn the deep ins and outs of the program, go for it. Those books are great to have, but using them to learn a program for the first time is like buying an investment-banking book to learn to use the ATM.

Part VII: The Part of Tens

This is the water-cooler part of the book. It's chock full of tidbits, advice, trivia, and other data about PageMaker that you can share with your colleagues during a work break or tell your friends at Tuesday bowling night. (On second thought, maybe not. But you *can* use these tidbits to help, impress, dazzle, or amuse your coworkers.) Some of this part's contents may seem obvious, some not, but all are based on remembering those little details and lessons that only experience can provide. Save yourself some bumps along the road and check out this part.

Icons Used in This Book

To alert you to special passages of text that you especially may want to read (or avoid), we've put in a bunch of modern hieroglyphics (proudly known as *icons*) to help guide you.

Here's an example of something you might want to avoid. (Not that it's bad or anything.) This icon highlights one of those nitty-gritty techno-details or background explanations that you shouldn't have to know but that will come in handy (a) if something goes wrong and you have to ask an expert for advice or (b) you want to impress your boss.

Here's some information that you should put on a Post-it note and stick to your monitor. You never know when it will come in handy and save you some effort or time. Look for these icons in your spare time.

Here's something that you should remember but could easily forget because the information may seem unimportant at first. Trust us when we say that you'll need it later.

Not everything works the way it should, or at least the way you expect. These icons let you know when an action (or lack thereof) might cause a problem, such as destroying your data.

Not everything works . . . oops, already said that. Anyhow, these icons are a cross between tips and warnings; they describe ways in which PageMaker acts in a manner other than what you might expect. You're in no danger of losing data, but may be unnecessarily perplexed. This information shows you how to get things back to normal or work around the oddity.

Where To First?

As mentioned earlier, everyone reads differently. Some folks read left to right, some right to left, some upside down.

Read this book left to right. It'll make more sense that way.

But even if you and your neighbor both read left to right, you may not agree on how to read a book. Should you diligently go through each page? Should you open pages at random and hopscotch from chapter to chapter? Or perhaps read the middle and skip the other sections?

Ultimately, it's up to you. If you have a specific question, go to the index. If you want to know more about one type of feature, use the table of contents to find the appropriate chapter. If you're experienced in manual layout and paste-up but you've been forced to switch to a computer by evil forces bent on cyborg domination of the earth, skim through Chapter 1, skip to Chapter 3, and keep on reading. And if you're totally new to the whole shebang, just move on to the next page and begin reading at a comfortable pace.

Remember, always consult a physician before beginning any new training program. (Jane Fonda taught us that one!) Then again, in this case, you may want to consult with a licensed psychologist.

No, really, we're just kidding. We promise that this book, unlike some others on the subject, won't leave you in a PageMaker panic. So if you have any fears about your ability to use this powerful program, put them aside. With this book by your side — for easier reading, you may want to prop it up against that stack of unpaid bills on your desk — you, too, can turn out sensational documents from your very own computer.

Part I
How to Start (Before You Even Launch PageMaker)

The 5th Wave   **By Rich Tennant**

"YES, WE STILL HAVE A FEW BUGS IN THE PAGE LAYOUT PROGRAM. BY THE WAY, HERE'S A DIRECT MAIL PACKAGE FROM MARKETING."

In this part . . .

1magine that you're taking a camping trip. You wouldn't just hop in the Miata or on your motor scooter and toddle off. No, first you'd figure out what you need to take with you, and then figure out how to get there — maybe taking a taxi to the airport or just piling your camping gear into the Westfalia. Likewise, before you launch PageMaker or your word processor, spend a few minutes to figure out exactly what you want to accomplish and then how you want to do it. This part shows how to find the road map to your destination.

Chapter 1

Why Can't I Just Use My Word Processor?

In This Chapter

▶ Word processors vs. PageMaker: Which is better when?

▶ How to prepare your word-processor file for use in PageMaker

▶ What word-processing features *not* to use

▶ What PageMaker offers that a word processor can't

*W*hether you use Microsoft Word or WordPerfect, you have all the tools you need to produce your documents, right? After all, both programs let you import pictures, display multiple columns, go crazy with fonts, and do all sorts of layout tasks. What the heck do you need another program for?

Well, to put it in layman's terms, to keep you from going bonkers. Sure, you can do rudimentary layout with a word processor, but using one to publish a newsletter or catalog is like using a bicycle to go from San Francisco to Boulder. It's slow, it's exasperating, it requires lots of preparation, and you probably won't make it. When it comes to layout, Word is a bicycle with a flat tire and WordPerfect is a tricycle with streamers on the handle bars.

By contrast, PageMaker is a corporate Learjet with all the amenities of home. It transforms page layout into a relatively painless and sometimes even pleasurable experience. Best of all, you'll find yourself trying things that you'd never dare attempt in a word processor (and would regret if you did).

The Face-to-Face Challenge

Don't misunderstand: There's nothing wrong with Word or WordPerfect. Both are fine word processors. There's nothing wrong with a bike, either, but you wouldn't use it for a cross-country business trip. So how do you know when to use PageMaker and when to use a word processor? The answer depends on what sort of document you're creating. Here's a quick look at how PageMaker stacks up against word processors when it comes to handling various document-creation tasks.

Formatting text

Both PageMaker and your typical best-selling word processor let you format text with little effort. Switching to italics is as simple as pressing Ctrl+Shift+I, while going to boldface is as simple as Ctrl+Shift+B. (You can use the same keystrokes to switch italics or boldface off.) You can also use the menus or palette options provided in either program. So if all you're doing is writing letters or memos that use a little text formatting, don't bother with PageMaker — a word processor is fine. Going back to the bicycle/plane analogy, simple formatting tricks amount to no more than a jaunt to the corner store. Taking a plane is hardly the solution, even if there's one parked in the driveway.

In a word processor, you generally press Ctrl+B instead of Ctrl+Shift+B to get bold text and Ctrl+I instead of Ctrl+Shift+I to get italic text. But in PageMaker, you have to press the Shift key. So just keep in mind that the keystrokes mentioned here apply specifically to PageMaker, not necessarily to other programs.

When you move beyond basic text formatting, the scales quickly tip in PageMaker's favor. You can handle drop caps, leading, paragraph spacing, kerning, and a bunch of other formatting options that are examined in Chapter 2 and other future chapters much more expediently in PageMaker than in a word processor. Figures 1-1 and 1-2 show examples of text printed from PageMaker and Microsoft Word, respectively. Which would you rather show to your boss? Which would you rather show to a client? Which would you rather show to the rest of the gang in the quilt club? Which would you just plain rather create?

Figure 1-1:
Text looks much nicer when printed from PageMaker, thanks to the program's better typographic controls.

Press Awards
continued from page 1

Overall Works
Best Computer Magazine (100,000 or more circulation)
- ■ WINNER: *Macworld.*
- □ RUNNER-UP: *NewMedia.*
- □ RUNNER-UP: *PC Magazine.*

Best Computer Magazine (less than 100,000 circulation)
- ■ WINNER: *Upside.*
- □ RUNNER-UP: *Computer Artist.*
- □ RUNNER-UP: *VAR Business.*

Best Computer Newspaper (100,000 or more circulation)
- ■ WINNER: *Computerworld.*
- □ RUNNER-UP: *Communications Week.*
- □ RUNNER-UP: *Computer Reseller News.*

Computer Press Awards Judging

To select the best of each year's body of work, the CPA solicits entries in print,

The CPA Awards Committee also formalized some judging practices: First, a

Figure 1-2:
Word's output quality is not as good as PageMaker's, particularly in its spacing — a typical disadvantage of word processors.

Ninth Annual Computer Press Awards
Semifinalists: San Francisco screening

Judges:
- Deborah Branscum, executive editor, *Macworld*
- Roberta Furger, senior user-issues editor, *PC World*
- Galen Gruman, senior associate features editor, *Macworld*
- Tom Halfhill, senior editor, *Byte*
- Audrey Kalman, free-lancer
- David Kalman, editor-in-chief, *DBMS Magazine*
- Carol Person, senior reviews editor, *Macworld*
- Charles Piller, senior associate features editor, *Macworld*

1. News Story in a General-Interest Publication
- *Business Times:* "IBM a Key Player in Automation of Indianapolis 500" by David
- *Business Week:* "Novell: End of an Era?" by Kathy Rebello, Robert D. Hof, and Russell Mitchell
- *Inc.:* "World without Wires"

Using multiple columns

Look at a professionally produced magazine or newsletter. Chances are that the text is organized into multiple columns. Even the text in this book — which is laid out in PageMaker, by the way — features a second, much slimmer column on the left side of the page for figure captions and the like.

Now look at a report in your In basket. Chances are it has only one column that's almost as wide as the entire page.

But so what? Who needs columns? You've never understood why anyone uses them in the first place, and you certainly don't need them.

Well, think again. Multiple columns are part and parcel of publishing because they make it easy to integrate multiple elements — both graphics and stories — into a layout. Having multiple columns means that you can change the width of a graphic freely without wreaking havoc on your layout. Multiple articles (an article is known as a *story* in PageMaker) can fit on a page without interfering with each other. Each page is a balancing act, and columns provide the structure needed to keep it from flying apart at the seams. (And here you thought it was just because artists like to do things that the rest of us can't.)

In the early days, the ability to create multiple columns alone was enough reason to invest in PageMaker. Today, you can create multiple columns in a word processor. But the process is awkward, even in a powerful program such as Word. You have to do a lot of formatting in dialog boxes. With all the mousing and clicking that's required, you feel like you're in the gym doing power training on your hands.

But check out PageMaker. It lets you drag columns around, repositioning and resizing them at will, just as if they were physical objects floating above the surface of your page. And although it's easier to change the number of columns in a word processor after you've set up multiple columns than it is in PageMaker, it's much harder to arrange the columns when you have two or more independent stories together on the page. Finally, in a word processor, it's a bear to place two stories on a page so that a four-column article starts above a three-column article — simple as that task may sound. Yet it's hardly a problem in PageMaker, as demonstrated in Figure 1-3. Clearly, PageMaker wins the multiple-column contest.

Importing graphics

Uh-oh, the gap between the capabilities of word processors and PageMaker is about to grow into a chasm. The Windows versions of Word and WordPerfect are certainly capable of importing graphics. But now try working with those graphics. The fact is, just because a program can do something doesn't mean that it can perform the task well enough to make it worth your while.

Say that you want to reposition a graphic at the beginning of a paragraph and have the text wrap around it. In PageMaker, you just drag the graphic to where you want it and turn on the text wrap feature. (Chapter 7 shows you how.) You can even make the wrap follow the shape of the graphic, as shown in Figure 1-4. If you want to do the same in Word or WordPerfect, get ready for some major work. It will take you so long that you may as well draw each character by hand.

Of course, PageMaker also lets you draw lines, squares, and circles, as well as apply shades of gray to boxes and other elements. You can also draw lines and other basic shapes in a word processor, but just try to put a shaded box behind some text to create, say, a sidebar.

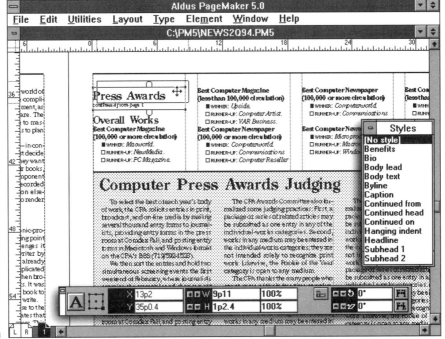

Figure 1-3: PageMaker makes it easy to set up and arrange different numbers of columns on the same page.

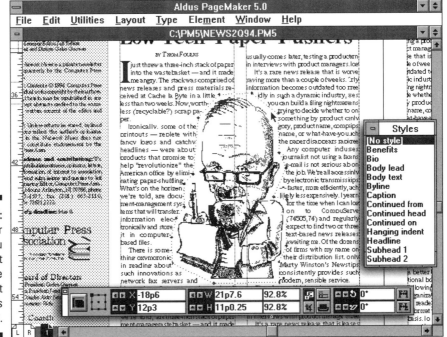

Figure 1-4: PageMaker lets you wrap text around the exact boundaries of a graphic.

Also, a word processor gives you no control over how images print. For example, you can't adjust a scanned-in photo so that it looks more crisp and identifiable on the printed page. Defining colors is another big disappointment in a word processor. And rotating graphics is much more difficult in a word processor than in PageMaker. As shown in Figure 1-5, you can rotate graphics to any angle in PageMaker by twirling them right there on the page. In Word or WordPerfect, the same simple operation involves a 12-step program that'll leave you wound up tighter than a knot.

Although word processors are constantly adding more graphics controls, it's pretty clear that if you really want to use graphics effectively in your document, you need a page-layout program like PageMaker.

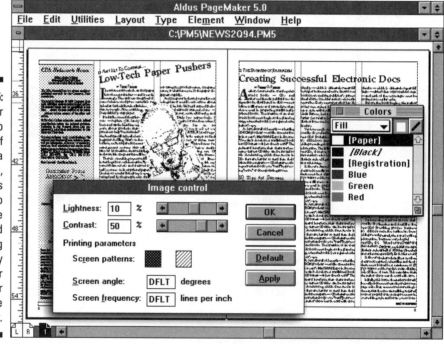

Figure 1-5: PageMaker lets you do all sorts of things with a graphic, such as rotating it to any angle and changing the gray values for sharper image output.

Combining multiple elements

Word processors are really good at handling a long, single document, whether or not it has headlines and bullets. But they're very bad at combining multiple stories that start on one page and continue on other pages. In fact, the only way to create such a document in Word or WordPerfect is to cut and paste the contents of each page. Then, if you need to edit the text, you have to remember which page each story jumps to and cut and paste the text among the pages. In PageMaker, the text for each story is linked from page to page, so if information is added at the beginning, the text is automatically shuffled onto the subsequent pages.

The best way to illustrate this feature is with a newsletter. Figure 1-6 shows the newsletter's opening page, which contains two stories plus a contents box. Figure 1-7 shows an interior set of pages, on which several stories continue from previous pages and some continue on to later pages. Word processors simply don't provide the kind of features you need to produce layouts like these. This is a case in which PageMaker wins by a knockout.

Figure 1-6:
In PageMaker, you can wrap multiple columns of text around graphics and balance the whole shooting match in a way not permitted by word processors.

Figure 1-7:
Mixing multiple stories in neighboring columns on a two-page spread is something you just can't do in a word processor.

Generating tables of contents, indexes, and page numbers

You'd expect a word processor to be good at handling business needs such as generating indexes and tables of contents. But you might not expect a page-layout program to offer similar features. PageMaker does. In fact, Word, WordPerfect, and PageMaker are about evenly matched in this regard.

And PageMaker offers a feature that Word does not: the ability to combine a series of documents into a *book*. Every chapter in this book is a separate PageMaker document, but the whole thing is part of a larger structure, enabling the designers to renumber pages, add index entries, and generate a table of contents automatically. If you're working on a multiple-chapter report with some colleagues, for example, you can use PageMaker's book functions to renumber all the pages of each chapter after you add a page to, say, Chapter 3. There's no need to open each chapter individually and renumber its pages manually.

Even if you don't use PageMaker's sophisticated typographic and graphics features, you may find it highly useful in creating indexes and tables of contents in business documents. By combining its page-layout skills with its business-document skills, you can go far beyond what a word processor can do. Forget the hype about *document processors* — that's just a fancy name for a word processor that's stuffed with features that still don't match what PageMaker can do. As your grandma used to say, "You can bring a donkey to the race track, but you can't make him win." (She never said that? Well, she probably would have if properly coerced.)

A word processor offers some pretty sophisticated controls for footnotes, headers, footers, and endnotes. PageMaker concentrates on headers and footers. If you want to use footnotes, you'll have to do it the old-fashioned way, adding them by hand. Fortunately, PageMaker can import your word processor's footnotes as endnotes — they all appear at the end of the story, rather than at the bottom of the page where the footnote occurs — so you won't lose any footnoting or endnoting done in your word processor.

Working Together

PageMaker, Word, and WordPerfect are all good tools. And although in some cases one type of program is clearly better than the other, you don't always have to choose between them. You can do a lot of work in your word processor and then import that work into PageMaker for further refinement, especially for layout. Think of the advantages: Layout artists can keep editors from messing in the PageMaker layouts by restricting them to features in Word or WordPerfect, and editors can make sure that layout artists don't skip over the text formatting to focus on the graphics. (Artists sometimes look at text and consider it to be the stuff that holds the graphics together, sort of like the Wonder Bread that holds the good-tasting peanut butter and jam.)

Which formatting should I do in PageMaker?

If you're working on a text-heavy layout — and most layouts, from newsletters to reports, use a lot of text — use your word processor to create and edit that text. That's what it's for, after all. Save PageMaker's built-in Story Editor for touch-ups, minor edits, and those documents that are mostly graphics with little text, such as advertisements.

Go ahead and apply the following formatting in your word processor:

- ✔ **Boldface**
- ✔ *Italics*

> ✔ Underlines
>
> ✔ Bullets: •
>
> ✔ Special symbols: ¶ Ç * _ ‡
>
> ✔ SMALL CAPS
>
> ✔ Superscripts
>
> ✔ Subscripts

You have to do this kind of local formatting work in one place or the other, and it's easier to do it in the place where the editing happens. Why? Because such character formatting is almost always related to the content of the text, and it's the writer or editor who's familiar with that content. Sure, whoever is doing the layout can apply the formatting in PageMaker, but that person probably isn't the writer or editor and thus won't know what points should be stressed through italics or underlines or whatever.

For the same reason, it's good to use style sheets in your word processor if you'll be using styles in your layout. (Styles are explained in depth in Chapter 4.) The styles don't have to look the same in your word processor as they do in PageMaker, but they have to have the same names. For example, if you have a style named *Heads* in your word processor and one called *Headlines* in PageMaker, rename one or the other so you have one common headline style name. That way, a headline that you create in your word processor will be formatted automatically when you import it into PageMaker. You save the layout staff work and reduce the chances that they will incorrectly format a title (or other type of paragraph style). If you follow this technique, the imported text takes on the attributes defined in PageMaker's styles. So you can make the text look one way in your word processor (where, after all, the layout is different) and another in your PageMaker layout without any extra work.

Even if you're the one who will be doing both the writing and layout, do the character formatting in your word processor, which is the place where you're focusing on the meaning of your text. After all, when you get to the layout stage in PageMaker, you'll have more things on your mind than content — you'll be worried about things like how many columns of text you want and whether the headlines fit properly. Even if you have remarkable powers of concentration and coordination — you can walk and chew gum while rubbing your head and patting your tummy — it's still not a good idea to work on layout and meaning and editing and drawing all at once. You'll have more luck if you keep these different elements of the page-production process separate.

Another good reason to concentrate on one operation at a time is that it's usually easier to edit in your word processor. That's what a word processor is designed to do, after all. However, there are some formatting techniques you should not attempt in your word processor. The following document production techniques that have very little to do with the meaning of your text and so should be handled in PageMaker:

- ✔ **Drop caps:** Don't try to import a drop cap from your word processor into PageMaker. You get the big first character, but the text around it won't wrap as it should, and you'll have to reformat it in PageMaker anyhow.

- ✔ **Tables:** When you import a table from your word processor, PageMaker strips out the formatting — so don't bother creating fully functioning tables with individual cells and the whole rigmarole. However, you can use tabs between table elements and then do the tab formatting in PageMaker to create a table with your imported text.

- ✔ **Font and size formatting:** PageMaker will import these elements, but unless the formatting you're using in your word processor will be used in the final PageMaker layout, you're just making more work for the layout person, who will have to undo your formatting and then apply the correct formatting for the layout. So just use whatever combination of font and size is most legible on-screen.

- ✔ **Columns:** Don't do layout formatting such as creating multiple columns in your word processor, because PageMaker ignores all that formatting when you import your text. (If you want to do the layout in your word processor, why bother having PageMaker at all?)

When do I import graphics?

Another thing not to do in your word processor is import graphics. Yes, PageMaker supports embedded graphics — it calls them *in-line graphics* because they are inside lines of text, not because they are waiting for movie tickets — which it considers to be basically special symbols in your text.

The problem is that the quality of the embedded graphics may deteriorate. It's sort of like making photocopies. You copy a copy and you get what's politely called a *second-generation* copy — a yucky, blurry, fuzzy copy that you give to someone else only in desperation because you lost the original. Well, a similar thing can happen when using second-generation embedded graphics.

The reason graphics can lose quality when imported as part of a text document is similar to why making photocopies of a photocopy leads to poor image quality: You're not working with the original. Programs like Word don't always copy the original file when you import a graphic; they sometimes copy a lower-resolution placeholder and link it to the original image. When you print, the higher quality original gets sent to the printer. But when you import the text file into PageMaker, the lower-resolution placeholder is imported, not the higher-resolution original. Figure 1-8 shows how an image imported directly into PageMaker compares with the same image imported into Word, edited slightly in Word's picture editor, and then imported into PageMaker. This quality problem won't always happen, but it can, so why risk it?

Figure 1-8:
A graphic imported into PageMaker (left) and the same image edited in a word processor and imported with some text (right).

What if I want to combine lots of different elements?

If your PageMaker document will include multiple elements — tables, graphics, sidebars, bulleted lists, columns of text, and so forth — don't try to combine all those elements in your word processor. You'll just have to separate the various components and lay them out again in PageMaker.

That doesn't mean that you can't have multiple segments in your text file — just not elements that you will lay out separately. Here's a rule of thumb: If an element will be positioned independently of another element, it should be in its own file. Thus, your tables should each be in their own files. Your graphics should be in their own files. So should your sidebars (those little stories that are often in a box or have a shaded background). But your bulleted list can stay in the text because it's part and parcel of the story and will flow with the rest of the text. Your headlines (titles) and bylines (author credits) should stay with their text, too.

What about the table of contents, index, page numbers, and footnotes?

You can specify in Word or WordPerfect which words, phrases, or styles you want included in your table of contents and index. But don't actually generate the table of contents or index before importing the text into PageMaker — the chances of the page numbers being the same in the PageMaker layout as in your word processor are about the same as a finding a snowball on an Acapulco beach.

As mentioned earlier, PageMaker retains a word processor file's footnotes (notes placed at the bottom of the page) and endnotes (notes that are lumped together at the end of the chapter so that they don't get in the way of the rest of the pages). But PageMaker converts footnotes to endnotes when importing. Still, it's usually most convenient to do the footnoting in your word processor — which likely has a footnoting feature — and then either cut and paste each footnote into the appropriate location in your PageMaker layout or just accept them as endnotes at the end of your story.

As for headers and footers — elements that you want to place at the beginning and ending of each page, respectively — don't bother creating them in your word processor. PageMaker ignores them when you import your document. If you want to use headers and footers in your word processor document for your own organization, fine, but they won't appear in the PageMaker layout unless someone manually adds them.

Page numbering that you do in a word processor is also ignored in PageMaker. But you can use it anyway — it will help you keep track of the order of pages printed during the editing stage, before you import the text into PageMaker.

What PageMaker Offers You

Don't let this comparison of word processing and page layout obscure the strengths that PageMaker offers — the reasons you bought the program in the first place. Here's a quick recap of what you get for your PageMaker investment:

- You can do more precise text formatting, giving your documents a more sophisticated appearance.
- You can combine multiple stories, images, and tables to present complex information in a way that's easy for the reader to grasp.

✔ You can combine multiple chapters and create books with a common index, table of contents, and page numbering.

✔ You can output documents to high-resolution printers in order to create professional-looking publications.

✔ You can add color to your documents.

✔ You can use special effects to call attention to key points and to simply make your overall publication more attractive.

Chapter 2

All I Need to Know about Fonts and Type

● ●

In This Chapter

▶ Introducing the terms of typography

▶ Using scalable fonts

▶ The difference between typeface and type style

▶ Changing type size and horizontal scaling

▶ Applying leading and paragraph spacing

▶ Changing horizontal spacing using kerning and tracking

▶ The advantages of paragraph indents

▶ Aligning and justifying paragraphs

● ●

*I*f you've ever prepared a document for a client, a boss, a teacher, or any of life's other authority figures, you know that the appearance of your text can make as big an impression on your prospective reader as the quality of your writing and research. In high school, you were more likely to get a good grade if you typed your report and put it in a plastic binder than if you wrote it with crayon on a greasy paper bag that your mom threw out because it was too disgusting to even use as a trash-can liner. Nowadays, you're more likely to impress folks if you publish your report on a laser printer than if you sketch it out on a few Post-it notes and stick them on an associate's ink blotter.

But laser printing isn't good enough. Anyone with a PC whose Ctrl and P keys are working can print a document. The trick is to make your laser-printed text look better than the other guy's laser-printed text.

This book is full of design tips that will help you transform your plain document into something special. But before you can understand them, you need to learn a few terms of the typographic trade. The vocabulary of desktop publishing is based on the language of traditional typesetting, which has its roots in the 15th century. Somewhere near the middle of the century, one Johann Gutenberg invented movable type, an innovation that was as instrumental in bringing books and literacy to Renaissance Europe as the Model T was in bringing mechanized transportation to folks at the close of the Industrial Revolution. Thanks to its link with history, PageMaker offers the occasional obscure term, such as *font*, *leading*, and *kerning*. Long-dead geezers like Aldus Manutius and Claude Garamond may have understood these terms right off the bat, but you might not. Suffice it to say, if you want the lowdown on type, read this chapter.

A Beginner's Guide to Type

If your experience with page design or laser printing is limited or next to nil, you may have problems understanding how it is that so many people devote so much attention to the appearance of a bunch of letters. If you've seen one typeface, you've seen them all, right? What's all the commotion? Why not just enter your text, print it out, and be done with it?

This is probably the point at which some books on publishing would offer a flowery discussion about the rich heritage of typesetting and letterforms and all that other twaddle you so rightly don't care about. Instead, we'll lay it on the line as simply as possible: The purpose of good type design is to make people *want* to read your pages.

Many folks wrongly construe this to mean that you should sweat over your designs until you've rendered elaborate works of art that'll knock your readers' socks off. The truth is that a lot of nit-picking and worrying can result in some hideously ugly designs.

The best designs tend to be the most simple. Although stylish pages may elicit more oohs and ahs, loose, straightforward, unobtrusive type is more likely to be read by a wider variety of people.

So don't go thinking that you need to expand your font library or purchase a $10,000 typesetter. The road from word processing to type design is paved with little more than a few basic terms and concepts.

If this book had a Don't Freak Out icon, it would appear here. But the Remember icon will have to do in a pinch. Keep in mind that this is only an introduction to the terms and techniques of typesetting and desktop publishing. Everything discussed in this chapter is covered in more detail in later chapters. This is your chance to get your feet wet without getting in over your head. You'll have plenty of chances later to try out these techniques for real.

Font terminology

In computer typesetting, the term *font* is frequently used as a synonym for *typeface*. But back in the days of hot metal type, a clear distinction existed. Because characters had to be printed from physical hunks of lead, an entirely separate font of characters was required to express a change in typeface, style, or size.

Things have changed quite a bit since then. PC users now can access *scalable fonts*, which are mathematical definitions of character outlines. These outlines can be scaled to any size, independent of the resolution of your screen or printer. The scaling may be handled directly by your printer, as is the case for fonts built into laser printers equipped with PCL 5 or PostScript, which include the HP LaserJet III and the Apple LaserWriter, respectively. If you rely on a less sophisticated printer, you can purchase a font-management utility such as Adobe Type Manager, Bitstream FaceLift, or Intellifont. ATM and FaceLift can also be used to scale fonts accurately on-screen, thus eliminating jagged edges (see Figure 2-1).

Figure 2-1: Large text shown as it appears on-screen with Adobe Type Manager installed (top) and without (bottom).

Smooth type with ATM
Jagged type without ATM

But although a single font can satisfy any number of size requirements, it can convey only a single *type style.* The plain and bold styles of a typeface, in other words, are supplied as two separate fonts. Therefore, in computer typesetting, every font carries with it both unique typeface and type style information.

Serif and sans serif typefaces

The most common typefaces available to personal computer users are Helvetica (same as Arial) and Times, or generic equivalents such as Swiss and

Dutch, shown in Figure 2-2. These typefaces were chosen more for their differences than their similarities. For example, although it was created in 1931 for the London *Times* newspaper, Times derives much of its classic appeal from the so-called "transitional" faces of the 1700s. The lines of each character change gradually in thickness, a phenomenon known as *variable stroke weight*, and terminate in tapering — or *bracketed* — wedges called *serifs*. By contrast, Helvetica is a modern font. Influenced by the 20th-century Bauhaus school of design, which fostered a disdain for old-style ornamentation, the strokes of Helvetica characters are rigid and almost entirely uniform in weight. Helvetica also lacks serifs, making it a *sans serif* face.

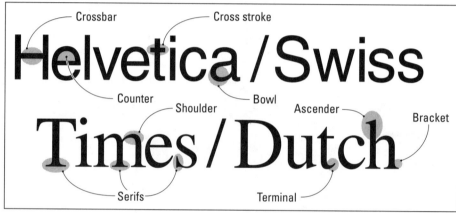

Figure 2-2: The anatomy of type, as applied to two popular laser printer fonts.

If you use a PCL 5-equipped printer, you'll most likely discover that the typeface Univers has been substituted for Helvetica. Although you might mistake this face for Helvetica on a foggy day, Univers offers specific differences in design and appearance, as demonstrated in Figure 2-3. The terminal of the Helvetica *a* loops to the right but remains straight on the Univers character; the middle bar of the Helvetica *E* is visibly shorter than the top and bottom bars while all bars are roughly equivalent in the case of the Univers *E*; the Helvetica *G* offers a terminal that the Univers *G* lacks; and so on. Still, Univers is close enough to Helvetica to get by. So if you own an HP LaserJet III or other PCL 5 printer, you have permission to substitute Univers for the frequent references to Helvetica in future chapters. Just be aware that your documents may look slightly different from the ones in this book when you print them out.

Designer type styles and families

To enhance the visual interest of a page, you could mix some Helvetica text with some Times text. Unfortunately, Helvetica and Times don't look so hot together. Helvetica is heavy and large; Times is more fragile and tends to appear smaller at similar type sizes. To help you spark up a page without mixing typefaces, type designers create variations on typefaces called *type styles*. Because these type styles are designed to be used together, you run no risk of mucking up a page as you diversify its text. For example, you can mix different styles of Helvetica together within a document to add some variety to a page without worry that the styles might clash.

Figure 2-3:
Two sans serif fonts with dissimilarities highlighted in gray.

PostScript Helvetica

abcdEFG!&@123

PCL 5 Univers

abcdEFG!&@123

Helvetica and Times can each be displayed in one of four designer type styles, as shown in Figure 2-4. Each type style is a separate font. Together, each set of four type styles makes up a *type family*.

Figure 2-4:
Different fonts from the Helvetica family are designed to be used together. The same is true of members of the Times family.

Helvetica
Helvetica Bold
Helvetica Oblique
Helvetica Bold Oblique

Times Roman
Times Bold
Times Italic
Times Bold Italic

Different type styles emphasize text in different ways. Plain text — sometimes called *roman*, meaning upright with serifs — is by far the most common variety. It is used to display *body copy*, which comprises the large blocks or columns of text that represent the heart and soul of information contained on a page. The *italic* (cursive) or *oblique* (slanted) style may be used within body copy to highlight a foreign or unfamiliar phrase or simply to stress a word. The *bold* style is relegated to special text, such as captions and headlines. The italic style may also be applied to special text; you may even italicize bold text to create a *bold italic* style.

Applying Typeface and Style

Mostly, this chapter is a lot of theory. But every once in a while you learn how to actually apply typefaces, type styles, and other *formatting attributes* to text. Never mind for a moment that you don't learn how to create text until the next chapter. Just know for now that you can select text in PageMaker by dragging over it with the Text tool. (For more information, read the section "Basic formatting methods" in Chapter 4.)

To assign a typeface and type style to a selected character, word, or paragraph, choose a command from the Type⇨Font submenu. Each command represents a different font. To apply a style, choose a command from the Type⇨Type Style submenu or press the corresponding keyboard equivalent. For example, to make a selected word bold, press Ctrl+Shift+B. To make it italic, press Ctrl+Shift+I. To make it both, hold down the Ctrl and Shift keys while pressing B and then I. (You can also use the Control palette, explained in Chapter 4, to apply formatting attributes.)

You can use these commands to de-bold and de-italicize as well. If the selected word is bold, pressing Ctrl+Shift+B makes it plain, and so on. To make all selected text plain, choose Type⇨Type Style⇨Normal or press Ctrl+Shift+spacebar. Is that enough options for you or what?

Note that when printing to PostScript printers, you cannot apply a style over a font that already includes that style. For example, if you choose the Helvetica Bold typeface and then choose Type⇨Type Style⇨Bold, PageMaker doesn't make Helvetica Double-Bold. Instead, it ignores the Bold command, leaving you with the familiar Helvetica Bold. You can, however, apply styles on top of styles with many non-PostScript printers.

PageMaker-imposed type styles

The Type⇨Type Style submenu also includes a collection of type styles that are not part of any scalable font definition. These *application-imposed* styles are applied by the program in order to achieve further emphasis or special effects:

- ✔ **Underline (Ctrl+Shift+U):** You may never want to use the first application-imposed style, Underline. Generally speaking, text that you would underline on a typewriter, such as a book title, is italicized in typesetting. The sentence, "After again reading Gone with the Wind by Margaret Mitchell, I had to lay off sugar substitutes for a week," for example, becomes "After again reading *Gone with the Wind . . . .*"

- ✔ **Strikethru (Ctrl+Shift+S):** The strikethru style — nice spelling, huh? — indicates text that is scheduled to be deleted from the final version of a document. Both on-screen and when printed, strikethru text is adorned by a horizontal line that runs midway through each character.

- ✔ **Reverse (Ctrl+Shift+V):** Choose this style to make your text the same color as the paper. If the text appears in front of a colored background, the effect is reversed type, just like the name suggests. If there is no object in back of the text, the text is invisible. This latter technique is useful for creating custom spaces.

The top-secret styles

A few styles aren't available from the Type⇨Type Style submenu. To access these styles, you have to choose Type⇨Type Specs (or press Ctrl+T) to display the Type Specifications dialog box, shown in Figure 2-5. Then select an option from either the Position or Case pop-up menu.

Figure 2-5: The Case pop-up menu in the Type Specifications dialog box contains two additional style options.

✔ **Superscript (Ctrl+Shift+backslash):** Selecting this option from the Position pop-up menu raises selected text slightly and makes it smaller, like the 3 in $6^3 = 216$. Superscripts are useful for creating mathematical equations, footnotes, and fractions.

✔ **Subscript (Ctrl+backslash):** Also found in the Position pop-up menu, this option lowers text slightly and makes it smaller, like the 1 in the equation $x_1 + y_1 = a$. Subscripts are used almost exclusively in equations. Do *not* use them to create fractions. The denominator (lower number) in a fraction should be positioned normally, not subscripted.

✔ **All Caps (Ctrl+Shift+K):** Selecting this option from the Case pop-up menu changes all selected characters, whether capital or lowercase, to capitals. It does not affect numbers and other symbols.

✔ **Small Caps:** Also found in the Case pop-up menu, this option replaces all lowercase letters with miniature capitals, sized to the approximate height of a lowercase *x*. Small caps are generally used to represent familiar initials that sometimes pop up in body copy, such as 900 BC or 10:30 AM. The small caps don't interrupt the natural flow of the text as they might at full size (900 BC or 10:30 AM).

If displaying the Type Specifications dialog box is too much trouble — and it *is* — just press the key combinations listed above. To change a bit of text to all caps, for example, just select it and press Ctrl+Shift+K.

To return the text to its original lowercase state, press the keyboard equivalent again. For example, Ctrl+Shift+backslash changes selected superscripted text to normal. If the first press doesn't work, try it again. In other words, if the first few characters are already in the normal position, you may have to press Ctrl+Shift+backslash twice in a row to return all the text to normal.

Enlarging and Reducing Type

After you choose a font to govern the fundamental appearance of your text, you can further enhance and distinguish elements of your page by changing the size of individual characters and words. Large type indicates headlines, logos, and the like; moderately small type serves as body copy; very small type indicates incidental information including copyrights and disclaimers. Combined with type style, the size of your text directs the attention of your readers and helps them to find the information that is most important to them.

Type size terminology

In order to understand how to size type, you must first understand how it's measured. To begin with, there are four basic kinds of characters. The horizontal guidelines that serve as boundaries for these characters are labeled in Figure 2-6.

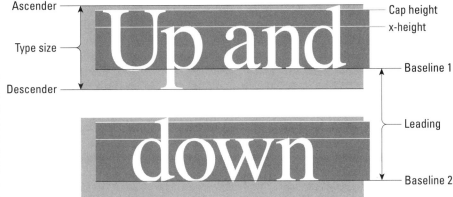

Ascender — Cap height
— x-height
Type size
— Baseline 1
Figure 2-6: Descender
Type is
measured
using a — Leading
series of
horizontal
guidelines.
— Baseline 2

- ✔ *Capital letters* extend from the *baseline* upward to the *cap height* line. Examples include *A*, *B*, and *C*. Numerals (*0123456789*) also qualify as capitals.

- ✔ *Medials* fit entirely within the space between the *baseline* and the *x-height* line. Examples include *a*, *c*, and *e*.

- ✔ *Ascenders* are lowercase characters that extend above the cap height line. Examples include *b*, *d*, and *k*.

- ✔ *Descenders* are lowercase characters that extend below the baseline. Examples include *g*, *j*, and *p*.

Not every character fits snugly into one of these categories. For example, the lowercase characters *i* and *t* violate the x-height line but are nonetheless considered medials; the dot of the *i* isn't considered an integral part of the character and the *t* doesn't extend even so far as the cap height line. Other times, a letter qualifies as both an ascender and a descender, as is the case for the italic *f* in a serif font. Non-letters such as %, #, and & are generally capitals, but several violations exist — among them, *$*, *§*, and many forms of punctuation, including parentheses.

Hot stuff, huh? Well, for those of you who are worried that we're delving too deeply into the territory of typo-dweebology, let's get straight to the point, which is this: The size of a character — known predictably as its *type size* — is measured from the topmost point of the tallest ascender to the very lowest point of the deepest descender. Type size is calculated in a unit of measure called *points*, where one point equals $^1/_{72}$ inch (just over $^1/_3$ millimeter), which is why you frequently see type size called *point size*. So a character that measures 0.167 inch from tip to tail becomes 12-point type, the equivalent of pica type on a conventional typewriter.

Changing the type size

To size type in PageMaker, choose an option from the Type⇨Size submenu. Although these options represent the most commonly used type sizes — based on sizes used back in the old hot-lead days — they are no more acceptable than thousands of other possible type sizes you can use in PageMaker. To specify your own custom size, choose Type⇨Size⇨Other, enter a value in the option box, and press Return. You can even enter decimal values such as 11.3 and 21.5.

If you want to experiment with a few different type sizes, highlight the desired text and press Ctrl+period to enlarge the type or Ctrl+comma to reduce it. PageMaker enlarges or reduces the type size to the next option in the Type⇨Size submenu. For example, press Ctrl+period to enlarge 24-point type to 36-point type; press Ctrl+comma to reduce 12-point type to 10-point type. If you want to be even more exact, you can enlarge or reduce text in 1-point increments by pressing Ctrl+Shift+period or Ctrl+Shift+comma.

Horizontal scaling

By changing the type size, you scale text proportionally; that is, you enlarge or reduce it the same amount horizontally and vertically. But you can also scale the width of selected characters independently of their height by choosing options from the Type⇨Set Width submenu. Choose a value larger than 100 percent to expand type; choose a value lower than 100 percent to condense it. You can also choose Type⇨Set Width⇨Other to enter a custom percentage value.

If you don't like the way your expanded or condensed text looks, just choose Type⇨Set Width⇨Normal (or press Ctrl+Shift+X) to restore it to its proportional type size.

The Many Facets of Character Spacing

Another way to improve the appearance of a page is to adjust the amount of vertical and horizontal space between characters. Spacing is one of the most important aspects of page design because it determines the visual relationship between individual characters and entire lines of type.

Figure 2-7, for example, shows two paragraphs of text, identical in content, font, type style, and size. Only the spacing is different. The left paragraph uses tight vertical spacing and loose horizontal spacing between words. The paragraph isn't entirely illegible, but it's difficult to read because your eye is tempted to read downward, in the direction of least resistance: "We United mined…people Nations, save from war…of deter- succeeding the which…" and so on. In the right-hand paragraph, the vertical spacing was increased and the space between words was decreased, eliminating any question as to the direction in which words should be read.

Figure 2-7:
Two identical columns of text subjected to different vertical and horizontal spacing.

> We, the people of the United Nations, determined to save succeeding generations from the scourge of war, which twice in our lifetime has brought untold sorrow to mankind, and to reaffirm faith in fundamental human rights, in the dignity and worth of the human person, in the equal right of men and women and of nations large and small, and to establish conditions under which justice and respect for

> We, the people of the United Nations, determined to save succeeding generations from the scourge of war, which twice in our lifetime has brought untold sorrow to mankind, and to reaffirm faith in fundamental human rights, in the dignity and worth of the human person, in the equal right of men and women and of nations large and small, and to establish conditions under which justice and re-

The concept of character spacing is pretty straightforward, but the actual process is more involved. You can specify the amount of space between lines of type, the amount of space between one word and the next, the amount of space between individual letters within a single word, the amount of space between paragraphs and columns — well, you get the idea. Spacing is a lot of work.

Leading is the space between the lines

As diagrammed back in Figure 2-6, *leading* (pronounced *ledding*) is measured from the baseline of one line of type to the baseline of the next line of type. Because it is orderly, predictable, and exacting, leading is the perfect tool for desktop publishing. Also, leading is measured in points, just like type size.

Back in the old days, printers used to space out lines of type by inserting horizontal strips of lead between them. More lead strips meant more space between lines. Hence, the space between lines came to be known as *leading*.

Now lead is dead, but its legacy lives on. In an effort to make the idea a little more straightforward to new users, some programs call the space between lines of type *line spacing*. But PageMaker, possibly in reverence to Aldus Manutius and all those other dusty old gaffers, sticks with *leading*. Long live tradition, even if it does require two paragraphs of explanation.

To change the leading between selected lines of text, choose an option from the Type➪Leading submenu. These options change depending on the size of the text. The bold option represents *solid leading*, which is leading that exactly matches the type size. For body text, solid leading is too tight. But it's just right for headlines and other large type.

To space body text, you generally should stick with the Auto setting, which is 120 percent of the type size. This amount of leading gives the text more room to breathe and makes it easier to read.

Using the Auto setting can create a problem if a line of type contains differently sized characters — for example, a drop cap mixed with regular body text. PageMaker bases the Auto leading amount on the largest character, which can result in unevenly spaced lines of text. If you're working with this sort of text, turn off Auto leading and choose a leading setting from the Leading submenu.

If you want to double-space the text — say, for a copy-editing draft or a preliminary report — choose the second-to-last option in the Type➪Leading submenu. Choose the last option to triple-space the text.

Paragraph spacing

The other form of vertical spacing available to desktop publishers is *paragraph spacing*, which allows you to insert additional space between the last line of a paragraph and the first line of the next paragraph. When you enter text, a *carriage return* — created by pressing the Return or Enter key — indicates the end of one paragraph and the beginning of the next.

To access PageMaker's paragraph spacing options, choose Type➪Paragraph or press Ctrl+M. The Paragraph Specifications dialog box appears, as shown in Figure 2-8.

Figure 2-8:
You can add vertical space before and after a paragraph by choosing Type➪ Paragraph and entering values into the spotlighted options.

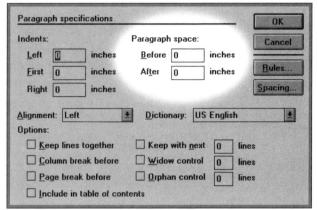

The Before and After values (spotlighted in the figure) control the amount of vertical space inserted before and after a paragraph. Why would you need to worry about both? After all, if you insert space after one paragraph, it automatically adds space before the paragraph that follows it. The reason is to gain greater control.

Suppose that you're creating *styles,* which you use to apply a set of custom formatting attributes to different kinds of paragraphs (described in the Chapter 4). You might want the heading style to include Before spacing so that a big gap always appears before the headline. But you might want the caption style to include After spacing so that a gap follows every caption. If PageMaker offered only Before spacing or After spacing, you wouldn't have this kind of flexibility.

Unlike type size and leading, the Before and After values are not measured in points. Instead, they're measured in the current unit of measure, which may be inches, picas ($1/6$ inches), or millimeters, as discussed in the "Setting rulers and guides" section of Chapter 3. The unit in force is listed to the right of each option box.

Don't just insert extra carriage returns to add space between paragraphs. Doing so can screw up your layout — if one of those extra carriage returns ends up at the top of a column, for example, you'll be left with unwanted space. So always use the Before and After spacing options to put space between paragraphs.

Horizontal Spacing Options

In the realm of horizontal spacing, word spacing and letter spacing first come to mind. *Word spacing* determines the width of the space between each word and its neighbor; *letter spacing* determines the horizontal space between individual characters (whether they're letters, numbers, punctuation, or some other kind of symbols).

To access PageMaker's word and letter spacing options, click on the Spacing button inside the Paragraph Specifications dialog box. The Spacing Attributes dialog box shown in Figure 2-9 appears.

Figure 2-9:
Click on the
Spacing
button in the
Paragraph
Specifications
dialog box to
display this
dialog box.

Spacing attributes

Word space:			Letter space:			
Minimum	75	%	Minimum	-5	%	OK
Desired	100	%	Desired	0	%	Cancel
Maximum	150	%	Maximum	25	%	Reset

Pair kerning: ☒ Auto above 4 points

Leading method: ⦿ Proportional ○ Top of caps ○ Baseline

Autoleading: 120 % of point size

Looks confusing, huh? Well, in fact, it *is* pretty confusing. What with all those Minimum and Maximum values to set, you can get mired down in this dialog box pretty quickly. So instead of giving you the long, drawn-out facts, here's the short story: Each value represents a percentage of a normal, everyday, space character. A value of 100 percent is a standard space, a value of 200 percent is the width of two spaces, and so on. The default letter spacing is 0 percent because characters in the same word don't usually have any spaces between them.

PageMaker likes to have room to wiggle, so rather than setting the word and letter spacing to exact values, it asks you to specify a range. Tell it the Minimum space it can use when space is tight, the Maximum space it can use when there's plenty of room to maneuver, and the Desired space to hit when conditions are ideal. Consider *justified* text — text that lines up exactly on the left and right margins, like in a paperback novel. To justify type, PageMaker needs to change the space between words and letters on the fly to accommodate each line of type. The Minimum and Maximum values represent the range PageMaker can work in.

Figure 2-10 shows text subject to different word and letter spacing values. Notice that the word spacing changes from one row to the next but remains constant throughout each row. Meanwhile, the letter spacing changes from one column to the next but remains constant throughout each column. Cool, huh? The values in the figure represent the values entered into the Desired option boxes.

<table>
<tr><td>

W: 50%, L: 75%

We, the people of the United Nations, determined to save succeeding generations from the scourge of war, which twice in our lifetime has brought untold sorrow to mankind, and to reaffirm faith in fundamental human rights, in the dignity and worth of the human person, in the equal right of men and women

</td><td>

W: 50%, L: 100%

We, the people of the United Nations, determined to save succeeding generations from the scourge of war, which twice in our lifetime has brought untold sorrow to mankind, and to reaffirm faith in fundamental human rights, in the dignity and worth of the human person, in the equal

</td><td>

W: 50%, L: 125%

We, the people of the United Nations, determined to save succeeding generations from the scourge of war, which twice in our lifetime has brought untold sorrow to mankind, and to reaffirm faith in fundamental human rights, in the dignity and worth of the

</td></tr>
<tr><td>

W: 100%, L: 75%

We, the people of the United Nations, determined to save succeeding generations from the scourge of war, which twice in our lifetime has brought untold sorrow to mankind, and to reaffirm faith in fundamental human rights, in the dignity and worth of the human person, in the equal right of men and women

</td><td>

W: 100%, L: 100%

We, the people of the United Nations, determined to save succeeding generations from the scourge of war, which twice in our lifetime has brought untold sorrow to mankind, and to reaffirm faith in fundamental human rights, in the dignity and worth of the human person, in the equal right of men and

</td><td>

W: 100%, L: 125%

We, the people of the United Nations, determined to save succeeding generations from the scourge of war, which twice in our lifetime has brought untold sorrow to mankind, and to reaffirm faith in fundamental human rights, in the dignity and worth of the

</td></tr>
<tr><td>

W: 150%, L: 75%

We, the people of the United Nations, determined to save succeeding generations from the scourge of war, which twice in our lifetime has brought untold sorrow to mankind, and to reaffirm faith in fundamental human rights, in the dignity and worth of the human person, in the equal right of men and

</td><td>

W: 150%, L: 100%

We, the people of the United Nations, determined to save succeeding generations from the scourge of war, which twice in our lifetime has brought untold sorrow to mankind, and to reaffirm faith in fundamental human rights, in the dignity and worth of the human person, in the equal

</td><td>

W: 150%, L: 125%

We, the people of the United Nations, determined to save succeeding generations from the scourge of war, which twice in our lifetime has brought untold sorrow to mankind, and to reaffirm faith in fundamental human rights, in the dignity and worth of the

</td></tr>
</table>

Figure 2-10: Three varieties of word spacing meet with three varieties of letter spacing. The center example shows unaltered text.

When text is not justified — like the paragraphs in Figure 2-10 — PageMaker spaces text according to the Desired value alone. This fact brings up one more rule: The Desired value must be smaller than the Maximum value and larger than the Minimum value. So to lower the Desired word spacing to 50 percent in Figure 2-10, for example, the Minimum value had to be 50 percent or lower.

Cramming and spreading text

So now you know how to change word and letter spacing. But the real question is *why*, isn't it? Well, to be perfectly honest, letter and word spacing don't rate very high on the list of controls you may use frequently. In a pinch, when you need to cram lots of type into a small area or spread out sparse type to fill an empty page, word spacing and letter spacing can provide a quick solution.

But it's a forced solution at best. As you can see from Figure 2-10, most spacing alterations — especially changes in letter spacing — yield some pretty unreadable results. The more attractive *and* more convenient solution is to adjust type size and leading. If that's not practical — for example, you generally wouldn't want to apply a size and leading to one paragraph that is different from the size and leading of another paragraph in the same story — use letter spacing and word spacing as a last resort.

Letter spacing's more sophisticated cousin: kerning

But horizontal spacing isn't a total wash. In fact, letter spacing has a close cousin called *kerning* that can prove extremely useful for perfecting the proximity of neighboring letters. PageMaker's kerning feature allows you to change the amount of space between a single pair of characters. You can kern characters in two ways — automatically and manually.

Here's the lowdown on automatic kerning. Font designers specify that certain pairs of letters, called *kerning pairs*, should automatically be positioned more closely together than the standard letter spacing allows. The letters *T* and *o* are an example of a kerning pair. When placed next to each other, their normal side-by-side spacing results in an incongruously loose appearance, as demonstrated in the first example of Figure 2-11. By turning on the Pair Kerning checkbox in the Spacing Attributes dialog box — when on, the checkbox contains an X — you instruct PageMaker to automatically kern all kerning pairs so they fit more snugly together, as shown in the second example in Figure 2-11.

Figure 2-11: The *T* and *o* kerning pair when the Pair Kerning option is turned off (top) and on (bottom).

Tomato

Tomato

If you're not satisfied with the amount of letter spacing between any two characters — whether or not the characters are defined as a kerning pair — you can adjust the kerning manually. Click between the two characters in question to position the insertion marker and then press one of the following key combinations:

- ✔ Press Ctrl+minus (on the keypad) or Ctrl+Backspace to kern the character together $^1/_{25}$ of the type size.

- ✔ Press Ctrl+plus (on the keypad) or Ctrl+Shift+Backspace to kern the character apart by the same amount.

- ✔ For more precise work, press Ctrl+Shift+minus (on the keypad) to kern characters together $^1/_{100}$ of the type size.

- ✔ Press Ctrl+Shift+plus (on the keypad) to kern the characters apart by the same amount.

For example, if you have 10-point type, pressing Ctrl+minus moves the characters 0.4 point closer ($^1/_{25}$ of 10 points = 0.4).

What the heck is tracking?

You can apply kerning across multiple characters at a time using the options in the Type➪Track submenu. *Tracking* is the smartest kind of letter spacing because it varies the spacing of entire selected stories in general increments and according to the type size of the text. The Normal option, for example, loosens spacing by 1 percent when applied to 12-point type but tightens it when applied to 48-point type and larger. Even Tight loosens small text by half a percent but begins tightening spacing at 36-point and larger. Only Very Tight kerns text together regardless of size. Both Loose and Very Loose always loosen text to some degree or other.

What's that Autoleading option?

If you look closely at Figure 2-8, you'll notice an Autoleading option box near the lower right corner of the Spacing Attributes dialog box. Remember reading earlier that the Auto leading setting is equal to 120 percent of the type size? Well, that's the setting when you first use PageMaker, but it doesn't have to remain that way. If you decide that you prefer some other automatic leading amount, enter it into the Autoleading option box. All text formatted with Auto leading setting changes to your new specification.

Indenting Paragraphs

The last kind of space to cover, the *paragraph indent*, serves to distinguish one paragraph of text from others within a single story. As you can when you use a typewriter, you can indent the first line of a paragraph by pressing the Tab key. But PageMaker also provides more sophisticated means for indenting text.

To indent a selected paragraph, press Ctrl+M to display the Paragraph Specifications dialog box and enter new values in the Indents option boxes, spotlighted in Figure 2-12. The options work as follows:

- ✔ **Left:** Enter a value into this option box to indent the entire left side of a paragraph.

- ✔ **First:** This is the most useful option. Use it to indent only the first line of text in a paragraph, rather than using a tab.

- ✔ **Right:** Enter a value into this option box to indent the entire right side of a paragraph. If you enter values in both the Left and Right options, you can reduce the width of the paragraph, as you might want to do to indicate a long quote in a document.

Figure 2-12:
The spotlighted options control the indents assigned to a selected paragraph.

Paragraph specifications		OK
Indents:	**Paragraph space:**	Cancel
Left [0] inches	Before [0] inches	
First [0] inches	After [0] inches	Rules...
Right [0] inches		Spacing...

Alignment: [Left ▼]   Dictionary: [US English ▼]

Options:
- ☐ Keep lines together   ☐ Keep with next [0] lines
- ☐ Column break before   ☐ Widow control [0] lines
- ☐ Page break before   ☐ Orphan control [0] lines
- ☐ Include in table of contents

If you're like most new users, you're probably thinking, "Why not just enter a tab at the beginning of each paragraph? It's not like it takes a lot of time. It might even be easier than dealing with this weird dialog box." The answer is, indents are more flexible. Say that you set up first-line indents throughout your document. You show the finished result to your boss, who says, "Dang, that's good! Just one thing: I don't like the indents. Get rid of them."

If you used tabs, you have to delete every one of them manually. If you used indents, no problem. Just select all the text, change the First value in the Paragraph Specifications dialog box, and you're finished.

Either way, be sure to exclaim, "Wow, that was certainly a lot of work deleting all those tabs!" so that your boss thinks you're working hard.

Aligning Lines of Type

The last formatting attribute to touch on in this chapter is *alignment*, sometimes called *justification*, which determines the manner in which lines in a paragraph align with each other. Choose Type⇨Alignment to display a submenu containing five alignment commands. Examples of the results of choosing all but the last of these commands are shown in Figure 2-13. The only difference between the fourth command, Justify, and the fifth command, Force Justify, is that the fifth command justifies every line of type without exception, while the fourth command justifies all but the last line (as in the figure).

Figure 2-13: Four alignment options. The gray lines demonstrate the axes with respect to which the text blocks are aligned.

Flush left (ragged right)

We, the people of theUnited Nations, determined to save succeeding generations from the scourge of war, which twice in our lifetime has brought untold sorrow to mankind, and to reaffirm faith in fundamental human rights, in the dignity and worth of the human person, in the equal right of men and woman and of nations large and small, and to establish conditions under which justice and respect for the obligations arising from treaties and other sources of law can be maintained.

Centered

We, the people of theUnited Nations, determined to save succeeding generations from the scourge of war, which twice in our lifetime has brought untold sorrow to mankind, and to reaffirm faith in fundamental human rights, in the dignity and worth of the human person, in the equal right of men and woman and of nations large and small, and to establish conditions under which justice and respect for the obligations arising from treaties and other sources of law can be maintained.

Flush right (ragged left)

We, the people of theUnited Nations, determined to save succeeding generations from the scourge of war, which twice in our lifetime has brought untold sorrow to mankind, and to reaffirm faith in fundamental human rights, in the dignity and worth of the human person, in the equal right of men and woman and of nations large and small, and to establish conditions under which justice and respect for the obligations arising from treaties and other sources of law can be maintained.

Fully justified

We, the people of theUnited Nations, determined to save succeeding generations from the scourge of war, which twice in our lifetime has brought untold sorrow to mankind, and to reaffirm faith in fundamental human rights, in the dignity and worth of the human person, in the equal right of men and woman and of nations large and small, and to establish conditions under which justice and respect for the obligations arising from treaties and other sources of law can be maintained.

Now just because five alignment options exist doesn't mean that you have to use them all in the same document. Flush left body copy, for example, generally looks best when combined with a flush left headline. In fact, the only alignment option that's guaranteed to look great in any kind of document is flush left. Some designers even go so far as to argue that a flush left paragraph's ragged appearance lends visual interest to the text and helps to compensate for much of the back-and-forth monotony of reading.

Fully justified text is also very popular, but is applicable almost exclusively to body copy. And because of its rigidly formal appearance, fully justified text can be limited in its appeal; it looks great in the *Wall Street Journal* but can look square, stodgy, and downright uninteresting when used in a flier or advertisement. In the case of body copy, the general rule of thumb is this: Align short blocks of text flush left; reserve full justification for very long documents.

To align text from the keyboard, just press Ctrl and Shift with the first letter of the alignment option. For example, Ctrl+Shift+L aligns selected text left, and Ctrl+Shift+J justifies it. Press Ctrl+Shift+F (as in *force* justify) to justify every line of text, including the last.

Part II
There's a Blank Page: Now What?

The 5th Wave   **By Rich Tennant**

THAT'S RIGHT, THE UPPER CASE BUTTON WORKS ON-SCREEN, BUT THEY'RE NOT COMING OUT ON THE DANG PRINTER! HOLD? SURE, I'LL HOLD.

Poet e.e. cummings makes his last service call.

In this part . . .

Starting out right can make a huge difference in the effort it takes to lay out your pages — and the quality of your final document. When you start PageMaker, you're faced with a blank page that you need to transform into an effective layout. This part shows you how to take that blank page and build it up with text, graphics, and special formatting to create an effective result.

Chapter 3

Starting Your First PageMaker Document

Where Do I Begin?

PageMaker is sort of like Arnold ("Ahnüld") Schwarzenegger. No doubt you're thinking, "Oh, sure, and WordPerfect reminds *me* of Benji," but bear with us for a second. If you're like most people, the first time you saw Ahnüld on TV or whatever, you didn't think "actor" or "savvy businessman," you thought, "Get a load of this muscle-bound troglodyte. Is he a dim bulb or what?" And yet, despite the fact that no one over ten years old would select Ahnüld as his or her favorite actor, he remains the biggest box-office draw in this and almost every other country. Like him or not, we all shelled out the GNP of all the Soviet breakaway republics to see *Terminator 2*, and we'll no doubt repeat the process for *True Lies*. Furthermore, unlike dozens of other celebrity Neanderthals who made millions and then promptly squandered every cent before they turned 35, Ahnüld invests his money shrewdly. Reputedly, nearly every business deal that the guy makes turns to gold.

So as you might imagine, there's a school of thought that says, maybe Ahnüld's not nearly as dumb as he looks. Maybe he just acts dumb so that his audience won't feel threatened by the true Ahnüld, who is a thinker of Brainiac proportions.

The same is true for PageMaker. After you start the program (by double-clicking on the PageMaker icon in the Windows Program Manager), all you see are a few pull-down menus at the top of the screen. Nothing fancy. Nothing at all, in fact, to lead you to believe that you didn't waste some perfectly good money on another hopelessly rinky-dink piece of software.

Although lots of programs like to show off by displaying a whole bunch of garish palettes and scary options right off the bat — features that seem designed to make you shrink in terror and swear off computers for good — PageMaker genuinely wants to be your page-layout buddy. Oh sure, deep down inside, PageMaker knows that it's way smarter than anyone short of Arnold "The Brain" Schwarzenegger, but it *pretends* to be dumb so that you won't feel insecure. Then, as you warm up to the program, it reveals more and more of its power, until pretty soon, you're fooled into thinking that you're hot stuff. It's a stealth program just as surely as Ahnüld is a stealth intellectual.

It's a Brand New Page!

To get PageMaker revved up and raring to go, you have to either create a new layout or open one that you created earlier. (You also have one other option, which is to change the default settings, as described in the upcoming "Making changes to your defaults" sidebar.) For now, create a new document — by choosing File⇨New (or pressing Ctrl+N). The Page Setup dialog box appears, asking you to specify the size of the page and several other items. Click on OK or press Enter to accept the default settings. (You learn how to set up different page sizes and work with the other options in the dialog box later in this chapter, in the section, "Setting Up a New Document.")

PageMaker opens a new document (which it refers to as a *publication*), and you're confronted by a blank page and some tools. Before taking a look at options for new documents, you need a brief introduction to PageMaker's tools.

You use PageMaker by messing around with three types of functions: menu commands, tools, and palettes. Menu commands work just like those in any Windows program. You move your cursor to the menu name and click to display a list of commands. You choose a command by moving the cursor over it and clicking. If an ellipsis (...) follows a command name, it means that when you choose the command, PageMaker displays a dialog box filled with options to control exactly how the command is applied. You select the options you want to use and click on the OK button to execute the command.

Tools are the instruments you use to do your work. PageMaker's tools are stored in the *toolbox*, also called the *Tool palette,* shown in Figure 3-1. To select a tool, move the cursor to the toolbox and click on the icon for the tool you want to use. Notice that the selected tool becomes white on a black background, while the others are black on gray backgrounds. You'll also notice that the mouse cursor changes when you change tools. This gives you added information about which tool is active. Before you know it, you'll recognize all umpteen kinds of cursors.

The Arrow tool also goes by another name: the *Pointer tool.* We think *Arrow tool* is easier to remember, given the shape of the tool's icon, so we use that term in this book.

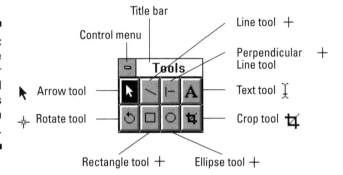

Figure 3-1:
The
PageMaker
toolbox and
the cursors
for each
tool.

PageMaker's other palettes, shown with the toolbox in Figure 3-2, give you easy access to certain layout and formatting options. If the palettes get in your way, you can move them around your screen by placing your cursor on the palette's title bar, holding the mouse button down, and dragging the palette to a new location.

If you want to get rid of a palette, double-click on its control menu icon (also called a *close box).* You can also use the Window menu to display or hide palettes. If a palette's name is checked in the menu, that means it's visible. Click on the option name to remove the check mark and hide the palette; click again to make the palette reappear.

Notice the page icons at the bottom left of the PageMaker screen, shown in Figure 3-2. Click on these icons to move from one page to another. (In the figure, the document has only one page — page 1 — plus its two master pages, which are covered in the next chapter). If PageMaker can't fit the icons for all of your pages on-screen, a scroll arrow appears on each side of the page icons. Click on the arrows to move to the other pages in your publication.

The other elements in PageMaker are standard Windows elements: pull-down menus, scroll bars, scroll boxes, and so forth. If you are new to Windows as well as to PageMaker, read Andy Rathbone's *Windows for Dummies,* published by IDG Books, for a primer on the subject.

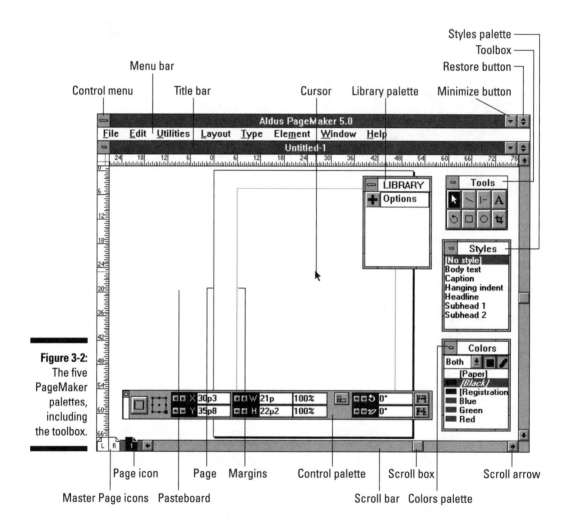

Figure 3-2:
The five
PageMaker
palettes,
including
the toolbox.

Making changes to your defaults

The simple interface that you get when you first launch PageMaker has an additional purpose (other than allowing you to think that you're smarter than the program). As it turns out, any command that you choose when no document is open becomes a default setting for all future documents. This is PageMaker's handy-dandy way of letting you adjust settings so that all new documents use them.

As you learn how to use the various options in this and other chapters, you may discover that you keep changing certain settings over and over again. To eliminate this utter waste of your time, close all open documents and implement your changes once and for all by choosing the appropriate command from the appropriate menu. Your revised settings become the new defaults.

You may be surprised to learn how many default settings you can change. The following list contains some examples. Don't worry if you don't know what even half of these items mean; they're just presented here to stick a few subliminal flags in your brain. When you come across comprehensive descriptions of one setting or another in a later chapter, the flag will go up, and you'll think, "You know, I could change the default for this option by closing the current document and choosing this here command." That's the idea, anyway. Whether or not it works is a matter for historians to discuss. Those historians that don't have anything better to do with their time, that is.

Anyway, in case you forgot the point of all this — it's easy to get caught up in this historical stuff if you're not careful — here's the aforementioned list of default settings that you can change in PageMaker when no document is open:

✔ General preferences, which include ruler measurement units, guide settings, the Story Editor font, and save options

✔ Page setup options such as page size, orientation, and numbering

✔ Multiple paste repeating values and offset amounts

✔ Index and table of contents formatting

✔ Number of columns, ruler display, and guide snap

✔ Automatic text flow

✔ Typestyle, font, size, tab, indentation, and other text settings

✔ Text wrap settings

✔ Line weights and fill patterns

✔ Style sheets

✔ Link settings

✔ Color definitions

✔ Which palettes are on-screen and where they appear

Setting Up a New Document

When you create a new document, you get the dialog box shown in Figure 3-3. This dialog box is where you give PageMaker basic instructions on how to set up your document. But nothing's set in stone; you can change these settings after you create your document by choosing File➪Page Setup.

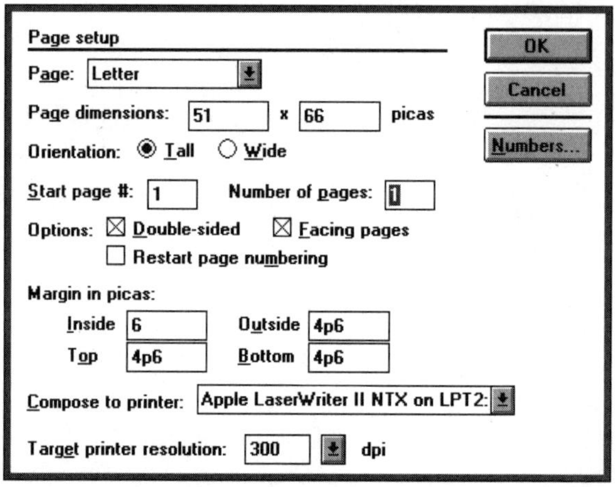

Figure 3-3:
You define
the basic
page
settings for
a new
document in
this dialog
box.

Remember that we told you that PageMaker doesn't like to overwhelm you? Well, that's not *always* true. The Page Setup dialog box is a prime example of PageMaker doing its absolute best to frighten you into an apoplectic fit. It's like Ahnüld grabbing one of his investment bankers by the lapels, sticking an uzi up the guy's nose, and shouting, "I want you to siphon off the equity from my multimillion dollar portfolio of no-load mutual funds and inject it into a development of non-qualifying HUD projects that we'll convert into luxurious high-rise office suites (after we displace the tenants under the guise of urban renovation) *and I want you to do it now!*" Sure, it's an everyday occurrence at the venerable institution of Schwarzenegger and Sycophants, Ltd., but you never quite get used to it.

So, to prevent you from entering some kind of computer-induced seizure, let's examine each of these options one at a time.

Page-size settings

You select your page size from the Page pop-up menu. Chances are, you'll want to select Letter ($8 \frac{1}{2} \times 11$ inches), but lots of other sizes such as Legal ($8 \frac{1}{2} \times 14$) and Tabloid (11×17) are also available. When you select a page size, its measurements appear in the Page Dimensions fields.

What's a pop-up menu and what do I do with it?

A *pop-up menu* is a type of menu that also goes by several other names, including *pick list* and *selection list*, depending on your particular dialect. For example, if you say *pick list*, be sure to say it like a hayseed, as in *paick laist*. But call them what you may, pop-up menus exist because there's a limit to how many options a programmer can cram into dialog box (and, as witnessed by the Page Setup dialog box, some programmers try awfully darned hard). Pop-up menus are a way to add options without taking a lot of space.

Take a close look at Figure 3-3. See the three options that have down-pointing arrows to the right of them? They're the Page, Compose to Printer, and Target Printer Resolution options. If you click on these arrows, you get a pop-up menu of choices. To select an option, just click on it.

If you want to lay out a document that has a different size than one of the predefined page sizes (for example, you're creating business cards or a fold-over brochure), activate the Custom option by simply entering the measurements in the Page Dimensions option boxes. (There's no need to select the Custom option from the Page pop-up menu, although you can if you want to waste some time.)

Tall or wide?

For Orientation, select Tall if you want the page to have the long side go from top to bottom. This option is called *portrait* in some programs because that's the way portrait paintings are generally oriented. Select Wide if you want the page to have the long dimension go from side to side (called *landscape* because that's the way paintings of landscapes are generally oriented). Generally, documents are created with a Tall orientation because standard publications — letters and magazines, for example — are traditionally published that way.

All pages in a document must be oriented the same way. Therefore, if you want both tall and wide pages in your layout (maybe there's a chart that you want to print in Wide orientation because its rows are really long), you'll find it easier to put your landscape pages in a separate PageMaker document from your portrait pages. (Of course, you could just rotate that really wide chart 90 degrees so that page appears horizontal when it prints, but then you have to twist your head on its side in order to read or edit the text on-screen. And although Ahnüld no doubt would recommend this type of aerobic workout, moving your mouse along one plane while your head is tilted on another requires a degree of hand-eye coordination that most 21st-century cyborgs lack.)

Number of pages and page numbers

You'll notice that the Number of Pages option box is highlighted when you first enter the Page Setup dialog box. That's because it's the setting most likely to be changed from one document to the next. You don't have to fill it in first, and you can change the setting later if you need to, but it's a good one to start with. Just enter the number of pages you plan to use, and move on.

The Start Page # option is set to 1 by default, which makes sense for most documents; the first page in the document is numbered as page 1. If you choose a different number, the first page in the document is assigned that number, and each page thereafter is numbered accordingly. So, if you use 2 as the Start Page # , the first page is numbered page 2, the second page is page 3, and so on. Why would you do this? Perhaps the first page of your document is laid out vertically while the rest of the publication is oriented horizontally. You would create a single-page portrait document for the cover, and a second landscape document that begins at page 2 for the rest of the publication.

Among the cluster of Options checkboxes is a Restart Page Numbering checkbox. It's normally deselected. It only comes into play if you use Page-Maker's book feature to number pages across a series of documents as explained in Chapter 8.

If you click on the Numbers button, PageMaker displays the Page Numbering dialog box. Here, you can choose the types of numbers that PageMaker uses to number your pages. Normally, people use Arabic numbers (1, 2, 3, and so on). But sometimes, Roman numerals (i, ii, iii, or I, II, III, and so on) or letters (a, b, c, or A, B, C, and so on) are more appropriate — such as for prefaces, indexes, and other subsidiary pages. By the way, you don't need to use this dialog box unless you want to change the default setting, which is Arabic numbers.

Keep in mind that whatever numbering scheme you pick for your pages, the numbers that appear in the page icons in the bottom left corner of the document window will always be Arabic numbers. These numbers have no effect on the printing of your document; they're only there to keep you abreast of what's happening on-screen. PageMaker figures that you're probably more used to reading Arabic numbers than Roman numerals.

Margins and side settings

PageMaker assumes that you'll be reproducing your finished documents on two-sided pages. That's what the Double-Sided checkbox means. However, if you'll only be printing on one side, uncheck the option.

What difference does it make whether a document is two-sided or one-sided? Often, none. But there's a good reason to have the option. Think about a report bound in a ring binder — the kind with three holes on the inside of each sheet of paper. When you're setting up such a document, you'll want to leave enough space on the inside of the sheet to account for the holes. So you'd make the left margin a little wider than the right margin to leave enough room, right? That's great for the right-hand pages. But if you're printing double-sided, the left-hand pages will be in trouble. Their right margins aren't wider, yet their right side is the side that is near the holes. Whoops. By having a double-sided option, PageMaker can track pages' *inside* and *outside* margins rather than their left and right. The inside margin for a right-hand page is the left margin, but for a left-hand page, it is the right margin. In this example, you would set a wide inside margin to accommodate those holes. PageMaker figures out which way to shift the text on each page for you.

You can see this feature in action by checking and unchecking the Double-Sided box. When the option is selected, the first two Margin options change to Inside and Outside (as in Figure 3-3); when deselected, they become Left and Right.

Whatever margins you set, keep in mind that you can still put any text or graphics anywhere on the page — the margins don't prevent that. They merely provide a visual clue for where more text and graphics should go. PageMaker also tries to keep text within the margins when it flows text inside a page.

The Facing Pages checkbox is dimmed (unavailable) unless Double-Sided is checked. The Facing Pages option lets you position text or graphics to straddle the gap between pages. In other words, a large page element goes to the edge of the left-hand page and continues onto the right-hand page, as demonstrated in the first example of Figure 3-4. If you're printing on a laser printer, don't select this option because all laser printers have a margin around the page on which they can't print. (It's where the printer grabs the page as it moves through the printer mechanism.) So text and graphics printed to the edge of the page get cut off. The bottom example in Figure 3-4 shows what happens to the text from the top example when the Facing Pages option is deselected.

Printer settings

In most cases, the Target Printer Resolution setting shown in the Page Setup dialog box corresponds to the resolution of the printer selected from the Compose to Printer pop-up menu. The problem with the Compose to Printer option, however, is that it only lists printers hooked up to your PC. So if you're working on a document that will be sent to an imagesetter or other high-resolution device for final printing but you're using a lower-resolution device like a laser printer for proofing, you should set the Target Printer Resolution option to match the final printer's settings.

Figure 3-4:
With Facing Pages checked (top), you can place elements across pages. With it unchecked (bottom), you can't.

The wonderful world of dpi

What is *dpi*? It's not pronounced *dippy*, by the way, but *dee pee eye*, and it stands for *dots per inch*. When you print to a laser printer, a dot-matrix printer, an imagesetter, an inkjet printer, or anything more advanced than two cans tied to a string, everything is converted to a series of black dots. The pattern of black dots on the white paper simulates the shades of gray that you see. But if you use a magnifying glass, you'll see the dots. (For color printing, there are four sets of dots per page: one cyan, one magenta, one yellow, and one black. The way these colors combine when overprinted creates the range of colors that you see.)

A printer's dpi number tells you the size of the dots. The smaller the dots, the finer the image, because it gets harder and harder for the human eye to see the dots as they decrease in size. Small dots fool your eye into thinking that it's seeing true shades of gray or color hues.

Take a look at the following figure. At left, it shows an image reproduced at 1270 dpi, which is what an imagesetter can achieve and the setting that is used for magazines and books. At right, it shows portions of the same image reproduced at smaller dpi sizes: 600, 300, and 72 dpi.

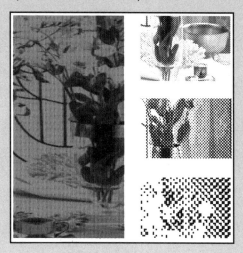

Suppose that you plan on printing the final document on a 1270-dpi imagesetter but you have a 300-dpi laser printer in your workgroup and you'll be using the laser printer to proof your document on a daily basis. To make sure that you're prepared for the final output device, enter the imagesetter's resolution, 1270, into the Target Printer Resolution option box.

Dividing Your Document into Columns

After you press the Enter key or click on the OK button, PageMaker presents you with one or more blank pages. How do you go on from here? How do you tell PageMaker your basic settings, such as the number of columns per page? Look to the Layout menu for the answer.

The first thing you'll probably want to set up is the number of columns and the amount of space between them (called a *gutter* by publishing types). Use Layout⇨Column Guides to do so. When you choose this command, PageMaker displays the Column Guides dialog box, as in Figure 3-5. The figure shows the dialog box with sample settings and the effects of those settings on the pages behind the dialog box.

The dialog box can change slightly, based on the following:

✔ If you selected both Double-Sided and Facing Pages, you can access separate Left and Right option boxes. To do so, select the Set Left and Right Pages Separately checkbox at the bottom of the Column Guides dialog box (as shown in Figure 3-5).

✔ If you deselected the Double-Sided checkbox in the Page Setup dialog box, you won't get separate fields for Left and Right pages.

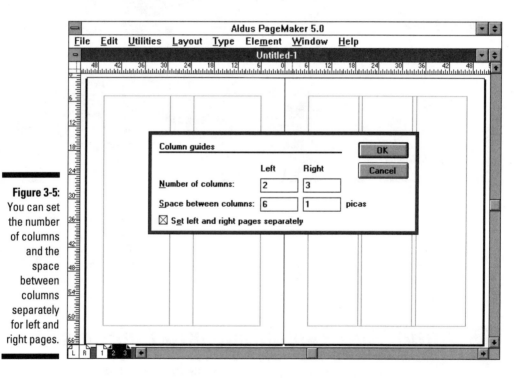

Figure 3-5:
You can set the number of columns and the space between columns separately for left and right pages.

Suppose that you have a three-page document, and you set the margins and columns for a *spread* (two facing pages). But if you move to page 3 by clicking on the page icons in the bottom left corner of the PageMaker window, you discover that no columns are set for that page. What gives? You told PageMaker what you wanted to do, and now it's ignoring you, just like your kids when you tell them to turn off that stupid Barney show and watch something that provides a realistic portrayal of dinosaurs, like "The Flintstones."

The problem is that the Column Guides command only affects the pages you're currently viewing. That may be okay when you're working in a small document, but what if you're creating a 112-page annual report? Choosing Column Guides 56 times may get a little repetitive. Luckily, you can set columns for your entire document by using something called *master pages,* which we'll get to in the next chapter (in the "Putting It All Together with Master Pages" section, to be exact).

Setting Rulers and Guides

Guides and *rulers* help you correctly position text and graphics on your pages. You can set up PageMaker so that page elements *snap* to guides and ruler positions. When the snapping function is turned on, page elements act as if they're magnetically attracted to guides and rulers. If you turn on Snap to Rulers, for example, and you drag a graphic near a ruler increment, the graphic jumps into alignment with the increment. You access snapping controls by choosing commands from the Layout⇨Guides and Rulers submenu, shown in Figure 3-6. A check mark next to an option means that it's enabled.

Rulers

Displaying the rulers makes it easier to place text and graphics accurately. There's really no reason not to display them.

However, you have to decide whether you want to enable Snap to Rulers (or Ctrl+Shift+Y, as in, "Yowsa, what the heck is *Y* doing here?"). When the function is turned on, PageMaker aligns anything that you draw or place on the page along one of the tick marks on the ruler (whether or not the ruler is displayed). If you select inches as your measurement unit (explanation upcoming), elements snap to the nearest $1/32$ of an inch; if you select picas, they snap to the nearest point. It's a great way to make sure that elements aren't positioned all cockeyed from one another, creating those slight disparities in alignment that make folks bug-eyed as their brains notice that something is amiss though they can't quite figure out what it is.

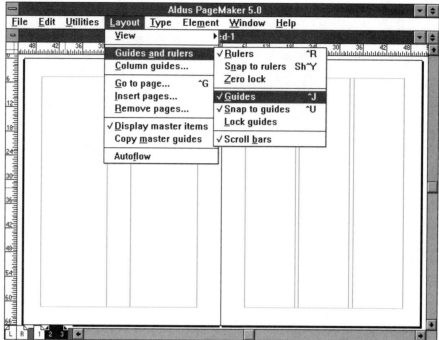

Figure 3-6:
Controls
over rulers
and guides
reside in the
Layout
menu.

So how do you decide what unit of measurement your rulers use? There's no option in the Layout menu; you need to open up the Preferences dialog box (File⇨Preferences), shown in Figure 3-7. Here's where you choose the measurement system as well as establish other preferences that affect the way that PageMaker implements a variety of options and commands.

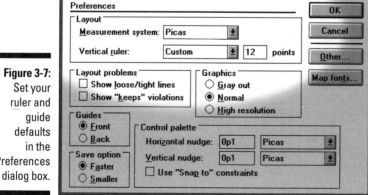

Figure 3-7:
Set your
ruler and
guide
defaults
in the
Preferences
dialog box.

For setting ruler preferences, you have two pop-up menus: Measurement System and Vertical Ruler. The Measurement System option determines what unit of measurement will be used throughout your layout — not only in the rulers, but also in dialog boxes, the Control palette, and so on. Chances are, you'll choose Inches or Picas; the inch is the basic measurement unit in the U.S., and the pica is the preferred system of measurement in U.S. publishing. But you can also choose Millimeters (the unit used in Canada and most of the rest of the world) and Ciceros (the unit used in European publishing). If you choose Inches Decimal, you get 10 tick marks per ruler inch rather than the standard 32. Use whatever you're comfortable with.

The Vertical Ruler setting lets you choose a different measurement system for the vertical ruler. It doesn't affect other parts of the PageMaker interface. Why does PageMaker give you this second measurement option? The answer is based on a publishing tradition that you probably won't ever care about. But here goes anyhow: In traditional publishing, layout artists measured text width in picas and length in inches. The text's column width was usually narrow, so using a finer measurement system made sense. But the text length could be tens or even hundreds of inches for a magazine or newspaper article — maybe thousands of picas. Thus the two measurements. You still hear the occasional reference to *column inches* at some crusty old newspapers, but you should avoid using the term in polite company.

One alternative is to use the Custom option and define your own ruler measurement units. You may want to use this option to establish a measurement unit that represents lines of text. Of course, because the height of a line depends on the text's leading — an amount that changes from document to document and even within a single document — you can't have a single measurement unit that would accurately reflect all lines of text throughout a publication. But you can set the Vertical Ruler measurement unit to Custom and make it the number of points used for the basic body text's leading. Then you can easily count lines or, if the text in your text blocks aligns to the vertical ruler's increments, you can make sure that graphics and other elements line up with the text's baselines.

The last ruler setting, found in the Layout⇨Guides and Rulers menu, is one you'll rarely use: Zero Lock. It's easier to show you this setting than explain it, so look at the ruler in Figure 3-8 and compare it to the ruler in Figure 3-6. Notice that the numbers are different: The numbers on the rulers have moved. At the upper left corner of the rulers is an icon that looks sort of like a cross. This is the *ruler origin box*. By dragging the box, you can move the zero points from their default location, which is the upper left corner of a page, as demonstrated in Figure 3-8. Choosing Zero Lock prevents you from making this change. If you do somehow move your zero points and want to put them back in their default positions, just double-click on that cross-like part of the ruler.

Ruler origin box

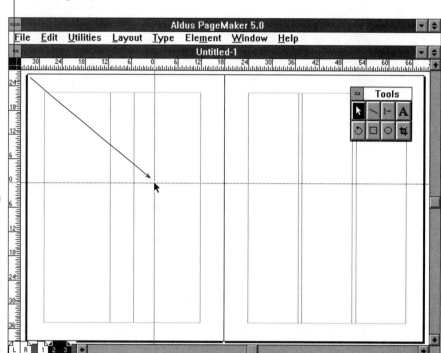

Figure 3-8:
Drag from
the ruler
origin box to
change the
locations of
the zero
points on
the rulers.

Guides

Rulers are great as general positioning aids. But what if you want to line an element up to something more specific? That's where ruler guides come in handy. Look at Figure 3-9 and notice the dotted horizontal line that extends along the bottom of the chart. That line is a *ruler guide*. Look below the ruler guide for a similar line and a special double-arrow cursor. That's a ruler guide in the process of being created.

To create a ruler guide, move the cursor to a ruler, hold down the mouse button, and drag a ruler guide out to where you want it to be. (You can drag from either ruler: The horizontal ruler at the top of the screen gives you horizontal guides and the vertical ruler along the left side gives you vertical guides.) These guides are best used to align elements to something inside a graphic or block of text. For example, Figure 3-9 shows guidelines placed between the bottom of the chart and the bottom of the chart's labels. Establishing this pair of guidelines made it easier to properly position the label text.

Ruler guides aren't the only sort of guides you can create in PageMaker. The lines that indicate column gutters are also guides (and you can select them and move them).

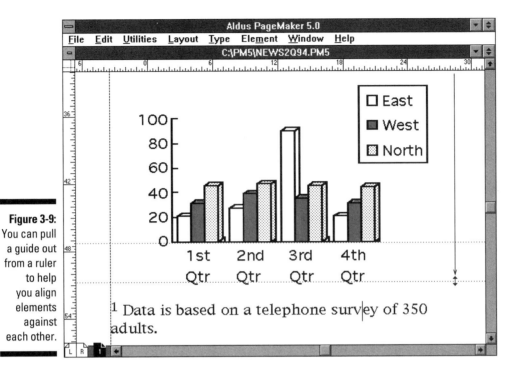

Figure 3-9: You can pull a guide out from a ruler to help you align elements against each other.

If you don't want guides — whether column guides or ruler guides — to be movable, select the Lock Guides command in Layout⇨Guides and Rulers. Alternatively, you can hold down the Ctrl key when selecting objects with the Arrow tool — this action makes guides inaccessible.

When you're positioning elements with your mouse, you can use guides to ensure alignment, not just as a general target. If you select Snap to Guides (found under Layout⇨Guides and Rulers), any text or graphic you place near a guide (column or ruler guide) jumps into alignment with that guide. You get instant, accurate alignment.

The last thing you should know about column guides is that you can control how PageMaker displays them. The Preferences dialog box (File⇨Preferences) offers a Guides option that gives you two choices: Front and Back. If you select Front, the guides display on top of every element they pass through. If you select Back, they display behind elements and so are visible only where there are no graphics or text on the page. In either case, the guides don't print when you print the document — they're only visible on-screen.

Let's see, now — you've got your pages, your margins, your columns, and your guides. Now, at last, you're ready to add text, which just happens to be the subject of the next chapter.

Chapter 4

The Joy of Text

*R*emember back in fourth grade, when the world's most evil teacher, Mrs. Sneets, made you write a letter to a senator in cursive writing? You had to use one of those cartridge pen thingies — the ones that leave big old blobs of ink on your paper if you're not careful. The Evil Mrs. Sneets insisted that each and every word of your letter be *perfect.* One ink blob, one cursive *S* without the appropriate curlicue, and you had to start all over from scratch. On the whole, it took about a zillion hours (including a few that you should have been able to spend at recess, playing murder ball) to create a document that pleased The Evil. And then the stupid senator didn't even write you a real letter back — just had his secretary send you some lame form letter that didn't even *mention* your request to have the F.B.I. do some checking up on one Mrs. Harriet M. Sneets.

Happily, those days are behind you forever. Now that you have PageMaker, you'll never again have to worry about ink blobs and making the perfect cursive *S.* You can generate a document full of fabulous looking words with hardly any trouble at all. And if you do make a mistake, correcting it is easy. Why, you're almost certain to get the job done way before recess time.

Importing Text vs. Entering Text Directly

There are two ways to put text into your PageMaker document: *import* it (PageMaker calls this *placing* text) or enter it directly.

To import text simply means to copy the contents of a word processor document into PageMaker. As an alternative, you can use PageMaker's own text-editing tools to compose your text in PageMaker. These aren't either/or options — you'll probably import some of your text and enter some directly.

✔ Compose your main text — the stories and the like that make up the bulk of your publication — in a word processor and import it into PageMaker. Why? Because a word processor is designed just for this kind of work. And almost everyone has a word processor, so a group of people can exchange drafts of stories for editing and approval purposes if necessary. Also, if different people are working on different stories for the publication, it would be pretty hard (not to mention downright chaotic) to have each person enter their text into the main PageMaker document. Instead, the different writers and editors should create and refine the stories in their word processors and then turn the whole batch over to the PageMaker layout person.

✔ Create the embellishments and adjustments — titles, tables of contents, and corrections — in PageMaker. It doesn't make a lot of sense, say, to type in a newsletter's issue date or to write a headline in your word processor and then import it into PageMaker. In the first case, it's more work to import such a small piece of text than it is to just create it in PageMaker. In the second case, chances are that the headline created in the word processor won't fit in the space allotted by the layout, so you'll have to rewrite it or at least edit it in PageMaker anyhow.

Importing text

To place text in PageMaker, follow these steps:

1. Use File⇨Place or the shortcut Ctrl+D.

PageMaker gives you the Place Document dialog box shown in Figure 4-1.

Figure 4-1: The Place Document dialog box lets you import text files into your layout.

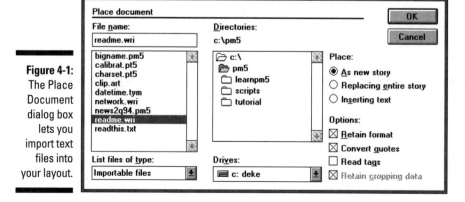

2. Navigate through the directories on your disk in the normal Windows fashion.

Double-click on a directory to open it. Then scroll through the text files and select the one you want.

3. Choose placement and formatting options.

First, the placement options. The three choices are pretty straightforward: As New Story brings the text in as a new, separate story, in addition to whatever you might have in your publication already. Replacing Entire Story substitutes the text for the text in the story that's currently selected — it can be selected with the Arrow, Text, or Rotate tools (the only tools that can select a text block). Inserting Text adds the text into the currently selected story, at the location of the text cursor — this option appears only if you have selected a story by clicking in it with the Text tool.

Second, the formatting options. You should be familiar with the text you're importing before selecting any of these options — you might look at the text first in a word processor to see, for example, whether it uses style sheets or includes character formatting. If it does, you must decide whether you want to retain the styles or formatting. (This issue is covered in more detail later in this chapter.)

4. Click on OK.

After you select a file to import and choose the importing options you want to use, PageMaker redisplays the current page and shows you a status box indicating that it's importing the text as you requested. When PageMaker finishes importing the text file, and you move the cursor onto the page or pasteboard, the cursor changes to a paragraph shape (📰) or a snake shape (🔟).

Note that when you choose the File⇨Place command to begin the importing process, you don't have to be at the page where you want the text to be placed. You can switch pages after importing the text but before clicking at a location at which it will be placed (as described in the next step.) But it's easier to be at the desired page before you import the text.

5. Click at the spot where you want PageMaker to place the text.

Depending on whether you turned on the Autoflow option in the Layout menu, the text flows across the page, within the current column, or through several pages (which PageMaker creates if needed), as described a little later.

The three faces of text insert

PageMaker is a big fan of using icons to tell you what it's doing or capable of doing. In the case of placing text, you have three possibilities:

- The paragraph icon lets you place just one column of text. To get this icon, make sure that Autoflow is unchecked in the Layout menu.

- By holding the Shift key when placing text, you get the semiautomatic flow icon, which lets you place one column right after another.

- By selecting the Autoflow option in the Layout menu before placing text, you tell PageMaker to place all the text in as many columns on as many pages as it takes.

Chapter 9 covers text placement in more detail.

Entering text directly in your PageMaker document

If you want to create text right in your PageMaker document instead of importing it from another source, just follow these steps:

1. **Select the Text tool.**

2. **Click where you want to type.**

3. **Start typing.**

After you enter some text, switch to the Arrow tool by clicking on its icon in the toolbox. Then click on some part of your text. PageMaker displays a pair of lines with little tabs on them. What you're seeing is called a *text box* or *text block* — which is simply a container that PageMaker created to hold your text. You can reshape or resize the text block at any time, as explained in greater detail in Chapter 9.

If your view or text size makes the text too hard to read while you're typing, you can zoom in by choosing Layout⇨View and choosing a bigger view size. Or you can switch to PageMaker's built-in word processor, the Story Editor, by pressing Ctrl+E or choosing Edit⇨Edit Story. (Use Ctrl+E or Edit⇨Edit Layout to get back to the layout.) Chapter 10 covers how to use the Story Editor in more detail.

Let Style Sheets Do the Formatting

With your text in place, you're ready to format it — to decide what font, size, spacing, and alignment it has. You can always format any text manually in

PageMaker, but you can also have PageMaker format a lot of text for you. The following sections explain both options.

Basic formatting methods

As in most Windows programs, the first step of formatting text is to highlight it. To do this, click on the Text tool in the toolbox, move the mouse cursor to the beginning of the text you want to format, hold the mouse button down as you move to the end of the text you want to format, and release the mouse button. Then go to the appropriate menu option to apply the text formatting. If you want to select all text in a story, click the text cursor anywhere in the story's text and choose Edit⇨Select All or Ctrl+A.

In PageMaker, the Type menu presents formatting options in a series of menus and dialog boxes. Figure 4-2 shows the Type menu's commands as well as those for one submenu, Type style.

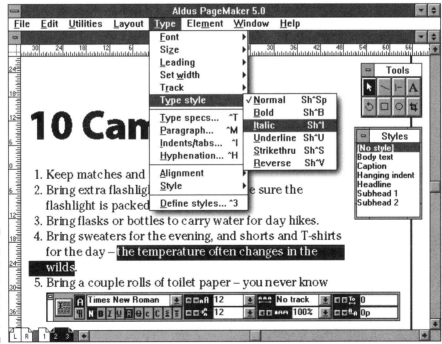

Figure 4-2: The Type menu and its Type Style submenu.

But constantly moving up to the Type menu and wading through its many submenus and dialog boxes is hardly the most efficient way to format text — you can quickly tire out your mouse hand. Fortunately, there's a better way — and sometimes two better ways — to do most common formatting.

One of the better ways is to use the set of keyboard shortcuts, such as Ctrl+ Shift+I for italics. It makes sense to use these shortcuts when you're editing text or doing other keyboard work because you don't have to move a hand to the mouse.

The other better way is to use the Control palette, shown at the bottom of Figure 4-2, which puts most formatting options in one place, for easy mouse access. The Control palette offers two modes: text mode (which PageMaker calls *character mode*) and paragraph mode. You switch between the two by clicking on the mode icons in the Control palette (labeled in Figure 4-3). When the palette is in text mode, it offers buttons for changing text size, leading, kerning, and character formatting (boldface, italic, superscript, and so on). When it's in paragraph mode, the palette provides buttons for setting paragraph formatting options such as paragraph alignment, spacing, and indents.

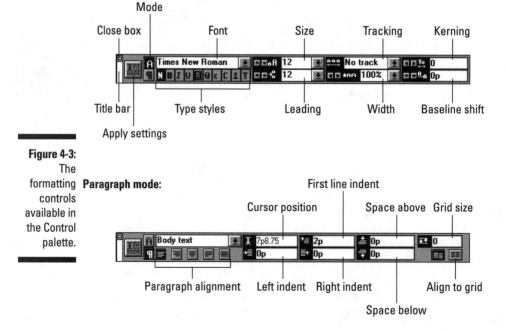

Figure 4-3:
The formatting controls available in the Control palette.

Figure 4-3 shows the Control palette for text and paragraph modes. (If you were to select a graphic, the palette would display yet another set of options, based on the type of graphic selected.) Text mode is the default setting when the Text tool is active, but if you switch to paragraph mode, the palette retains that mode the next time you select text.

Table 4-1 shows which formatting options are available where. Text settings are also available via the Type Specifications dialog box (Type⇨Type Specs, or Ctrl+T). Paragraph settings are also available through the Paragraph Specifications dialog box (Type⇨Paragraph, or Ctrl+M).

Keep in mind these tips when using the Control palette:

✔ The triangle symbols next to some options are *nudge icons*: clicking on the up and right triangles nudges the value to the next highest increment; clicking on the down and left triangles nudges the value to the next lowest increment. If you hold down the Ctrl key when clicking a nudge icon, PageMaker nudges the value to 10 times its current value.

✔ If you click on the big icon on the left of the palette (the one that indicates what type of element is selected), it applies any changes you have made in the palette to the selected text. Pressing Enter has the same effect, as does clicking the cursor on something outside the palette.

✔ The value for the baseline shift nudge controls is based on the value set for the Vertical Nudge settings in the Preferences dialog box's Control Palette section. (Use File⇨Preferences to get the Preferences dialog box.)

✔ The other nudge settings for text formatting are fixed and cannot be changed.

Table 4-1	Text Formatting Options		
Formatting	*Shortcut*	*Palette Mode*	*Menu Path*
Baseline shift	None	Text	Type⇨Type Specs⇨Options
Boldface	Ctrl+Shift+B	Text	Type⇨Type Style⇨Bold
Center-align	Ctrl+Shift+C	Paragraph	Type⇨Alignment⇨ Align Center
Color	None	None[1]	Type⇨Type Specs
Column break	None	None	Type⇨Paragraph
Font	None	Text	Type⇨Font
Force justify	Ctrl+Shift+F	Paragraph	Type⇨Alignment⇨ Force Justify
Hyphenation	Ctrl+H	None	Type⇨Hyphenation
Indent first line	None	Paragraph	Type⇨Paragraph
Indent left margin	None	Paragraph	Type⇨Paragraph
Indent right margin	None	Paragraph	Type⇨Paragraph
Italics	Ctrl+Shift+I	Text	Type⇨Type Style⇨Italic
Justify	Ctrl+Shift+J	Paragraph	Type⇨Alignment⇨Justify

(continued)

Table 4-1 *(continued)*

Formatting	*Shortcut*	*Palette Mode*	*Menu Path*
Keep lines together	None	None	Type⇨Paragraph
Kerning	None[2]	Text	Type⇨Track
Leading	None[3]	Text	Type⇨Leading
Left-align	Ctrl+Shift+L	Paragraph	Type⇨Alignment⇨Align Left
Letter spacing	None	None	Type⇨Paragraph⇨Spacing
Normal	Ctrl+Shift+ spacebar	Text	Type⇨Type Style⇨Normal
Orphan control	None	None	Type⇨Paragraph
Page break	None	None	Type⇨Paragraph
Reverse	Ctrl+Shift+V	Text	Type⇨Type Style⇨Reverse
Right-align	Ctrl+Shift+R	Paragraph	Type⇨Alignment⇨ Align Right
Ruling lines	None	None	Type⇨Paragraph⇨Rules
Size	None	Text	Type⇨Size
Space after	None	Paragraph	Type⇨Paragraph
Space before	None	Paragraph	Type⇨Paragraph
Strikethrough	Ctrl+Shift+S	Text	Type⇨Type Style⇨ Strikethru
Style	None	Paragraph[4]	Type⇨Style
Tab settings	Ctrl+I	None	Type⇨Indents/Tabs
Tracking	None[5]	Text	Type⇨Track
Underline	Ctrl+Shift+U	Text	Type⇨Type Style⇨Underline
Widow control	None	None	Type⇨Paragraph
Width	None[6]	Text	Type⇨Set Width
Word spacing	None	None	Type⇨Paragraph⇨Spacing

[1] Use the Colors palette

[2] If text cursor is between two characters and no other text is highlighted

[3] Ctrl+Shift+A sets leading to Auto

[4] You can also use the Styles palette

[5] Ctrl+Shift+Q sets tracking to No Track

[6] Ctrl+Shift+X sets width to 100 percent (normal)

The wonders of styles

Styles — also called *style sheets* — enable you to ap[ ]
formatting options (type size, style, paragraph inde
with just a keystroke or two. Using styles is a real ti
you decide that you want all your headlines to appe
and size, with a certain amount of leading, you can (
lines. Then, instead of formatting each headline one
type style, then the size, and then the leading, you j
to the appropriate heads. PageMaker automatically [ ] ....ig ioi
you in one fell swoop. You might create one style for your first-level headlines,
one for second-level heads, one for body text, and one for your picture captions. Styles not only give you more time to work on more important matters
than formatting, they ensure consistency. You don't have to remember from
one day to the next what formatting you're supposed to use for a particular text
element.

To create a style, you follow the same steps you use to format text through the
Text Specifications dialog box (Ctrl+T or Type⇨Type Specs) and Paragraph
Specifications dialog box (Ctrl+M or Type⇨Paragraph). You can even take
already-formatted text and have PageMaker create a style based on that text —
no need to specify that formatting again.

Here's how to define a new style.

1. Choose Type⇨Define Styles or use the shortcut Ctrl+3.

PageMaker displays the Define Styles dialog box shown in Figure 4-4. If you
selected text before opening up the dialog box, the [Selection] option is
highlighted, which means that PageMaker has collected all formatting
information for the selected text and will base the new style's characteris-
tics on it. If no text is selected, the new style is based on the characteris-
tics of a style called No Style, which every PageMaker document has.

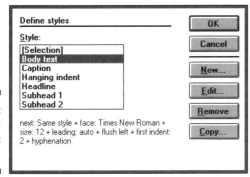

Figure 4-4:
The Define
Styles
dialog box.

2. Click on the New button.

You get the Edit Style dialog box, shown in Figure 4-5. Enter the name of the new style in the Name field. Notice that the Based On and Next Style fields are already filled in, either with No Style or whatever style was applied to the text that was selected when you entered the Define Styles dialog box. If you want to base the new style on a different style, select that style from the Based On pop-up menu.

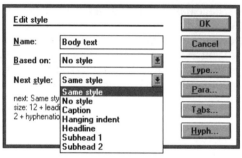

Figure 4-5:
The Edit Style dialog box is where you begin the actual definition of styles.

Microsoft Word defines a default style called Normal, and chances are that the text you create in Word has this style applied (it is, after all, the default). If you create a style in PageMaker called Normal, Word text using the Normal style will be redefined to use the PageMaker Normal style. Going this route saves you from having to apply your basic body style — the style used for the bulk of your text — in PageMaker. It's especially handy because there's no way to edit the settings for No Style, so you can't really use that as your body style. (The chances that the No Style formatting will match your body style's settings are close to zero.)

4. Choose the Next Style.

Some text elements are always followed by text that has a different style. For example, a byline may always be followed by text that uses the Normal style. In cases such as this, you should set the Next Style option box to that other style (use the pop-up menu to select any existing style). Otherwise, select Same Style.

5. Use the Type, Para, Tabs, and Hyph buttons to access the Type Specifications, Paragraph Specifications, Indent/Tabs, and Hyphenation dialog boxes.

This is the point at which you specify how you want to format any text to which you apply the style. (These options are all covered in detail in the next section.)

6. Click OK in each dialog box until all dialog boxes are gone.

Congratulations! You have a new style.

To modify an existing style, use the Define Styles dialog box just as if you were creating a new style, but click on the Edit button instead of the New button. You can delete a style by clicking on the Remove button.

If you want to use styles that were defined in another PageMaker document, click on the Copy button and find the document through the dialog box. After you select the document, click on OK. You may get a get a prompt asking whether it's okay to copy over existing styles. If you give PageMaker the go-ahead, any style in your current document whose name is the same as in the other document is replaced by the other document's style. So be careful when using this feature.

You can define styles based on the formatting of existing text. One way is to select some formatted text and go to the Define Styles dialog box as described above; the formatting of the selected text becomes part of the new style. Or you can use the Control palette instead. To use this method, click with the Text tool inside the paragraph whose formatting you want to turn into a style. Make sure that the Control palette is in paragraph mode, highlight the style name, enter a new name, and press Enter. The result is a new style.

A similar technique is to highlight the text, hold down the Ctrl key, and click on No Style in the Styles palette. This takes you to the Edit Style dialog box, in which you can enter the new style name and make changes. This method isn't as fast as the Control palette method, but it does let you make further changes to the style more easily.

You may notice that a paragraph's style name sometimes has a plus sign (+) after it. The plus sign means that the selected paragraph's formatting has been modified from the style's settings. Perhaps, for example, you italicized some text or changed the margin for that paragraph. Note that the text cursor has to be on the modified portion of the paragraph; the plus sign appears only if the current selected text in the paragraph is different from the style settings.

Importing styles

When you import text and check the Retain Format checkbox, PageMaker loads in any formatting defined in the word processor document. PageMaker adds many default formatting settings for options that the word processor doesn't offer, such as tracking. But the basics — such as font, size, indents, and alignment — are all brought into PageMaker along with the text. PageMaker can also import your word processor styles.

Sometimes, the text you're importing has a style name not defined in PageMaker. When this happens, PageMaker creates a new style (based on No Style). It adds an asterisk (*) to the style name so that you can tell that the style is undefined in PageMaker. For example, if you don't have a Credit style in PageMaker but there is a Credit style in an imported Word document, PageMaker applies a style called *Credit** to the paragraphs coded with Credit. Simply edit the style settings the normal way and change the name back to *Credit*.

Sophisticated Formatting

PageMaker's higher-level formatting options — such as tracking, widow and orphan control, and hyphenation — are found in four dialog boxes: Type Specifications, Paragraph Specifications, Tabs, and Hyphenation. You use these same dialog boxes whether you want to establish formatting for a style or simply format an individual block of text. If you're creating or editing a style, you access the dialog boxes by clicking on the Type, Para, Tabs, or Hyph buttons in the Edit Style dialog box. If you want to simply format a bit of selected text, you click on the appropriate dialog box name in the Type menu.

The Type Specifications dialog box

The options in the Type Specifications dialog box (displayed by choosing Type⇨Type Specs or pressing Ctrl+T) are fairly self-explanatory, especially if you read the typographic descriptions in Chapter 2. But three deserve a little explanation:

- ✔ The Track option should usually be set to Loose. If you think Loose is too spacey, choose Normal or Tight, but definitely stay away from No Track.

- ✔ The No Break option prevents a selected word from being hyphenated and breaking between lines.

- ✔ Reverse changes the text to its reverse color. For example, it changes black text to white text. However, it does not change the background color. So, if you have black text on white paper and you select this option, you get white text on white paper — which makes the text invisible. If you want white text on a black bar, you can do it by following the steps in Chapter 6.

The Options button brings up the Type Options dialog box, shown in Figure 4-6. This dialog box is full of options that you rarely alter. You can define how certain attributes are implemented — such as the size reduction for small caps, the size reduction and positioning of subscripts and superscripts, and the amount of baseline shift. Here are some recommendations:

✔ Leave Small Caps Size at 70 percent unless you want a different look than you're getting. This will typically happen only if you're using small caps on type that's larger than about 24 points.

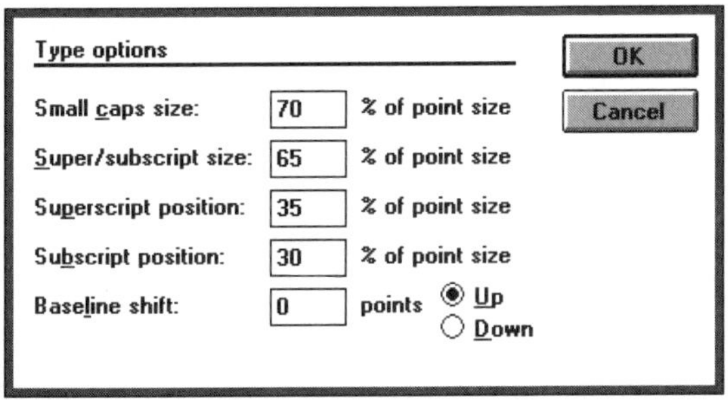

Figure 4-6:
The Type
Options
dialog box
showing
some
recommended
settings.

Type options		OK
Small caps size:	70	% of point size	Cancel
Super/subscript size:	65	% of point size
Superscript position:	35	% of point size
Subscript position:	30	% of point size
Baseline shift:	0	points ● Up ○ Down

✔ Change the Super/Subscript Size to 65 or 70 percent for most text under 14 points. PageMaker's default of 58.3 percent is definitely too small.

✔ Change the Superscript Position to 35 percent and the Subscript Position to 30 percent for typical text — where the point size is 8 to 12 points and the leading 1 to 2 points more than the text size. These settings keep your superscript and subscript characters readable while at the same time minimizing the chances that they'll bump into your normal text. For example, a subscript won't bump into the ascender (the part that sticks out from the top) of an *h* or *l*.

The Paragraph Specifications dialog box

As with Type Specifications options, the options in the Paragraph Specifications dialog box are fairly self-explanatory. Again, though, here is some advice regarding a few of the options:

✔ You'll get an error message if your left margin, or the combination of your first-line indent and left margin, is a negative number. PageMaker simply won't let you have the text extend to the left of the column margin.

✔ If you have multiple language dictionaries, you can select a hyphenation dictionary for a particular language. This feature is great for people working on multilingual publications. Most people will just have US English or their country's language.

✔ The Page Break Before and Column Break Before options force a page or column break before the selected paragraph, so that the paragraph will start at the top of a column or page. You might want to use this option in a headline style to ensure that headlines always appear at the top or a page or column. But use it judiciously, or you may find that you have only one or two paragraphs per page or column.

✔ It's considered a publishing faux pas when the last line of a paragraph appears in a different column or page than the rest of its paragraph. It's considered equally gauche to let a page break or column break separate the first line of a paragraph from the rest of the paragraph. When the solo line is the last line of the paragraph, it's called a *widow*; when it's the first line, it's an *orphan*. The Widow and Orphan Control settings keep you from making such gaffes. You can tell PageMaker that if it needs to put a page or column break in the middle of a paragraph, it must place the break a certain number of lines away from the first or last line. You specify the number of lines in the Widow and Orphan Control option boxes. Most of the time, though, you can just leave these options unchecked and say to heck with elitist publishing snobs. If it really bothers you to have a single line of a paragraph at the bottom or top of a column, set both values to 1 or 2.

✔ If the Include in Table of Contents checkbox is selected, the style that you're editing or creating will be included in any table of contents generated by PageMaker for this document. Chapter 12 explains how to generate a table of contents.

✔ Click on the Rules button to bring up a dialog box to apply rules above and/or below paragraphs. You can also draw rules with the Line tool.

✔ The Paragraph Specifications dialog box has a button labeled Spacing, which opens the dialog box shown in Figure 4-7. Most of these settings are pretty arcane for business users, although the typographically savvy in the crowd will want to adjust them to fit personal preferences. But even for everyday business documents, it's a good idea to make a few adjustments to whatever style it is you use for basic body copy. (Remember, if you want these settings to become the default settings for all future documents, you have to adjust them while no document is open.)

✔ Set the Maximum setting for Word Space to 125. Change Leading Method to Baseline. The adjustment to the Word Space setting will result in less space between words — PageMaker's default often results in a gap-toothed appearance. Changing the Leading Method to Baseline doesn't noticeably affect your document; the setting just requires the document to use the leading method that's used by typographers, which helps ensure good output when you send files to a typesetter or imagesetter.

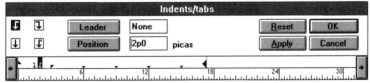

Figure 4-7:
The
Spacing
Attributes
dialog box.

Tabs

Although labeled Indents/Tabs, this dialog box (shown in Figure 4-8) is really best used for setting tabs. Instead of setting indents here, set them with the margin controls in the Paragraph Specifications dialog box. Using the ruler in the Indents/Tabs dialog box can be tricky, even if it is a more visual approach. Of course, if you feel more comfortable setting indents here, go for it. But it can get pretty confusing with all those little tab and indent thingamabobs floating around.

Setting tabs can be dicey because no matter how carefully you map out where you think tab stops should be for particular text, things often don't work out right the first time. That's why there's an Apply button in this dialog box: If you click on it after setting tab stops, PageMaker displays the currently selected text with these tab settings applied (the text will have to have tab characters in it, of course). If the tabs aren't right, just change them or click on Cancel to get out of the dialog box. (The Reset button puts back the default tab settings: a left-aligned tab every half inch.)

Figure 4-8:
The
Indents/
Tabs dialog
box.

To create tabs, follow these steps after opening the Indents/Tabs dialog box.

1. Click anywhere on the ruler to create a tab stop.

You can select the tab and drag it to change its location.

2. **Click on the icon representing the alignment you want the tab stop to have.**

The top two icons represent left alignment and right alignment, respectively; the bottom two icons are for center and decimal alignment. In a left-aligned tab, text after the tab character begins at the tab location and continues to the right. In a right-aligned tab, text typed after the tab character ends at the tab (and begins to the left). In a center tab, the tab becomes the center point for text entered after the tab. In a decimal tab, text (usually numbers) aligns on the first period found after the tab character.

3. **If you want a tab leader, select a leader type.**

A *leader* is a repeating sequence of characters, usually periods, that fills the space between the text before the tab and the text after the tab. Click on the Leader button to access a pop-up menu that offers four leader options: periods, dashes, underlines, and Custom, which lets you enter up to two characters. (If you enter two, they alternate, such as *+*+*+*+*+.)

4. **Repeat Steps 1 through 3 for each tab you want to create.**

You should know a few things about using tabs:

✔ Click on the Position button to access a pop-up menu that offers these choices: Add Tab, Delete Tab, Move Tab, and Repeat Tab.

✔ Don't bother using the Position pop-up menu for its first two options (Add Tab, Delete Tab). It's easier to just click on the ruler to insert a tab stop and drag a tab marker away from the ruler to delete it.

✔ The Move Tab option is good for precisely positioning a tab stop. Just click on the tab to select it, enter a new value in the option box to the right of the Position button, and then select the Move Tab option. The tab moves to the numerical location you indicated.

✔ The Repeat Tab option in the Position pop-up menu also comes in handy. Here's how it works: Suppose that you have a five-inch column. If you define a tab stop at the one-half inch mark and select Repeat Tab from the Position pop-up menu, you get a tab every half-inch across the column.

✔ If you have very wide columns, the entire column may not display in the Indents/Tabs dialog box. Use the arrow icons at the far left and right of the dialog box to scroll through the column.

✔ When setting tab stops in a paragraph style, set only those tabs you'll use frequently (see Chapter 5 for the examples of bulleted and numbered lists). You can always use Type➪Indents/Tabs (Ctrl+I) to set individual tab stops for specific paragraphs.

Hyphenation

Hyphenation is a mark of professionalism in publishing. It has nothing to do with proving that you remember how to properly hyphenate words such as *hy-phen-at-ed*. It has to do with the more mundane fact that hyphenation gives typesetters more opportunities to create even spacing, because they have more chances of having a similar number of characters on each line.

The narrower your columns, the more you'll want hyphenation, because the narrower the columns, the more chances that you'll get awkward spacing if you turn hyphenation off. Fortunately, PageMaker does the hyphenation for you.

This last component of a style, accessed via the Hyph button in the Define Styles dialog box, is one you'll rarely change once you've set it. As with Spacing attributes, it's a prime candidate for changing in the Normal style with no document open so that it becomes the default setting for all future documents. Figure 4-9 shows the Hyphenation dialog box. The options are simple:

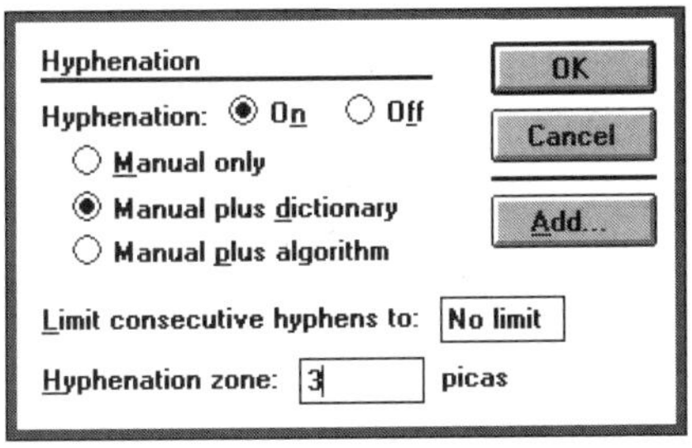

Figure 4-9:
The
Hyphenation
dialog box.

✔ Keep Hyphenation set to On for most text. Exceptions are headlines and other such large text.

✔ Select the radio button for Manual Plus Dictionary as the hyphenation method. PageMaker will look at a dictionary of words for your current language rather than trying to figure out where the hyphens go on its own. (That's what Manual Plus Algorithm does — and it's no match for using a dictionary, even if it is a little faster.) The Manual Only setting requires you to insert hyphens yourself using Ctrl+hyphen, which goes against the point of having automatic hyphenation in the first place.

✔ You could have a serious argument with a professional typographer over the best setting for Limit Consecutive Hyphens To. Choose a number between 2 and 4, and you'll be all right. The higher the number, the more consecutive lines can end with a hyphen. The more such lines, the harder it is for your eye to track which line to jump to next. Conservative typographers say to set this value to 2, while moderates say 3. The more adventurous among us say set it at 4. After all, if you have four hyphenated lines in a row and they're making the text hard to read, you can always manually override the hyphenation.

✔ Speaking of overriding hyphenation, the way to do it is by entering Ctrl+hyphen (called a *discretionary hyphen* or a *soft hyphen*) at your preferred hyphenation spot. That doesn't guarantee that the word will be hyphenated, only that *if* PageMaker needs to hyphenate the word, it will put the hyphen at the spot you indicated. (Entering Ctrl+hyphen right before a word tells PageMaker not to hyphenate it.) *Never* hyphenate by using the keyboard hyphen character — if the text wraps, the hyphen will move with it, and you'll have stray hyphens in your text.

✔ Set the Hyphenation Zone to between 0.2 and 0.6 inches — the default 0.5 is fine for most text, although for narrow columns (3 inches or less), a smaller value gives PageMaker more flexibility. PageMaker will not hyphenate a word that begins within the hyphenation zone. Hence, the rule is this: The larger the zone, the fewer hyphenations and the rougher the rag of the text; the smaller the zone, the more hyphenated words and the smoother the rag.

Sometimes, PageMaker doesn't know how to hyphenate a word — maybe it's a company name or a rarely used word, or maybe it's a word like *project* that is hyphenated different ways depending on whether it is a verb or a noun. You can add such words to PageMaker's dictionary by clicking on the Add button and entering the word. If you have multiple language dictionaries installed, make sure that you tell PageMaker which dictionary the word is supposed to be added to (there's a Dictionary pop-up menu). You can even tell PageMaker to pay attention to capitalization so that it hyphenates the word only if it is lowercase or only if it is a proper name.

You can also type in a word that you want PageMaker to delete from its dictionary — just click on the Remove button after entering the word. (You'd use this option if you incorrectly specified the hyphenation for a word.)

Putting It All Together with Master Pages

Okay, so now you know how to create margins, columns, text, and styles. That doesn't help you with other common elements. For example (quick, here's a pop quiz), remember that you learned in Chapter 3 that specifying the number of columns for one page doesn't specify the columns for other pages? You do? Then you may also remember that you can use *master pages* to specify basic layout elements like the number of columns just once in a document.

You may have noticed at the far bottom left of the PageMaker window that there are page icons labeled *L* and *R* (or just *R* if the document is not double-sided). These icons represent the left and right master pages. Anything that you put on these pages is added to all pages in a document — both those that you create after making up your master pages and those created earlier.

Here are the two most important things you can do with master pages:

✔ Set column settings for all pages

✔ Set repeating elements, such as page numbers or company logos

To establish your master pages, you just click on the L or R page icons to highlight them. Then you can create columns and enter text as you normally would.

You already know how to set columns (if you've forgotten, go back to the "Dividing Your Document into Columns" section in Chapter 3). This time, the columns you set will apply to any pages in your document for which you haven't already established column settings. Master page settings do not override settings you establish on individual pages.

Figure 4-10 shows a sample set of master pages. Elements on these master pages include a line at the bottom of the page (created with the Line tool); the name of the publication, *Environmental Weekly*, on the left side; and the letters *RM* on the right side (a right-aligned tab was used to set the *RM* text). That *RM* is PageMaker's code for the current page number. To access this code, press Ctrl+Shift+3. If you enter this code on a right-hand page, you'll see *RM* on the master page — *RM* for *Right Master*. If you enter it on a left-hand page, you see *LM*, for *Left Master*. But the real pages in your document will be numbered with regular page numbers.

You don't have to use just text as a repeating element. The line in Figure 4-10 is an example of using graphics as a repeating element.

 Anything on a master page appears under anything created on a standard page. Thus, if you place a colored rectangle on a master page, any text placed on a standard page in the same location is placed on top of that rectangle, assuming text wrap is turned off for the rectangle (see Chapter 7 for details). On a standard page, whatever was created most recently is placed on top of anything created before it in the same location. You can use this fact to create watermarks on pages. (Yes, you can shuffle elements to change their stacking order. You use the commands Element⇨Send to Back or Ctrl+B and Element⇨Bring to Front or Ctrl+F.)

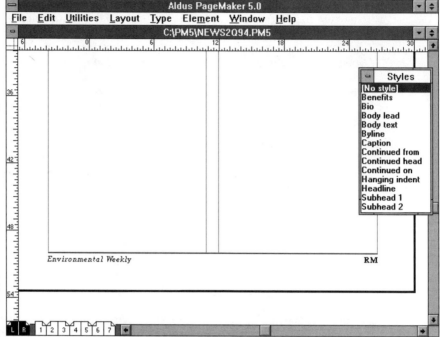

But what if you don't want a repeating element on every page? For example, you probably don't need a page number on the first page of a newsletter — it's obviously the first page — and you may not want one on the last page because you may want to leave the bottom blank for the address labels. You have three choices:

1. Don't use master pages.

2. Use master pages but hide all master page items when needed. To hide master page items on a particular page, uncheck Display Master Items (in the Layout menu) for that page.

3. Use master pages but cover up elements that you don't want to print on a particular page. Here's how: Create a solid white rectangle with the Rectangle tool. Then use the Fill and Line dialog box (Element⇨Fill and Line) to change the Fill setting to Solid, the Color setting to Paper (which is white), and the Line setting to None. (Use this technique when you want to hide some master page items but keep others.)

The approach you pick depends on how many pages don't use the master page elements. Chances are that most will, so the second and third options are the ones you'll use.

Believe it or not, you've now gone through the basic PageMaker features. Although there are others you'll want to learn to use, you're done with the basics of setting up a document and adding text. Now it's on to the fun stuff, like adding fancier text and graphics.

Chapter 5

I Have a Point to Make Here

● ●

In This Chapter

▶ How to choose between bulleted and numbered lists

▶ The best ways to create bulleted lists

▶ Cool symbols to use as bullets

▶ The best ways to create numbered lists

▶ Formatting hints for lists

● ●

*P*oint by point — that's a great way to make your message clear. Nothing grabs a reader's attention like a good, old-fashioned bulleted or numbered list. You know, the kind that lays out a series of facts one after the other, with each point introduced by a number, the ever-popular bullet, or, as in this book, a check mark. There's no mistaking where each point begins and ends. And it's easier for the reader to make sense of your message because it's broken down into easily digested, bite-size morsels of information.

This chapter shows you how to create your very own bulleted and numbered lists in PageMaker. By the time you're through, you, too, will be able to transform boring, hard-to-chew pages of facts and ideas into a tasty platter of information appetizers.

Should I Use Numbers or Bullets?

The choice is often subjective, but there are some guidelines you can follow:

✔ If the order of items is not important, bullets are typically best. Using numbers implies that the order of the items is meaningful.

✔ If the order of items is important — as in a top ten list that is organized from least to most important, or steps in an instructional guide (like this one) — use numbers.

✔ If you will refer back to each item, use a number so that the reader can tell which item you're discussing.

In PageMaker, the basic techniques for creating bulleted and numbered lists are the same. The first part of this chapter discusses bullets, and the second part explains how to adapt the same techniques to generate a numbered list. So if you're creating numbered lists, make sure that you read the text about bullets first.

The Wrong Way to Make Bullets

In your word processor, adding bullets is usually as simple as clicking on a bullet icon in a button bar. In PageMaker, the process is a bit more complex. To make the creation of bullets easier, Aldus includes an *addition* — a separate program that runs inside PageMaker — to add bullets to text.

By the way, additions are available only if you've installed them. If you don't find the Aldus Additions command in the Utilities menu, or if a particular addition covered here does not appear in the Aldus Additions submenu, you need to install the additions from your original PageMaker disks. You don't have to reinstall PageMaker, just the additions, so use the custom-install option. (See Appendix A for complete installation information.)

Although the Bullets and Numbering addition is supposed to make life easier, it can actually make life more difficult if you use it without doing some preliminary legwork, which is documented in the "How to Do Bullets Right" section. The following steps explain how to use the addition and demonstrate its limitations.

1. **Enter or place the text that needs bullets**.

   Each item should be its own paragraph.

2. **Make sure that the Text tool is selected.**

   Highlight all the paragraphs that should get bullets. Or, if the paragraphs in the story that need bullets all use the same paragraph style (and no other paragraphs use that style), just click anywhere in the story.

3. **Choose Utilities⇨Aldus Additions⇨Bullets and Numbering.**

   The Bullets and Numbering dialog box appears, as shown in Figure 5-1.

4. **Select one of the five bullet types or access any character in the current font by clicking on the Edit button.**

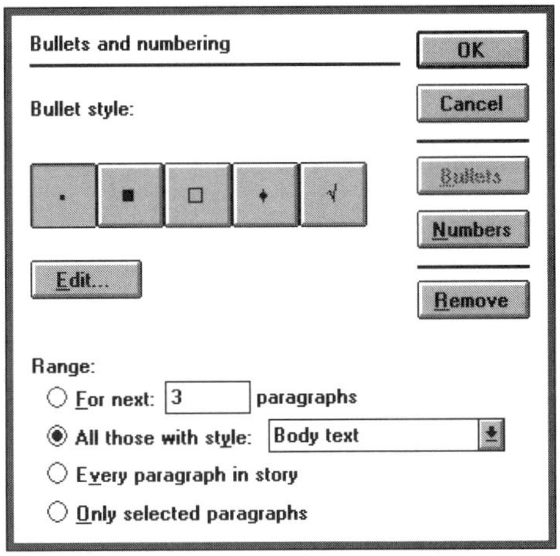

Figure 5-1:
The Bullets
and
Numbering
dialog box
lets you
apply a
bullet to
your list text.

If you click on the Edit button, you get the dialog box shown in Figure 5-2. (If the Bullets and Numbering dialog box doesn't seem to offer an Edit button as in Figure 5-1, first click on the Bullets button at the right side of the dialog box.) Notice that the default font and size may not match that of your text; you may need to experiment with this setting to get the bullets to look right. After selecting a character, press Enter to return to the Bullets and Numbering dialog box.

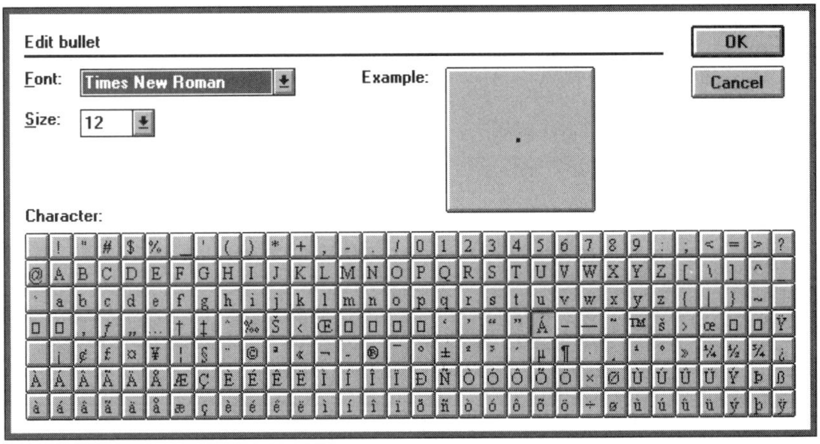

Figure 5-2:
The Edit
Bullet dialog
box lets you
select a
character
from the
current font.

5. Select a Range radio button.

You can apply bullets to a range of paragraphs, to all text formatted with a specific style, to all paragraphs in the selected story, or to the selected paragraphs only.

6. Click on OK to apply the bullets.

What's so bad about this addition? The obvious problem is that the bullets it displays are hard to read, so it's difficult to know exactly what the bullets will look like until you apply them. (Another irritant is that after you've used the addition, it switches you from the Text tool to the Arrow tool, even though you're more likely want to remain in text mode.)

But the bigger problem is that it doesn't indent your text correctly, as shown in Figure 5-3. Notice the huge gap between the bullet and the text? Not very attractive. And did you see any controls for this spacing in the Bullet and Numbering dialog box? Nope. Instead, the space after the bullet is determined by the tab setup for the paragraph's style. If your paragraph style happens to indent the first line of text in each paragraph, the resulting bullets are not as bad (see Figure 5-4), but still not very attractive.

Fortunately, there's a <u>R</u>emove button in the Bullets and Numbering dialog box that can get rid of those unsightly bullets. Now might be a good time to use it.

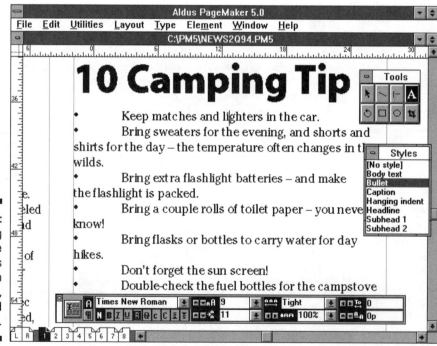

Figure 5-3:
The spacing
of the
bullets
creates an
unattractive,
gap-toothed
look.

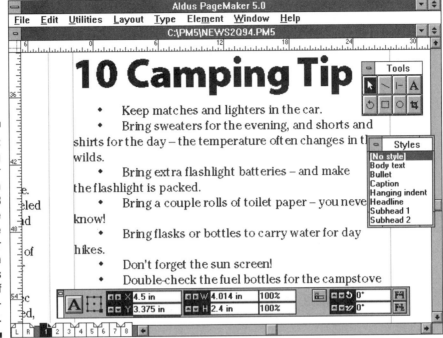

Figure 5-4:
This spacing
is better
than that in
Figure 5-3
because the
bullets are
shifted over
to the right a
little, but it's
not much of
an improve-
ment.

✔ If you choose a large-size bullet in the Edit Bullets dialog box, you get mispositioned bullets, as Figure 5-5 shows.

✔ The default size for bullets is 12 points; the default font is Times. Those choices are fine if your current text is also 12-point Times. But chances are, it isn't. And after you change the font and size of the bullets, the settings are retained for the next time you use bullets. That's great if the next set of bullets you want happens to be for the same type of text. If not, you need to change the size and font again. So in most cases, you have the extra step of going to the Edit Bullet dialog box and changing the bullet settings to better match your text settings.

✔ If you use the addition to add bullets and then add new paragraphs later that also need bullets, you have to highlight the new paragraphs and have the addition add bullets only to them. If you use the option to apply bullets to all paragraphs with a certain style, it adds an extra bullet to any paragraph that was already bulleted — it can't check to see whether a bullet is already there.

Therefore, the time to use this addition is after you've created all your paragraphs and indented them properly. The following section explains how to create bullets and indent text the old-fashioned way (that is, manually). Later on — in the "Good-looking bullets" section — we'll revisit the Bullets and Numbering addition and show how it can come in handy.

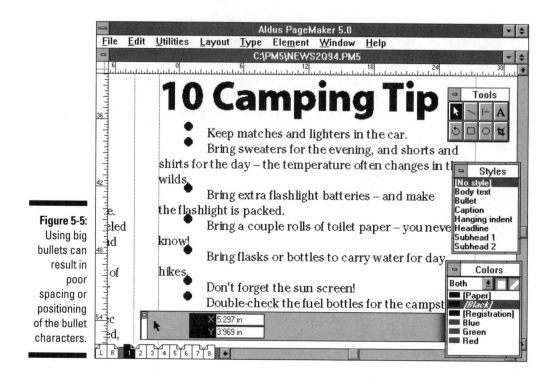

Figure 5-5:
Using big
bullets can
result in
poor
spacing or
positioning
of the bullet
characters.

How to Do Bullets Right

Before you learn the techniques for easy bullet entry, you should know the two best ways to present bullets:

- **As a lead-in:** In this case, the bullet is simply the first character in the paragraph, followed by a space. The space can be a standard space or one of PageMaker's special space characters, such as the em space (Ctrl+Shift+M) or en space (Ctrl+Shift+N), both discussed in Chapter 6. You can also use a tab, provided that you define the tab location to put the text close to the bullet. The paragraph usually has the first line indented when the bullet is formatted as a lead-in style.

- **As an hanging indent (also called an indent hang):** In this case, the bullet hangs out to the left of the text's left margin. Typically, the bullet aligns with the leftmost point of the column, and all text in the paragraph is indented to a point a little to the right of the bullet. Often, the space between the bullet and the text is an en space (Ctrl+Shift+N).

Figure 5-6 shows the two styles in action. Usually, it makes no difference which one you use — they both look good and are easy to read. However, the longer the bulleted paragraphs are, the more awkward the hanging-indent technique can look.

Now it's time to see how to create these bulleted paragraphs easily.

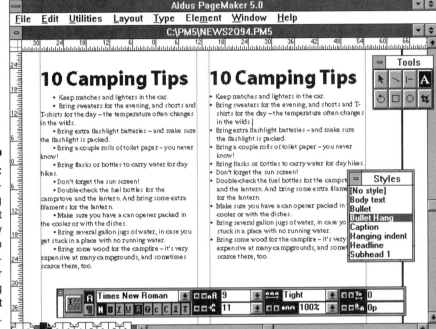

Figure 5-6:
Good-
looking
bulleted text
is usually
one of two
types: lead-
in (left) or
hanging
indent
(right).

Creating bullets in your word processor

You may have had a nagging question in the back of your mind about bullets: Why not just enter them in your word processor? After all, programs such as Word automate the entering of bullets (and numbers) with their bullet (and number) buttons. Or, for that matter, why not just enter the bullet the standard Windows way? Press and hold the Alt key while typing the numbers 0149 on the keypad. The result is a nice, round bullet. And for a numbered list, why not just type in the number?

Why not indeed? Using Alt+0149 works particularly well for the lead-in style of bullet because all it does is add a bullet. You can also add the en space in your word processor.

If you want to use the hanging indent style of bullets, either insert an en space or tab character after the bullet. If you use Word, its bullet tool automatically puts that tab in after the bullet. Use a separate style in your word processor for your bulleted paragraphs, and have a style with the same name in PageMaker that sets up the paragraph so that the hanging indent works properly (this technique is described shortly).

Creating bullets in PageMaker

If you're entering text in PageMaker, use the same techniques described above for creating bullets in a word processor. The only difference is that you can access the bullet character by pressing Ctrl+Shift+8. (Alt+0149 also works, if you find that easier to remember.) After your bulleted text is entered — whether placed from your word processor or created directly in PageMaker — you're ready to format it, as explained in the upcoming sections.

Lead-in bullets

For lead-in bullets, there really is no formatting to do: The text typically uses the basic text style. After all, it's just standard text that begins with a bullet and a space.

However, in order to make bulleted text appear more distinct, some folks vary their bulleted text slightly from their standard text. For example, if the standard text has the first line of each paragraph indented, the bulleted text might not be indented. Or if the standard text has no first-line indent, the bulleted text might have the indent. There's no right or wrong — it's just a question of personal taste and effective communication.

If you want to make your bulleted text slightly different from your standard text, create a new style based on your standard text's style (see Chapter 4 for details). Make the changes to the style's formatting and apply the new style to your bulleted text.

If you're using this style for multiple documents, like each issue of a newsletter, create a style with the same name in your word processor and apply it to your bulleted text there. That'll save you the work of going through your layout looking for bulleted text that needs to have the bullet style applied.

Hanging-indent bullets

Because using a hanging indent means setting paragraph margins that are different from those in your standard text, you need to set up a style for bulleted text that uses a hanging indent. The actual settings will depend on your text's font and size, but the steps are the same.

You can create a style with the same name in your word processor that simulates how the bulleted text will look in PageMaker. That saves production time and gives you an idea of what the text will look like when it's laid out in PageMaker.

Chapter 4 covers the creation of styles in detail; the following steps concentrate just on creating a hanging-indent bullet style.

1. **Choose Type⇨Define Styles (or press Ctrl+3).**

   PageMaker opens the Define Styles dialog box.

2. **Select the style that you want to base the bullet style on**.

   This typically is the Normal style or whichever style is used for the standard text.

3. **Click on the New button.**

   You get the Edit Style dialog box.

4. **Enter a name for the style (such as *Bullet*).**

   Note that the Based On pop-up menu shows the standard text's style. (If it doesn't show the style you want to base the bullet style on, use the pop-up menu to select another style.) Chances are that bulleted text will be followed by bulleted text, so make sure that Next Style option is set at Same style (the default).

5. **Click on the Para button.**

   PageMaker displays the Paragraph Specifications dialog box.

6. **Set the First value to a negative number, moving the bullet out past the text's left margin.**

   Set the Left value to the same number, but make it positive. For example, if you set First at -0.1, set Left at 0.1. This setting moves the entire paragraph back to the right so that the bullet stays inside the column and the text remains indented to the right of it. Figure 5-7 shows the settings for a sample style.

7. **Continue editing as required**.

   Chances are, getting the correct amount of indent so that everything lines up will take some experimentation, so you'll have to edit the bullet style several times until you get settings that work. Note that the First setting determines the distance between the bullet and the indented text on subsequent lines of the paragraph. The key is to find a value that equals the distance between the left side of the bullet and the right side of the space that follows.

Figure 5-7:
Sample
settings for
creating a
hanging
indent.
Notice that
the First and
Left settings
have
opposite
values.

Paragraph specifications		OK

Indents:

Left [0.1] inches

First [-0.1] inches

Right [0] inches

Paragraph space:

Before [0] inches

After [0] inches

Cancel

Rules...

Spacing...

Alignment: [Left ▼]   Dictionary: [US English ▼]

Options:

☐ Keep lines together   ☐ Keep with next [0] lines

☐ Column break before   ☐ Widow control [0] lines

☐ Page break before   ☐ Orphan control [0] lines

☐ Include in table of contents

Using tabs with bullets

As mentioned earlier, you could use an en space or a tab to separate a hanging-indent bullet from the text that follows it. For that matter, you could use a tab with lead-in bullets, too. Using a tab gives you more control over the space between the bullet and the text that follows because you can define that tab amount to be whatever you want.

If you're going to use tabs with bullets, keep in mind that you have two options: Put a tab after the bullet or put a tab both before and after the bullet. In the first case, you're just trying to control the distance between the bullet and the text that follows it. In the second case, you're trying to position the bullet relative to the column's left margin as well as determine the space between the bullet and the text that follows it. You'll use the second approach more often if you're using nonstandard bullet shapes (described in the next section). But it also comes in handy if you have long bulleted items or bulleted text that could be buried in a sea of text and you want to create some break in the left margin to compensate. Figure 5-8 shows examples of bullets with tabs.

The indent values should match the tab value. If you set the tab stop to be 0.188 inches, for example, set the First indent of the paragraph to be -0.188 inches and the Left indent to be 0.188 inches.

To set up the tab stops, first experiment with the tab ruler (it's shown in Figure 5-9). (Use Type↷ Indents/Tabs or Ctrl+I to access it.) Try different settings and click on the Apply button to preview them. When you like what you have, write the settings down and click on OK. Then add the settings to your bullet style if you created one as explained in earlier sections.

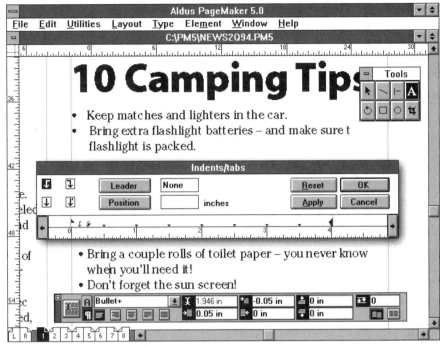

Figure 5-8:
The top two bullets use a tab after the bullet character to increase the space. The bottom two bullets have a tab before the bullets to indent them slightly.

PageMaker has a counterintuitive response in setting tab stops that affects how your bullets look. When using inches, you're restricted to certain settings if you position the tab markers with the mouse. For example, you can set tabs to 0.156 but not 0.15, at 0.188 but not 0.175, or at 0.219 but not 0.2. What's happening is that PageMaker is moving the tab markers to the nearest tick mark on the ruler, overriding your ostensibly WYSIWYG placement. (Even more oddly, this doesn't happen for indents or other paragraph settings.) The solution is to select each tab stop one by one and enter the value you want in the Position field — which can be a lot of work — or to switch your measurement system to picas and points, the system used by professional layout artists. A pica is ¹/₆ inch and is made up of 12 points (so there are 72 points in an inch).

Good-looking bullets

Filled circles aren't the only kind of bullets, although they're the most common kind. You can use all sorts of characters and symbols as bullets. Some are variations on traditional bullets — such as squares and triangles — while others are more distinct — such as arrows, logos, and stylized letters. Figure 5-9 shows a sampling of bullet characters that were created using the ornamental font Zapf Dingbats.

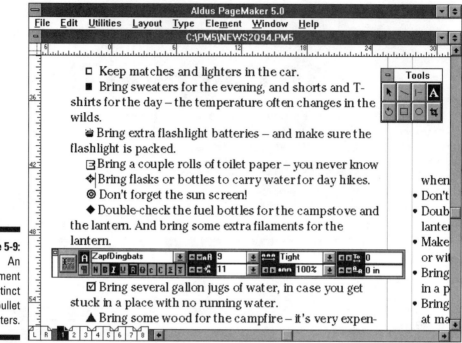

It's the moment you've been waiting for! Here's where we demonstrate a good use for the Bullets and Numbering addition. Basically, it's good for locating bullets and — as you'll see in the next section — assigning numbers. To search through a few amazing bullets in Zapf Dingbats or some other wacky font, select your properly indented paragraphs with the Text tool, choose Utilities⇨Aldus Additions⇨Bullets and Numbering, and click on the Edit button. Select Zapf Dingbats or some other font from the Font pop-up menu and peruse the symbols available to you. (If you're having problems recognizing the symbols because they're too small, you can select a larger size from the Size pop-up menu to view a bigger version of the bullet in the example box. Just be sure to reduce the size to the desired setting before returning to the Bullets and Numbering dialog box.)

When you've selected your special bullet, press Enter to go back to the Bullets and Numbering dialog box. Then select the Only Selected Paragraphs radio button and press Enter again. All selected paragraphs get the new bullet.

Working with Numbered Lists

Numbered lists aren't all that different from bulleted lists. So if you skipped here directly and didn't read the first part of the chapter, which covers bulleted lists, go back and read it. Okay, now we can continue.

The Bullets and Numbering addition has most of the same limitations for numbering as it does for bullets, so using it isn't the best choice in all circumstances.

The addition can automatically add numbers to selected text. Choose Utilities⇨Aldus Additions⇨Bullets and Numbering to display the Bullet and Numbering dialog box. Then click on the Numbers button to display the Numbering Style options shown in Figure 5-10.

Figure 5-10:
This second group of options in the Bullets and Numbering dialog box lets you automatically number paragraphs.

Bullets and numbering

OK

Numbering style:
- ● Arabic numeral 1,2,3...
- ○ Upper roman I,II,III...
- ○ Lower roman i,ii,iii...
- ○ Upper alphabetic A,B,C...
- ○ Lower alphabetic a,b,c...

Separator: None
Start at: 1

Range:
- ○ For next: 3 paragraphs
- ● All those with style: Body text
- ○ Every paragraph in story
- ○ Only selected paragraphs

Cancel

Bullets

Numbers

Remove

Like the bullet feature, the numbering feature uses tab stops after the numbers, so you have to define those tab locations in your style to make sure that space between the numbers and the text that follows is not ungainly.

Unlike the bullet feature, the numbering feature gives you more control over the formatting. You get a choice of numbering styles; separators (the characters that appear after the number: a period [.], colon [:], close bracket []], close parenthesis [ )], or none); and the number that the numbering starts with. And this feature uses the current font and size (the bullet feature uses a default setting or the last setting used, not the current paragraph's settings).

Again, manually numbering your list items or using your word processor's numbering option is probably the better way to do things. Some word processors offer numbering features that automatically add numbers in front of each paragraph in a document and correctly number each paragraph as you enter it. They may even renumber paragraphs if you insert new ones or delete existing ones. Alas, if only PageMaker's numbering addition or Story Editor was this smart.

However you enter the numbers, here are a few design tips to follow:

✔ It's best to put at least an en space (Ctrl+Shift+N) after a number to help set the number apart from the text.

✔ If your numbering goes beyond 9, make sure that the numbers align where the decimal point would be (or actually is, if you use a period after the numbers). The easiest way to do this is to put an en space before items 1 through 9, because an en space is the same width as a numeral in most fonts. You could also set up tabs so that the numbers are right-indented to a tab stop and then set up a left-aligned tab stop at whatever distance you'd like for the text that follows (your paragraph settings should also reflect this indent so that subsequent lines in the paragraph indent to the same spot). For numbers created by your word processor's numbering tool or through the Bullets and Numbering addition, this is the simplest way to format the text.

The technique for defining tab stops in a numbered list is the same as for a bulleted list, with one exception. The first tab is a right-aligned tab that indicates where the numbers align to, rather than a left-aligned tab that indicates where the number begins (as it is for bullets). The second tab, as for bulleted lists, is a left-aligned indicator of where the text begins. Use the value of that second tab as the value for the First and Left indent settings for the numbered paragraphs (remember that the First value should be a negative number; the Left value should be a positive number). Figure 5-11 shows an example of how a numbered list should look, with the tab settings displayed on the tab ruler.

Making Lists More Effective

Now that you know how to create bulleted and numbered lists, one more topic needs to be addressed before moving on: how to make lists look more attractive. Good-looking bullets and numbers are a start, but they're not the end.

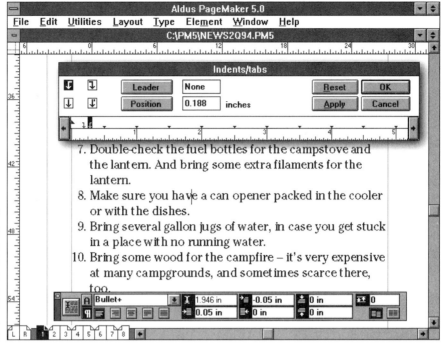

Figure 5-11:
Use tabs in
a numbered
list to align
numbers on
the decimal
point.

For simple lists, plain bullets and plain numbers are fine. But if you have lots of text or long items in a list, you can do more. For example, put the numbers in boldface and follow them with a two- or three-word summary (maybe in boldface, too) of the paragraph's contents. That's a great way to drive home the points, especially in a list of steps or rules. You can do the same with bullets.

You might also use different bullet characters or styles. For example, if you're listing winners in a contest, you might make the winner's bullet solid and the finalists' bullets hollow. Or you might use lead-in bullets for short items in one list and use hanging-indent bullets for a series of multiple-line explanations in another list.

No matter how you do it, the thing to consider is whether it's important to differentiate types of lists and then figure out how to do so in a way that is pleasing and not confusing or distracting — the differences should be obviously tied in to differences in the types or contents of text.

Chapter 6

Fancy Type Tricks

• •

In This Chapter

▶ Starting off with initial caps and drop caps

▶ Setting white text against a black background

▶ Creating a hanging indent

▶ Using real quotes and other symbols

▶ Experimenting with paragraph rules

• •

*N*ow that you've read about all the practical-but-boring stuff you can do with text, it's high time to learn a few fancy text tricks. This chapter explains how to create and use drop caps, reverse text, special symbols, and a bunch of other neat stuff. Every effect you're about to learn is either very difficult or darn near impossible to pull off using traditional typesetting and paste-up techniques.

But before we begin, a little cautionary note is in order: Use these effects sparingly. Why? Well, a document filled with fancy text tricks is kind of like a barking dog. A few tricks, like a few barks, attract attention and get people to read your document, which is always job number one. But if you throw in too many tricks, the document starts barking so loudly and so frequently that your reader is unable to focus on your message. An overly fancy document can appear pathetic and even irritating in its desire to attract attention. As any dog learns after it chews up your favorite pair of slippers, there's good attention and there's bad attention, and the quality of the attention generally works inversely to the quantity. In other words, a little goes a long way.

Begin with a Big Cap

One of the easiest ways to make your document look a little more lively is to start each story off with a bang. A big capital letter at the beginning of an article can help set it apart from neighboring articles. It also serves as a visual guide-post, clearly showing where the article begins.

There are two kinds of big caps: the initial cap, which is basically just a big capital letter at the beginning of a story, and the drop cap, which is lowered into the article. Examples of both appear in Figure 6-1.

Figure 6-1:
The initial cap rests on the baseline with the rest of the text on the first line (top); the drop cap drops below the baseline (bottom).

Initial cap —

We, the people of the United Nations, determined to save succeeding generations from the scourge of war, which twice in our lifetime has brought untold sorrow to mankind, and to reaffirm faith

Drop cap —

We, the people of the United Nations, determined to save succeeding generations from the scourge of war, which twice in our lifetime has brought untold sorrow to mankind, and to reaffirm

Big cap maintains high profile

Making an initial cap is only slightly harder than it looks. When you make the first character of text larger than the others, PageMaker has a habit of messing things up a bit, which necessitates a little fixing up on your part. Here's how it works.

1. **Select the first character in your story.**

   Drag over it with the Text tool. Presumably, you start your sentences with a capital letter, so this letter will serve well as an initial cap.

2. **Select a larger type size.**

Either select it from the Type⇨Size submenu or enter the new size into the size field in the Control palette. You can also press Ctrl+period or Ctrl+Shift+period a few times to enlarge the cap incrementally.

3. **Change the font.**

This step is optional, but sometimes initial caps look a little more distinctive if you select a different font. In Figure 6-2, for example, the initial cap font is Berkeley Black, which contrasts nicely with the Helvetica text. In typography, *Black* means bolder than bold.

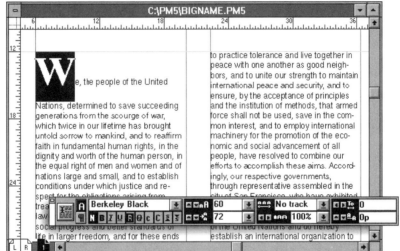

Figure 6-2: The result of changing the type size to 60 points and the font to Berkeley Black.

4. **Record the leading.**

As you can see in Figure 6-2, there's now a big gap between the first line of type and the ones that follow. This is because the leading is set to Auto, which changes the leading to 120 percent of the type size. Because the size of the first character grew, the leading grew, too. To equalize the leading, select some text in the paragraph — make sure that the initial cap is not selected — and note the value in the leading field of the Control palette. For example, if you have 12-point type, you will have 14.4-point leading.

5. **Adjust the leading.**

Press Ctrl+A to select all the text in the story. Then change the leading value in the Control palette to the one you noted in the preceding step and press Enter. The leading equalizes, but as shown in Figure 6-3, the top of the initial cap is cut off. This bit of weirdness doesn't affect the printing of the character, but it doesn't look right on-screen.

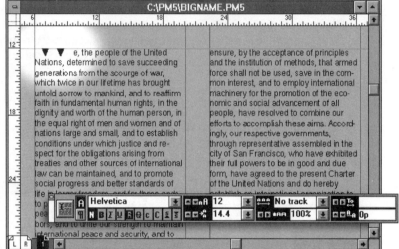

Figure 6-3:
After you
equalize the
leading, the
top of the
initial cap
appears to
be cut off.

6. Add some carriage returns.

Remember back in Chapter 2, when we said that you should never use carriage returns to insert space between lines of text? Well, here's an exception to that rule. To fix the screen appearance, you need to bring the initial cap back into the text block. Move the insertion point to the beginning of the text block by pressing the left arrow key and then press the Enter key a couple of times. To complete the effect, force the screen to redraw. You can do this by pressing the keyboard shortcut for the current view size, scrolling the cap off and then back onto the screen, or changing the view size. In Figure 6-4, for example, the view size is magnified to 200 percent.

7. Kern the cap closer to the rest of the text.

The last thing to do is to eliminate that awful gap between the initial cap and the other letters in the word. Click just to the right of the initial cap with the Text tool, as shown in Figure 6-4. Then press Ctrl+minus (be sure to use the minus key on the keypad) a few times to kern the letters closer together. If you kern too far, press Ctrl+plus (also on the keypad) to spread the letters.

See, we told you that this was more complicated than you thought it'd be. Who'd have thought that increasing the size of a single letter could entail so much wiping of the old brow?

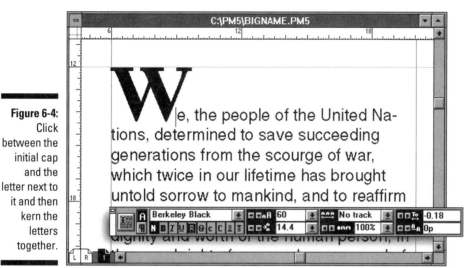

Big cap gets down with the little letters

Drop caps are about a zillion times — give or take a few million — easier to create because PageMaker 5 automates the process. The program ships with an addition that automatically creates drop caps to your specifications. All is not perfect in the world of drop caps — they're difficult to edit, PageMaker doesn't always size your text correctly, and it won't work if your text is already kerned — but as long as you prepare your text correctly, the process is swift and straightforward.

1. **Make your text all the same size.**

   If you changed the size of your first letter as described in the preceding steps, return it to its original size. The first cap should be the same size as the rest of the text in your story.

2. **Unkern the first character.**

   If you kerned between the first and second characters, select the first two characters and change the kerning value in the Control palette to 0.

3. **Change the font.**

   Now that we're done with those optional, what-if steps, let's move on to move essential issues. Change the font of the first character as desired. For the example, the *W* was changed to Berkeley Black in Figure 6-5.

4. Apply the Drop Cap addition.

With the first letter selected, choose <u>U</u>tilities⇨Aldus <u>A</u>dditions⇨Drop Cap to display the Drop Cap dialog box shown in Figure 6-5.

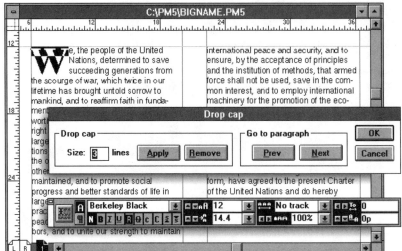

Figure 6-5:
The Drop Cap addition automatically converts a selected character into a drop cap.

5. Specify the size of the cap.

In the Drop Cap dialog box, specify the size of a character in terms of lines of type. Enter the number of lines you want to fill into the Size option box and then click on the Apply button. In Figure 6-5, the Size value is 3, so the drop cap is three lines of type tall. PageMaker automatically sizes the character, subscripts it, and tabs the surrounding text so that the characters don't overlap.

6. Press the Enter key to close the dialog box.

That's all there is to it.

One unfortunate aspect of this addition is that it eliminates hyphens in the lines that contain the drop cap. Frankly, there's not a whole lot you can do other than manually change words. For example, if you wanted to hyphenate the word *Nations* in Figure 6-5, you'd have to enter *Na-* on the first line, and delete *Na* from the second line.

If you ever want to get rid of the drop cap, select the character, choose <u>U</u>tilities⇨Aldus <u>A</u>dditions⇨Drop Cap, and click on the <u>R</u>emove button. Then press the Enter key to again close the dialog box.

Be careful, though, if you have modified any lines of text affected by the drop cap. Any kerning, line breaks, tabs, and so on, other than those put in by the Drop Cap addition won't be removed when you remove the drop cap. Also, if you made modifications to your text after creating the drop cap, the addition may screw up the text in the process of removing the cap.

Reverse Text Tricks

Chapter 2 mentioned how the Reverse command (Type⇨Type Style⇨Reverse) works. But it didn't go into much detail about how and when you should use it.

The Reverse command is most useful for setting white text against a colored background. The following steps describe how to use the command to create a logo that is half black against a white background and half white against a black background, as shown in the upcoming Figure 6-7. It's a simple effect, but it's guaranteed to add some visual interest to just about any page.

1. **Enter some text.**

   Create a new text block and enter two words.

2. **Set the font and type size.**

   Press Ctrl+A to select the entire text block. Then change the font and type size as desired. In the example in Figure 6-6, the font is Helvetica Compressed and the size is 60 points. As is always the case when creating special text effects, big text is best.

3. **Draw a rectangle around the second word.**

   Select the Rectangle tool (Shift+F6) and drag around the second word, as shown in Figure 6-6. If you don't draw it exactly right the first time, don't worry. You can edit the shape by dragging one of the corner handles with the Arrow tool.

4. **Make the rectangle black.**

   With the rectangle selected, choose Element⇨Fill⇨Solid. This changes the rectangle from transparent to black. You can no longer see the second word.

5. **Reverse the second word.**

   Select the Text tool (Shift+F4) and then double-click on the second word to select it. Even though the rectangle is in the way, the word becomes selected. Then choose Type⇨Type Style⇨Reverse (or press Ctrl+Shift+V) to change the second word to white.

6. Send the rectangle behind the text.

Still can't see the second word? That's because the rectangle is in front of it. Select the Arrow tool (Ctrl+spacebar), click on the rectangle, and choose Element⇨Send to Back (Ctrl+B). Your text should look something like that in Figure 6-7.

Figure 6-6:
Draw a rectangle around the second word by dragging with the Rectangle tool.

Figure 6-7:
The finished text reversed out against a black background.

Your more adventurous types may be wondering, "Can I do the same thing to a single letter? Can I make a letter half black and half white?" Nope, you sure can't. Sorry. You have to use a drawing program like CorelDraw to pull that off. And then you have to read *CorelDraw! for Dummies*, published by this same publisher. It's the perfect companion book for the perfect companion product. (The fact that one of the authors of the book you're now reading wrote *CorelDraw! for Dummies* is purely coincidental.)

However, you *can* do something almost as cool. If you set a reverse version of a text block in front of a standard version of it, you get an engraved effect like the one shown in Figure 6-8. The effect is subtle, but it's worth learning.

Figure 6:8:
Engraved
text created
by setting
reversed
text in front
of a black
version of
itself,
against a
white (top)
and light
gray
(bottom)
background.

The following steps make the process crystal clear.

1. Create some new text.

Make it big. If you want to work from the text in the previous steps, select all the text and choose Type⇨Type Style⇨Reverse or press Ctrl+Shift+V twice in a row.

2. Copy the text.

Switch to the Arrow tool and click on the text block to select it. Then choose Edit⇨Copy or press Ctrl+C to copy it to the Windows Clipboard. This saves the text for later use.

3. Press Ctrl+Shift+P.

This wonderful and little-known keyboard equivalent pastes what you just copied to the Clipboard at the exact location where it was when you copied it. So what you get is one text block positioned directly in front of another.

4. Nudge the text block down and to the right a little.

Or down and to the left, or up and to the left, or whatever. The point is, nudge it. You can nudge a selection by pressing the arrow keys. Each press of the arrow key moves the selection 1 point in the direction indicated on the key. The effect shown in Figure 6-8 required pressing the right-arrow key twice and the down-arrow key twice. (If 1-point nudges are too large, you can change nudge settings in $^1/_{10}$-point increments by choosing File⇨Preferences.)

5. **Reverse the text.**

    Select the Text tool (Shift+F4), click inside the text, and press Ctrl+A to select it. Then choose Type⇨Type Style⇨Reverse to change it from black to white.

The result is the effect shown in the first example of Figure 6-8. If that effect is too subtle for you, draw a rectangle around the text, fill it with light gray (by choosing Element⇨Fill⇨20%), and send the rectangle to the back of the document (Ctrl+B). The second example in Figure 6-8 shows the outcome.

Locating Those Special Typographic Symbols

Chapter 5 explained how to create numbered or bulleted lists using indents. The bullet (Ctrl+Shift+8) is only one of the many special characters and symbols that you can access inside PageMaker. The following sections describe these special characters and provide a little background about them.

Curly quotes and apostrophes

"Trevor, get back in the house this instant!" screamed Mary, ready to throttle the child.

"Trevor, honey, time to come in," Mary called casually.

See the difference? The straight quote (") is wooden and severe, while the curly quotes (" and ") are expressive and frankly more interesting to look at. It's also worth noting that the straight quote looks the same regardless of which side of the quotation it appears on; the curly quotes provide visual clues as to whether you're starting a quotation or finishing one.

But most folks use the straight quote because the key is properly labeled. Right there next to the Enter key is the straight quote, the one you remember from your typewriter days. The curly quotes are hidden.

✔ To access the open curly quote ("), press Ctrl+Shift+left bracket.

✔ To access the close curly quote ("), press Ctrl+Shift+right bracket.

✔ To access the open single quote ('), press Ctrl+left bracket. Single quotes are frequently used to indicate quotes inside quotes, as in, "So Henry said to me, 'Darla, don't you ever wear that perfume again.' I mean, who does he think he is? Calvin Klein?"

✔ To access the close single quote ('), press Ctrl+right bracket. This is also the preferable symbol for an apostrophe — *don't* is better than *don't*.

If you can get in the habit of using these keyboard locations, you'll be able to use curly quotes and apostrophes at your own discretion. In other words, you can use curly quotes when you want quotes and straight quotes when you want feet and inch (or minute and second) symbols. But if you can't quite manage to stop using the old straight quote key, all is not lost. PageMaker is capable of automatically inserting curly quotes when necessary.

Choose File➪Preferences and click on the Other button inside the Preferences dialog box. After the Other Preferences dialog box appears, select the Use Typographer's Quotes checkbox, spotlighted in Figure 6-9. From now on, PageMaker will automatically substitute the correct curly quote symbol whenever you press the straight quote key. This goes for apostrophes as well.

Figure 6-9:
Select the
spotlighted
checkbox to
insert curly
quotes auto-
matically.

Other preferences

Autoflow: Printer name:
☐ Display all pages   ☐ Display PPD name

Maximum size of internal bitmap: 64 kBytes
Alert when storing graphics over: 256 kBytes

┌ Text ──────────────────────────
☒ Use typographer's quotes
◉ Preserve line spacing in TrueType
○ Preserve character shape in TrueType
Greek text below: 9 pixels

┌ Story editor ──────────────────
Font: Times New Roman ▼   ☒ Display style names
Size: 12 ▲▼ points   ☐ Display ¶

OK
Cancel

PageMaker does not, however, change the straight quotes that you have already entered into your document. To change existing quotes, you have to re-enter them or replace them by using the Find and Change feature in the Story Editor (explained in Chapter 10). Furthermore, to access feet and inch symbols, you have to turn the Use Typographer's Quotes checkbox off.

Nonbreaking spaces and hyphens

We're all familiar with the space character. You're no doubt also familiar with the hyphen, also known as the small dash. But you might not know that you can access four additional kinds of spaces and four additional kinds of dashes inside PageMaker.

The first variation on the space and dash is the *nonbreaking* character. Standard spaces and hyphens allow words to "break" from one line to the next. If you bind the two with a nonbreaking space or hyphen, however, PageMaker treats the two words as a single word and breaks them down to a second line together, as demonstrated in Figure 6-10. Both characters are useful for improving the appearance of ragged right (flush left) text by cutting down on the raggedness a little. In Figure 6-10, for example, the word *was* in the second-to-last line really sticks out there. Joining it to the word *the* with a nonbreaking space cuts the line short.

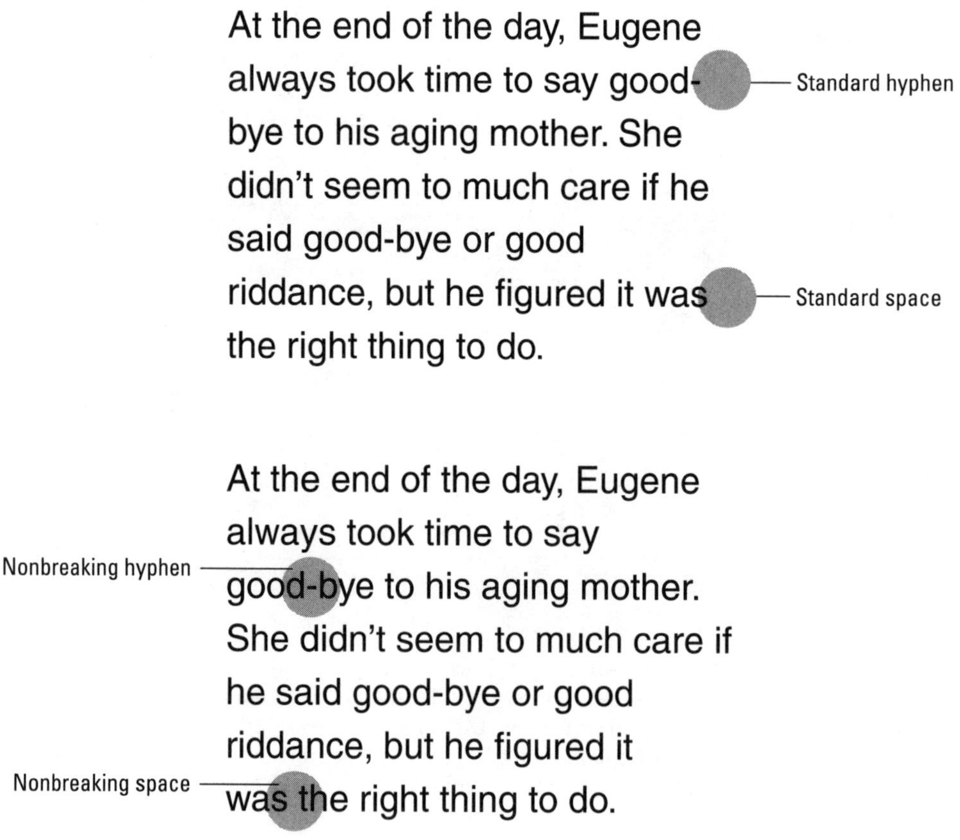

At the end of the day, Eugene
always took time to say good-   —— Standard hyphen
bye to his aging mother. She
didn't seem to much care if he
said good-bye or good
riddance, but he figured it was   —— Standard space
the right thing to do.

Figure 6-10:
Standard
hyphens and   Nonbreaking hyphen ——
spaces can
break
across lines
(top) but
nonbreaking
characters
do not
(bottom).   Nonbreaking space ——

At the end of the day, Eugene
always took time to say
good-bye to his aging mother.
She didn't seem to much care if
he said good-bye or good
riddance, but he figured it
was the right thing to do.

To access a nonbreaking space, also called a *hard space,* press Ctrl+Shift+H. To access the nonbreaking hyphen, press Ctrl+Shift+hyphen.

Avoid using nonbreaking spaces in a justified paragraph. PageMaker can't vary the width of a nonbreaking space the way it can a standard space character, so nonbreaking spaces may look too thin or too fat compared with their standard space neighbors.

Fixed-width spaces

Another kind of space is the fixed-width space, introduced in the "How to Do Bullets Right" section of Chapter 5. PageMaker provides three kinds of fixed-width spaces, all of which are nonbreaking:

- ✔ Press Ctrl+Shift+M to access the *em space*, which is as wide as the type size is tall — so a 12-point em space is 12 points wide, roughly the width of a capital letter *M.*

- ✔ Press Ctrl+Shift+N to access the *en space*, which is half the width of an em space (about the width of a small letter *n).*

- ✔ Press Ctrl+Shift+T to access a *thin space*, which is one quarter the width of an em space, or about the width of a lowercase *t.*

Use fixed spaces when tabs just won't work. In Figure 6-11, tabs separate the days from the text in the left-hand paragraphs. Because the tabs line up, as shown by the dotted line, the result is a huge gap after *Tuesday* and a smaller gap after the longer word *Wednesday.* Using em spaces instead of tabs equalizes the gaps, as shown on the right side of the figure.

Minus signs and em dashes

As mentioned earlier, there are four kinds of special dashes (above and beyond the standard hyphen). In addition to the nonbreaking hyphen, there's the discretionary hyphen (Ctrl+hyphen), discussed in the "Hyphenation" section of Chapter 4. This hyphen only appears when PageMaker needs it to break a word across two lines.

The remaining dashes are the *en dash* and *em dash*, the same widths as their en and em space counterparts. Use the en dash (Ctrl+equal) to represent a minus sign in mathematical equations. Use the em dash (Ctrl+Shift+equal) to separate thoughts, as in, "So, anyway, I was hiking with Mark — you know, the guy with the mousy brown dreadlocks — when this giant badger attacked us and started gnawing on Mark's ankle."

Tuesday I don't	**Tuesday** I don't know
know how to tell Ted the	how to tell Ted the
engagement is off. He	engagement is off. He
was so sweet today that	was so sweet today that
I almost regretted	I almost regretted
falling in love with Bob.	falling in love with Bob.
Wednesday What a	**Wednesday** What a
jerk Ted is! He was so	jerk Ted is! He was so
full of himself this	full of himself this
morning, I just had to	morning, I just had to
let him have it. "I love	let him have it. "I love
Bob!" I shouted so all	Bob!" I shouted so all

Figure 6-11:
Text
separated
with tabs
(left) and em
spaces
(right).

Fractions

Like all Windows programs, PageMaker provides access to three fraction characters, $^1/_4$, $^1/_2$, and $^3/_4$. Each of these characters is an exact fraction — no superscripting or subscripting is required to create them. Accessing these characters, however, is a little tricky. You have to enter *ASCII codes,* which are the numerical addresses of the characters. To enter an ASCII code, press and hold the Alt key and then type 0 followed by the three-digit ASCII code. You must use the keypad to type the numbers. After you type the last digit, you can release the Alt key.

The ASCII codes for the fractions are as follows:

$^1/_4$ 188

$^1/_2$ 189

$^3/_4$ 190

For example, to create the $^1/_2$ character, press and hold Alt, type **0189** on the keypad, and then release Alt. That's all there is to it.

But what if you want to create some other fraction, like $^{31}/_{56}$? Well, you're in luck. PageMaker ships with a Fraction script that you can implement using the Run Script addition. Here's how it works:

1. **Place the insertion point immediately after the denominator.**

   The denominator is the bottom number in the fraction. So in the case of $^{31}/_{56}$, you'd click after the 6 with the Text tool.

2. **Start the script.**

   Choose Utilities⇨Aldus Additions⇨Run Script. PageMaker displays a dialog box asking you which script you want to run. Locate and select the FRACTION.TXT file, which is in the SCRIPTS subdirectory inside the PM5 directory, and press Enter.

3. **Sit back and relax.**

   PageMaker does the rest of the work for you.

Other unusual characters

So far, we've explained a lot of characters that you didn't even know you needed. But what about all those characters that you *are* searching for? Like the degree symbol, the cent sign, the copyright symbol, and so on? Table 6-1 shows how to access these characters inside PageMaker.

Alt+key equivalents — you know, the ASCII codes — are applicable to all Windows applications. The Ctrl+key equivalents can only be used in PageMaker.

Keep in mind that Table 6-1 is but a brief listing of the characters available. Nearly all ASCII codes from 130 to 255 produce some character or other, the exceptions being 141, 142, 143, 144, 157, and 158. Feel free to hunt around if you need a character not included in this list. (We would have listed them all, but we really must be moving on to the next topic.)

Table 6-1	Accessing Special Symbols	
Symbol	*What It Looks Like*	*How to Create It*
Degree	°	Alt+0176
Cent	¢	Alt+0162
Pound	£	Alt+0163
Yen	¥	Alt+0165
Florin	ƒ	Alt+0131
Copyright	©	Ctrl+Shift+O (or Alt+0169)
Trademark	™	Alt+0153
Registered trademark	®	Ctrl+Shift+G (or Alt+0174)
Paragraph	¶	Ctrl+Shift+7 (or Alt+0182)
Section	§	Ctrl+Shift+6 (or Alt+0167)
Dagger	†	Alt+0134
Double dagger	‡	Alt+0135
Plus or minus	±	Alt+0177
Multiply	x	Alt+0215
Divide	÷	Alt+0247
A grave	à	Alt+0224 (capital, Alt+0192)
C cedilla	ç	Alt+0231 (capital, Alt+0199)
E acute	é	Alt+0233 (capital, Alt+0201)
O dieresis	ö	Alt+0246 (capital, Alt+0214)
O slash	ø	Alt+0248 (capital, Alt+0216)
N tilde	ñ	Alt+0241 (capital, Alt+0209)
German double S	ß	Alt+0223
Down question	¿	Alt+0191
Down exclamation	¡	Alt+0161
Ellipsis	…	Alt+0133

Chapter 7
Adding Pretty Pictures

● ●

In This Chapter

▶ Preparing graphics files for import

▶ Placing graphics

▶ Sizing and cropping graphics

▶ Wrapping text around graphics

▶ Creating special effects with text wrap

● ●

*T*his chapter is about graphics, the one thing you can't create in PageMaker. Oh sure, you can draw lines, rectangles, and ellipses, but unless you intend to limit yourself to crude drawings of smiley faces and Mr. Potato Head, you need more sophisticated tools.

That's why PageMaker lets you import graphics. You can create a picture in just about any graphics program you choose, save the artwork to disk using one of several different file formats, and insert it into your PageMaker publication. Inside PageMaker, you can stretch the graphic, label it with text, or wrap text around it to create irregular columns and other fancy effects.

This last option is particularly great. Why? Well, back in the days before PageMaker and desktop publishing, it cost serious money to wrap text around graphics because each line of text had to be individually measured and typeset — sometimes even placed on the page by hand, one line at a time. If the text changed, the whole expensive and time-consuming process had to begin again. Even rectangular wraps were expensive because they required fairly complex typesetting codes. So only big, glossy, state-of-the-art magazines with big staffs did text wrap with any frequency, and even then you could expect the art director and production staff to spend about 6,000 meetings discussing how to make sure there was enough time to do it. Today, even a lowly word processor can do rectangular text wrap, and any desktop publishing program worth its weight in rubber cement can do nonrectangular wraps, the kind that follows the contours and shape of an image.

But before you get to have fun with text wrap, you have to understand how to place the graphics you're wrapping around. So let's start there.

Preparing Graphics for PageMaker

Just as you need to prepare text in your word processor for use in PageMaker, you need to prepare your graphics for importing. And naturally, the preparation you need to do depends on the program you used to create the graphic and the type of graphic you created.

Graphics come in two basic types: *bitmap* and *vector*. Bitmap graphics are made up of square dots called *pixels,* and vector graphics are made up of lines. For example, everything printed by your laser printer becomes a bitmap graphic on the page because the entire page is composed of a series of black dots on the white paper — take a magnifying glass and check! Some programs create their images the same way, using a pattern of colored or black dots to render an image. Paint programs, scanners, and photo editors generally create bitmaps. Adobe Photoshop, Aldus PhotoStyler, and Fractal Design Painter are probably the most popular paint and photo-editing programs, but there are another dozen or so programs in use.

Bitmapped images are good for representing continuous ranges of colors with soft edges, such as impressionist paintings and photographs. But because they are made up of patterns of dots, enlarging or reducing them too much can make the dots ungainly or too fine to reproduce well.

Vector drawings, on the other hand, are great for high-contrast art such as weather maps, architectural plans, logos, charts, informational graphics, and all kinds of other bright, colorful artwork you might see in *USA Today*. A vector drawing is composed of lines, circles, and other shapes that can be stretched, combined, and otherwise manipulated, all without appearing the least bit jagged. Eventually, when they're printed to paper, these drawings are converted to bitmaps, but in the computer, they are vectors, which means that they can be resized without any loss in quality. CorelDraw, Adobe Illustrator, and Aldus FreeHand are the best-known drawing programs, but, again, other programs provide the same capabilities.

Keep in mind that most vector programs can export a bitmap version of their drawings, and that some programs let you combine bitmap and vector images in one file. The words *bitmap* and *vector* are techie terms, and many people are now using the terms *image* and *drawing* to refer to these types of formats. This book calls them *image* and *drawing* as well, and uses the term *graphic* to mean both. (Figure 7-1 shows examples of bitmap and vector art.)

Figure 7-1:
The two
types of
graphics:
bitmap (left)
and vector
(right). The
top center
graphic is
also a
vector
drawing,
illustrating
that this
type of
graphic
appears
smooth
when
printed
small or
large.

What formats can PageMaker import?

PageMaker can import many formats of graphics — as long as you have the right filter installed. The following list explains the formats that PageMaker supports; if you try to load a file in one of these formats and get a message saying that PageMaker doesn't know how to place it, get your install disks, run the Aldus Installer program, and check the Filters box before clicking on the Install button to install the missing filter. (You do *not* have to reinstall the entire PageMaker program, so make sure that the All box is unchecked. You also do not have to reinstall previously installed filters — just the new ones.)

PageMaker can import any of the following formats. (All the formats support color and grayscale graphics, unless noted.)

Image formats

- **TIFF:** TIFF, the Tagged Image File Format, can be produced by most graphics programs. TIFF is the standard image format on most personal computers, including PCs and Apple Macintoshes. It's also the best format for images you want to import, because PageMaker has the most control over how TIFF images print.

- **PCX:** The PC Paintbrush format, PCX is a PC standard similar to TIFF. It's been around forever and was definitely the de facto standard before TIFF came along.

- **BMP:** BMP, the Windows bitmap format, is the format used by Windows' built-in screen shot program as well as that little Paintbrush program found in the Accessories program group. Most programs support it, but because the TIFF and PCX formats came along earlier and are more standardized, BMP is rarely used by professionals.

- **MacPaint:** The first image format for the Macintosh computer, MacPaint remains a black-and-white-only format to this day. In fact, it's highly unlikely that you'll run into MacPaint images unless they're very old and come from the Mac.

Drawing formats

- **EPS:** The Encapsulated PostScript format is the standard drawing format for professionals. Almost every program that supports PostScript printers can create it, and it's incredibly reliable. The only problem is that only PostScript printers can print EPS graphics. If you use a PCL printer or some other non-PostScript device, don't use EPS.

- **AI:** PageMaker also supports the Adobe Illustrator format, a variation on the EPS format. The advantage of the AI format is that drawing programs — including CorelDraw, Illustrator, and FreeHand — can edit AI drawings while they may not be able to edit EPS.

- **DCS:** DCS, the Desktop Color Separation format, is another variant of EPS in which each of the four colors used in professional printing — cyan, magenta, yellow, and black — has its own file. These four files are then coordinated by a fifth file (the DCS file), which is what is actually imported into PageMaker. Don't worry about this format unless you want to print professional-quality, full-color graphics.

- **WMF:** The Windows Metafile Format was the first Windows drawing format and is still common for low-end and midrange graphics programs. Note that WMF also supports images.

- **PICT:** The Macintosh Picture format, PICT is the Macintosh equivalent of WMF.

- **DXF:** The Digital Exchange Format is used by CAD (computer-aided design) programs on PCs and workstations.

If PageMaker doesn't support your graphics program's native file format (the one that's used by default), chances are that the graphics program allows you to save files in a format that PageMaker does support. For example, PageMaker cannot import the CorelDraw (CDR) format, but CorelDraw can save files in the EPS, AI, and WMF formats, all of which PageMaker accepts. Similarly, Photoshop has its own format but can save images in the TIFF, PCX, BMP, or even MacPaint formats.

What to do before you import

In most cases, you can just import a graphic file as is, with no preparation. But in some cases, you need to do something special.

Preparing images

For images, the most important thing to do is get rid of any extraneous information. For example, if the image area is 3×5 inches and the bottom 2 inches are blank, crop out those bottom inches in your paint program before saving the file. Similarly, if you want only a portion of the image used in the PageMaker layout, crop out the parts you don't want (save the cropped file to a new name if you want to have a copy of the original file for use elsewhere.)

Why crop? Because you will have to crop it in PageMaker when you place the file. Cropping in PageMaker is easy, so you may be tempted to do the cropping there instead. But there's another reason to crop the image in the original program: That 2 inches of blank space is actually a series of white dots. Those dots take up disk space and space inside the PageMaker file. When you crop in PageMaker, you're not changing the actual image file, just hiding part of it, and the hidden portion continues to consume disk space. Another advantage to cropping in the source program is that you are ensured that whoever does the layout has only the part of the image you want them to use.

Mac file names vs. PC file names

On the PC, files get extensions to show what format they were saved in. CAT.TIF is a TIFF file, DOGGIE.DXF is a DXF file, and so on. If you're working with files originally created on the Mac, however, you'll soon find that this is not the case. On the Mac, files can have up to 31 characters and include any amount of periods. A filename such as *Steve's Flower 7/95.Tuscon* is not the least bit uncommon. You'll have to change the name to something like FLOWER.EPS before PageMaker will recognize it.

What is *cropping*? Cropping is selecting the part of an image that you want to keep and getting rid of the rest — like clipping a photo from a magazine and throwing the rest of the page away. Most photo editors have cropping tools.

Here are a few additional image preparation issues to keep in mind:

✔ **Color type:** If your source image is color, and you will be producing it in grayscale or black and white, convert the file to a grayscale or black-and-white image before importing it into PageMaker. (Again, save the altered file with a new name if you want to preserve the original.) There are two reasons to do this. One, the file will be smaller, which saves disk space and decreases print time. Second, although PageMaker can convert color images to grayscale or black-and-white images on its own, your photo editor is likely to do a better job.

✔ **Size and resolution:** For color and grayscale images, make sure that the image size is the same as it will be in your PageMaker layout. Enlarging or reducing an image can make it hard to read or just downright ugly. Enlarging more than 25 percent can result in very blocky images. Reducing more than 25 percent can cause distortions called *moirés.* It can also increase print time because the dots that make up the image get smaller as you reduce the image. Often, the dots are smaller than the printer can reproduce, which means that PageMaker has to combine some dots to make them printable, a process that can take some time.

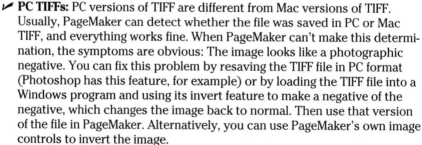

You can resize a TIFF image without risk of moiré by using PageMaker's *magic stretch* feature, which requires only that you press the Ctrl key while resizing. This feature snaps the image to sizes that are compatible with the resolution of your printer.

✔ **PC TIFFs:** PC versions of TIFF are different from Mac versions of TIFF. Usually, PageMaker can detect whether the file was saved in PC or Mac TIFF, and everything works fine. When PageMaker can't make this determination, the symptoms are obvious: The image looks like a photographic negative. You can fix this problem by resaving the TIFF file in PC format (Photoshop has this feature, for example) or by loading the TIFF file into a Windows program and using its invert feature to make a negative of the negative, which changes the image back to normal. Then use that version of the file in PageMaker. Alternatively, you can use PageMaker's own image controls to invert the image.

Preparing drawings

The following information applies to EPS files because those are the most complex. For other types of drawings, there's really nothing to prepare ahead of time for import into PageMaker.

✔ **Colors:** If you defined colors in an EPS file created in, say, Illustrator or FreeHand, PageMaker imports those color definitions along with the file and adds them to the list of colors in the Color dialog box (see Chapter 15 for more details). If a color already defined in your PageMaker file has the same name as a color in the imported EPS graphic, you'll see a dialog box asking whether you want to preserve the existing PageMaker color definitions or use the EPS file's definitions. Sometimes, neither answer is right — you want both. So make sure that you use unique names in PageMaker and your drawing program. (For non-EPS drawings, this is not a problem because all colors in imported files are immediately translated to a mix of red, blue, and green and no longer have names.) Also, make sure that the color model used to create the color — RGB or CMYK — matches that of your output device. RGB-to-CMYK conversion and CMYK-to-RGB conversion are hardly exact sciences, and colors can be altered.

✔ **Fonts:** EPS drawings that include text formatted with typefaces that are not built into your printer may not print correctly. Here are two solutions: Download the fonts to the printer before printing from PageMaker, or convert the text to curves in the drawing program before importing the file into PageMaker.

✔ **Previews:** EPS drawings from Macs may display as a gray box. This happens because an EPS file is actually a program that tells the printer how to draw the image. What you see on-screen is actually a bitmap preview, and the preview format created by a Mac program may not be PC-compatible. But not to worry, the file will print correctly.

What's a color model, anyway?

RGB (red, green, blue) and CMYK (cyan, magenta, yellow, black) are the two main ways to create colors in most programs. RGB is the set of colors used in computer monitors and in inkjet printers, slide makers, and thermal-wax printers. CMYK is the set of colors used in commercial printing presses. When creating colors, programs like Illustrator and FreeHand ask you to choose the color model you want to base the colors on. Pick the one that your final output device uses to get the closest color match possible in the final output. PageMaker converts between these two models when you print, depending on the printer selected, so if you use an intermediary printer for proofing, you may notice some color shift. Unfortunately, there's no way to know at this proofing stage whether the shift will be reflected in the final version. That's why publishers ask for a color proof — often called by their trade names, such as Matchprint and Fujichrome — before sending the negatives to the commercial printer. There are other models — such as Pantone and Trumatch — in addition to RGB and CMYK, and these caveats apply for them as well.

Bringing Graphics into Your Layout

After your image is ready, just follow these steps to import it:

PageMaker calls importing *placing*, but placing is really just the second part of the process: positioning the graphic. This book tends to use the word *import* but does use *place* when referring to the PageMaker commands or when the focus is on the positioning of the graphic.

1. **Go to the page in your layout where you want to place the graphic.**

   (Note that any graphic placed in a master page, described in Chapter 4, will appear on all pages in the document.)

2. **Change your view so that you can see the whole page or at least the area in which you want to place your graphic.**

3. **If you want the graphic to be free-standing, so that it doesn't move with a particular piece of text, select the Arrow tool.**

   If you want it to be an *in-line graphic* — one that moves with a particular piece of text — select the Text tool and click on the location in the text where you want the graphic to be inserted. (Think of an in-line graphic as a special character that happens to be a graphic.)

4. **Use File⇨Place (Ctrl+D) to get the Place Document dialog box.**

   Use the dialog box to find the graphics you want to place. Select the first graphic. Note that PageMaker displays only the files for which it recognizes the format *and* has the appropriate import filter. Figure 7-2 shows the dialog box.

Figure 7-2:
The Place
Document
dialog box
lets you
import
graphics
into
PageMaker.

Place document			OK
			Cancel

File name:
pmw3_25.tif

Directories:
a:\

pmw3_20.tif	a:\
pmw3_21.tif	resource.frk
pmw3_22.tif	
pmw3_23.tif	
pmw3_24.tif	
pmw3_25.tif	
pmw3_26.tif	
pmw3_27.tif	
pmw3_28.tif	
pmw3_29.tif	
pmw3_30.tif	

Place:
◉ As independent graphic
○ Replacing entire graphic
○ Inserting text

Options:
☒ Retain format
☒ Convert quotes
☐ Read tags
☒ Retain cropping data

List files of type:
Importable files

Drives:
a:

5. **Check to see whether the Ꭺs Independent Graphic or Replacing Ꭼntire Graphic button is selected.**

   If you selected (clicked on) a graphic in your layout just before opening the Place Document dialog box, PageMaker gives you the option of replacing it with a new graphic — select the Replacing Ꭼntire Graphic option to do so.

6. **Click on the OK button.**

   If PageMaker has trouble importing the graphic, it displays a dialog box telling you that the filter does not support the file format. Open the graphic in the program that created it to make sure that it's OK, and resave it before trying to import it again. You may also get a dialog box that says the file is very large and asks you to confirm whether to copy the graphic into PageMaker, as shown in Figure 7-3. Whether you answer yes or no, PageMaker places the graphic; by *copy*, it means bring a copy of the graphic file into the PageMaker file. Chapter 8 provides more information about this option.

Figure 7-3:
PageMaker
sometimes
asks
whether you
want to
copy the
graphic
into the
publication.

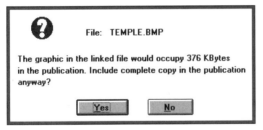

File: TEMPLE.BMP

The graphic in the linked file would occupy 376 KBytes in the publication. Include complete copy in the publication anyway?

[Yes]   [No]

7. **The cursor changes to an icon that represents the graphic.**

   The icon depends on the type of graphic; Figure 7-4 shows the various icons and the file formats they represent. The upper left corner of the icon represents the upper left corner of the graphic. Move the cursor to where you want to place the graphic and click the mouse button. Your graphic appears.

Figure 7-4:
The various
icons for
imported
graphics.

MacPaint, BMP

WMF, PICT

TIFF, PCX

EPS, AI, DCS

Fine-Tuning a Graphic

When placed, a graphic is the same size as in the originating program. You may not like that size. Fortunately, you can change it. Notice the little black rectangles at the corners of the graphic. These rectangles are called *handles*, and you can use them to resize or crop a graphic. Figure 7-5 shows a graphic's handles, as well as the cursor you see when you select one.

Figure 7-5:
Select an imported graphic to display eight tiny square handles (left). Drag one of the handles to scale the graphic (right).

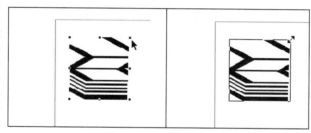

Resizing

If the Arrow tool is active, you can resize a graphic by clicking on one of its handles, holding the mouse button down, and dragging the mouse. Depending on which way you drag, the graphic gets smaller or bigger — dragging away from the graphic makes it bigger, and dragging toward the graphic makes it smaller. Note that the handle you choose is significant. Choosing a midline handle resizes the graphic in one dimension (the handles on the side resize its width, while those on the top and bottom resize its height). Choosing a corner handle resizes both dimensions.

You can easily distort a graphic by resizing it along one dimension or by dragging a corner handle at any angle but 45 degrees. Most mere mortals don't have the kind of coordination that's required to precisely calculate the angle that they're moving the mouse. Fortunately, there is a way to resize a graphic proportionally, so that it does not become distorted: Hold down the Shift key while dragging.

Resizing by mouse makes a lot of sense when you're experimenting. But you can resize graphics more precisely by using the Control palette, as Figure 7-6 shows. If you know the degree of enlargement or reduction, you can specify it in the palette and have PageMaker apply it for you. Or you can enter the new dimensions or click on the Nudge icons to change the values gradually, until the size looks right to you. A good technique is to use the mouse to do a rough resizing and then use the Control palette to fine-tune it.

Figure 7-6:
The Control palette lets you resize a graphic by entering the percentage of enlargement or reduction.

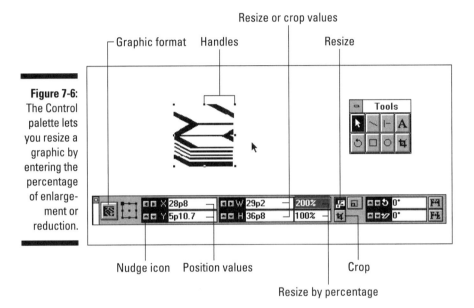

Take a careful look at the figure. To the right of the Resize icon is an icon that indicates proportional resize, which means that if you change one of the resize percentages (to the left of the Resize icon), both the horizontal and vertical percentages are changed to the same value. If you click on that Proportional Resize icon, you get a different icon, one that represents independent resizing along the horizontal and vertical axes. You can have this icon active and make proportional changes to both values, but switching to the Proportional Resize icon makes it easier to resize most graphics because most people resize graphics proportionally. For some graphics — monochrome bitmaps — PageMaker displays a third icon that resizes the graphic to a resolution that is compatible with the selected printer (if the image does not match, the printer icon has an *X* in it). Figure 7-7 shows the three icons.

Proportional resize

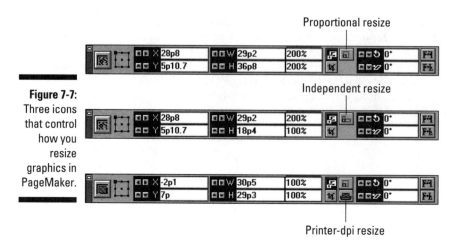

Independent resize

Printer-dpi resize

Figure 7-7:
Three icons
that control
how you
resize
graphics in
PageMaker.

Cropping

To crop a graphic, you need to select the Crop tool (⊔). Now, position the tool
over the graphics handles and hold down the mouse button. Move the cursor
toward the graphic's center to crop out part of it; move away from the center to
uncrop a previously cropped graphic. Just as with resizing, the handle you pick
determines whether the crop is along one dimension or two, and holding the
Shift key while cropping ensures a proportional crop (although most crops are
not proportional because you usually want to get rid of a particular portion).

As with resizing, you can also use the Control palette to crop. Just make sure to
click on the crop icon (identified in Figure 7-6). When you use this palette for
cropping, you'll notice that the percentage fields disappear — you can crop
only by using the increase and decrease icons or entering the crop values. Note
also that the crop occurs from the currently selected handle within the Control
palette (the square to the right of the icon that represents the file type). The
selected handle is the larger one.

Setting Up Text Wrap

When you place a graphic over some text, one of two things happens: the
graphic overprints the text, or the text *wraps* — moves out of the way of the
graphic. It's extremely rare that you'd want to obscure text with a graphic, so
it'd be nice if PageMaker could automatically wrap text around graphics you
place. Lucky for you, PageMaker can.

Before you learn how to set up automatic text wrap as the default setting, keep in mind that the controls for text wrap can also be applied to a specific graphic (whichever one is currently selected with the Arrow tool). Thus, you can enable text wrap for graphics placed before you set wrap to be automatic. You can also change the wrap settings for specific graphics. (You learn why you might do that later.)

By changing settings in PageMaker when no documents are open, you set defaults for all documents created in the future. Thus, by altering text-wrap settings with no documents open, you ensure that all future documents will use those text-wrap settings. And, of course, the next time you change those default settings, they become the new defaults.

To establish automatic text wrap as the default setting, follow these steps.

1. **Open PageMaker but don't open any documents.**

2. **Use Ele<u>m</u>ent⇨Text <u>W</u>rap to get the Text Wrap dialog box.**

   Figure 7-8 shows the default settings.

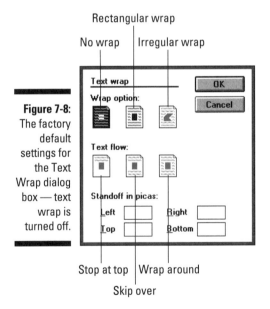

Rectangular wrap

No wrap | Irregular wrap

Figure 7-8:
The factory
default
settings for
the Text
Wrap dialog
box — text
wrap is
turned off.

Stop at top | Wrap around

Skip over

3. **Select the wrap icons you want.**

   The icons in the dialog box represent different text wrap options, which are described in more detail later in this section. Select the ones that match your needs. Most people select the top middle icon (rectangular wrap) and the bottom right one (wrap around), as shown in Figure 7-9.

Figure 7-9:
Common
settings in
the Text
Wrap dialog
box:
Rectangular
text wrap is
turned on
and text is
set to wrap
around both
sides of the
graphic.

4. Enter the standoff settings.

The *standoff* is the margin between the graphic and the text. A dotted box appears around the graphic to represent the standoff area. The diamonds in the corners are the standoff box's handles. The default settings — 0.167 inches, or 1 pica — are fine for most uses.

You rarely would have a standoff of 0, which would eliminate any space between the graphic and the text. In multicolumn text, a pica is the standard margin between related elements such as graphics and text or between columns. But in some cases, you'll want more space — for example, if you have a single, page-wide column and large graphics and thus want a fairly large space, perhaps 0.3 to 0.5 inches, between elements so that they don't seem too crowded. Note that you can set the standoff separately for all four sides. Do so when it makes sense, such as when it looks better to have, say, more space along the sides than at the top and bottom of the graphic.

The icons in the top row of the Text Wrap dialog box, from left to right, represent no wrap, rectangular wrap, and irregular wrap. No wrap is self-explanatory, and rectangular wrap means to wrap around the invisible box that contains the imported graphic. No matter the actual shape of the graphic, PageMaker places it in an invisible box, which is what the handles are attached to. The last option, irregular wrap, is grayed out. Figure 7-10 shows the various results for these options.

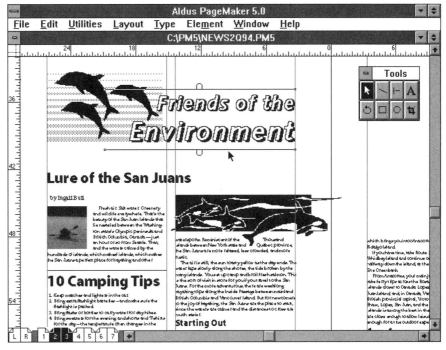

Figure 7-10:
Samples of
the three
kinds of text
wrap — no
wrap (top),
rectangular
wrap (left),
and
irregular
wrap (right,
around the
whale's
tail).

That's the top row of icons. Now the bottom row, which is labeled Text Flow. From left to right, the icons are stop at top, skip over, and wrap around. If you choose the stop at top icon, the text box stops above the graphic. Use this option only if you want the text to stop above a graphic, such as in a single-column document where the graphics are at the bottom of the page, or when graphics and their captions will extend to the bottom of the page.

The skip over option stops the text block at the top of the graphic and resumes the text block below. Use this option if your graphic is not as wide as your text column *and* if it is not aligned against one side of the column. Otherwise, you'll get text that's split vertically by the graphic, not just horizontally. This option is typically used in documentation and simple business reports.

The last option — the one you'll likely use most often for newsletters and fancier documents — is wrap around, which makes sure that the text flows any place in the text block where the graphic isn't. Thus, it can be used to make a graphic the equivalent of a drop cap or to have two columns wrap around a graphic placed between them. Figure 7-11 shows the various results, good and bad, for these text-wrap options.

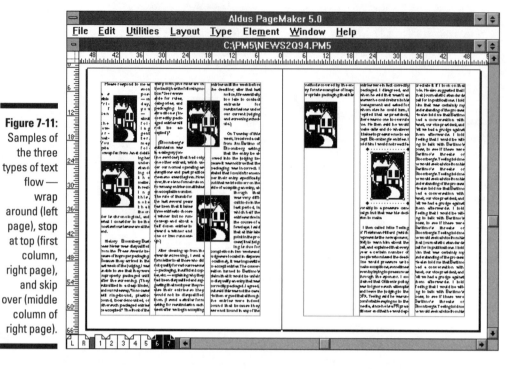

Figure 7-11:
Samples of
the three
types of text
flow —
wrap
around (left
page), stop
at top (first
column,
right page),
and skip
over (middle
column of
right page).

That's all there is to it, at least for setting the defaults.

When you move a graphic, the text that wraps around it reflows as needed based on the graphic's new position. If the graphic moves into a new area of text, that text wraps around the graphic. Similarly, if you place, modify, or resize text where a graphic is located, that text wraps as well. The whole point of desktop publishing is to automate the layout process — and here's proof that PageMaker does.

You can select multiple graphics and apply text-wrap settings to all simultaneously.

Special Effects with Text Wrap

The one setting you can't set as a default is irregular text wrap. PageMaker needs to have a particular graphic selected to apply this option. The following steps walk you through the process of using irregular text wrap on a graphic-by-graphic basis.

1. **Select the graphic.**

2. **If the default text flow setting is not wrap around, use Element⇨Text Wrap to open the Text Wrap dialog box.**

   Make sure that the lower right icon (wrap around) is selected. Set the Standoff values and click on the OK button.

   But wait! What about that icon in the Text Wrap dialog box for irregular wrap? The truth is, you don't need it. In fact, you can't ever select this icon — it's not selectable. Its only real purpose is to indicate when you have an irregular wrap, although that's obvious from just looking at the graphic.

3. **The dashed box that indicates the standoff margin appears.**

4. **Drag a diamond-shaped handle to a new location.**

   Notice how the text wrap follows the new shape of the standoff box.

5. **So far, you're limited to just four corners — a trapezoid.**

   What if you want the wrap to be something else, perhaps circular, or star-shaped? Just move the cursor to a spot on the standoff box's line and click. A new handle appears, which you can position as you want. By adding handles and moving them, you can create any sort of polygon shape, and by having enough points, you can simulate a circle or rectangle.

Figure 7-12 shows how text was set to wrap around one image.

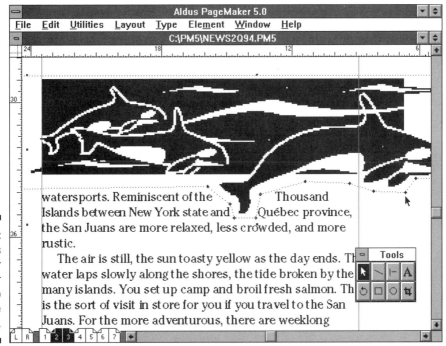

Figure 7-12:
The handles created for an irregular wrap around one image.

Tips for text wraps

What if you create a truly horrible irregular text wrap and want to cancel it? Go to the Text Wrap dialog box and select the rectangular wrap icon (top middle). Your standoff box and its handles revert to the rectangular settings.

Text blocks cannot be set to wrap around other text blocks. If you want to create this effect, you have to create text blocks of the needed sizes to simulate text wrap. Another, easier method is to place an invisible graphic that does have text wrap on behind the text block you want to wrap other text around. (An invisible graphic is a line, rectangle, or ellipse, created in PageMaker, that has no line or fill, as discussed in Chapter 14.)

If you want text to overprint a graphic, make sure that text wrap is turned off for the graphic. Then make sure that the text block is in front of the graphic — use Element➪Send to Back (Ctrl+B) if the graphic is selected or Element➪Bring to Front (Ctrl+F) if the text block is selected. You can use this technique in reverse if you want to obscure text with a graphic, perhaps when creating a piece of artwork within PageMaker.

You can wrap text around graphics created in PageMaker, such as lines and circles. Chapter 14 covers PageMaker's graphics tools.

Finally, screen redraw can be a pain while you're editing a custom text-wrap boundary. Every time you release the mouse button, the screen redraws. To keep that from happening, depress the spacebar while you alter custom text-wrap boundaries.

The 5th Wave   By Rich Tennant

"YOU KNOW THAT GUY WHO BOUGHT ALL THAT SOFTWARE? HIS CHECK HAS A WARRANTY THAT SAYS IT'S TENDERED AS IS AND HAS NO FITNESS FOR ANY PARTICULAR PURPOSE INCLUDING, BUT NOT LIMITED TO, CASHING."

Chapter 8

Keeping Track of It All

● ●

In This Chapter

▶ How to control the automatic updating of graphics

▶ What are your link options?

▶ When to use live links — and when to avoid them

▶ How to combine multiple documents via books

● ●

*G*raphics here, text files there, chapters everywhere. You soon can lose track of the elements that make up your publication. So before you move on to learn more about layout, take a moment to read this chapter. The topic may seem a bit obscure and unsexy, but knowing about how to keep track of the various elements of your PageMaker creations will make your layout life a lot easier. Promise.

What are Links — and Why Should You Care?

When you place a graphic or text, a lot goes on behind the scenes. Here's a look at what happens:

1. First, PageMaker checks the format of the file you're importing and then tries to import the file. For text, it translates the word processor format into its own format. For graphics, it builds an image of the graphic that it will use to display the graphic on-screen (EPS drawings come with their own prebuilt screen images).

2. Second, PageMaker checks to see where the file resides — the disk and directory — and records that information, along with the file name and the last modification date.

3. Third, it lets you place the file in your layout.

It's at the second step where *links* come into play. Links are basically tags that show PageMaker where to find the original file. With links, PageMaker can tell if, say, a graphic has been modified and thus know to import the newer version. PageMaker also needs links when printing graphics because in many cases it substitutes the original graphic for the on-screen display image to get the best-quality output.

All this can happen automatically if you let it, which can be good and bad. It's good if you want PageMaker to always use the latest version of a graphic, bad if you don't. It's also bad if you think that PageMaker is automatically importing the latest version of a graphic but in fact the option that tells the program to do this is turned off, or vice versa. So get in the habit of checking the link settings, as explained in the upcoming sections.

Setting link defaults

The time to set your link options is when you first create a new document. To do so, use Element⇨Link Options with nothing selected. (If you establish link settings when no document is open, your settings become the defaults for all future documents.) Figure 8-1 shows the dialog box that appears. Note that there are two sets of options — one for text and one for graphics. Also note that the options are indented from each other — that's because in order for an option to be available, the one above it must be checked. This indentation is meant to remind you of that fact.

Although Figure 8-1 shows the dialog box for setting a document's defaults, you can also display a similar dialog box for a particular element and establish settings to control that element's behavior. (You won't get both the text and graphics options, just the set appropriate for the selected element.)

There's no reason to have the same linking rules apply to all your elements — it would be silly, for example, to link a logo that never changes to an outside graphic, and it would be equally silly not to link a graphic that changes every month (such as for a calendar). That's why you can set link options individually.

The Store Copy in Publication option

The first option in the Link Options dialog box is Store Copy in Publication. This option, strangely enough, copies the text or graphic file into your PageMaker document. In other words, the text or graphic is actually inserted into the PageMaker file. You'll notice that this option is checked and dimmed for text — that's because text is always stored in the publication. PageMaker gives you no choice in the matter.

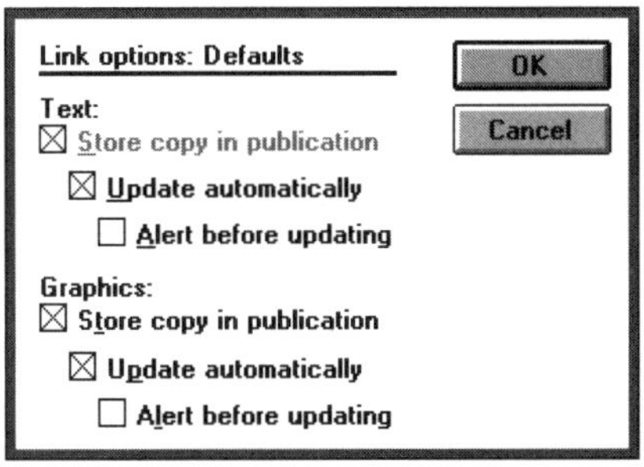

Figure 8-1:
Use these
options to
specify how
and when
imported
text and
graphics are
updated
from disk.

Link options: Defaults

OK

Cancel

Text:
☒ Store copy in publication
  ☒ Update automatically
    ☐ Alert before updating

Graphics:
☒ Store copy in publication
  ☒ Update automatically
    ☐ Alert before updating

For graphics, checking this option is no guarantee that a particular graphic will be copied into PageMaker. Another dialog box allows you to override the Store Copy in Publication setting: In the Other Preferences dialog box (File⇨Preferences⇨Other), you set the Alert When Storing Graphics Over amount (see Figure 8-2).

Suppose that you want to store a copy of the graphics in the publication. Your Alert When Storing Graphics Over value is 32K, but you import a graphic that takes 67K. PageMaker displays a dialog box, shown in Figure 8-3, that gives you the choice of whether to copy the graphics file internally into PageMaker or not. (The reason to set this threshold is to prevent the PageMaker document from getting too big; after all, if you're linked to the original graphic, you don't really need that graphic copied in PageMaker.)

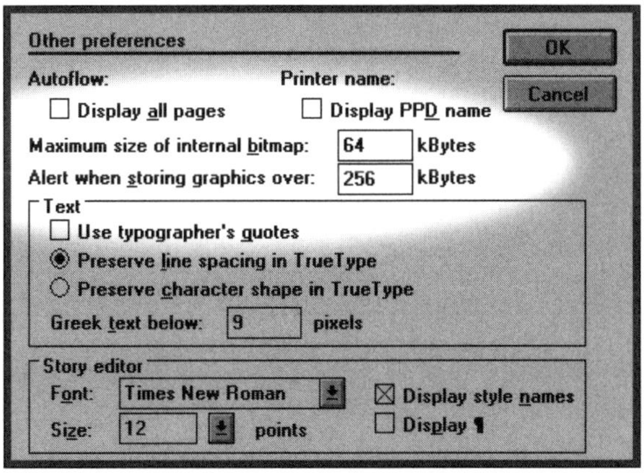

Figure 8-2:
Use the
Alert When
Storing
Graphics
Over setting
in the Other
Preferences
dialog box
to avoid
copying
huge
graphics
files into
your
PageMaker
file.

Other preferences

OK

Cancel

Autoflow:
☐ Display all pages

Printer name:
☐ Display PPD name

Maximum size of internal bitmap: `64` kBytes
Alert when storing graphics over: `256` kBytes

Text
☐ Use typographer's quotes
◉ Preserve line spacing in TrueType
○ Preserve character shape in TrueType
Greek text below: `9` pixels

Story editor
Font: `Times New Roman`
Size: `12` points
☒ Display style names
☐ Display ¶

Should you check the Store Copy in Publication box? It depends. If you do, and the original files get lost, you still have a copy in your PageMaker layout that can be used for printing. If you don't, your PageMaker file stays smaller because the graphics won't have a duplicate inside the file. Our advice is to check the item but set a fairly low threshold in the Alert When Storing Graphics Over amount — for example, 32K. Thus, small graphics are copied in while the big ones remain just linked.

Files that are copied in are also linked — PageMaker still keeps a reference to the original file, for reasons that will soon become clear.

Figure 8-3:
PageMaker
gives you
the option of
not copying
large
graphics
files into
your
publication.

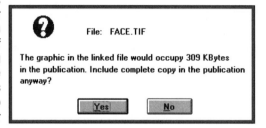

The Update Automatically option

The second option is Update Automatically. This option tells PageMaker that every time you open the publication, it should check to see whether the source files have been changed or moved. That's why PageMaker records the file information when it first places the file. Even if PageMaker previously copied a graphic or text file into the PageMaker layout file, it checks to see whether the source file has changed.

Select this option if graphics and text change frequently and you want to make sure that the latest version is used in the layout. For example, if you have a monthly newsletter with a guest columnist, you may want to save the columnist's photo under some generic file name like GUEST.TIF and simply substitute the latest photo each month. Thus, when the newsletter document is opened, PageMaker loads in the latest columnist photo. Of course, for this option to work, you need to make sure that the source file is changed only when planned — it's embarrassing to have the wrong photo for a particular columnist simply because someone changed the photo early or the newsletter was produced a little later than normal.

Note that if you decide not to copy graphics into the PageMaker file, the Update Automatically option is checked and grayed out. All such linked files are automatically updated because PageMaker must link to the source file each time you open the layout. There's no internal copy for PageMaker to use.

It's generally a good idea to disable the Update Automatically option for text files. If you have some text files that do change frequently, you can enable this option, but understand that any editing formatting you did in PageMaker gets lost when the layout is updated with the new word processor file. And don't think that you can export your current text (via File➪Export) to get around this loss — the exporting process loses special formatting such as tracking, kerning, drop caps, and other PageMaker-specific features not found in a word processor.

The folks at Aldus don't want you to accidentally override your text, so if this option is checked, PageMaker displays the alert box shown in Figure 8-4 to give you a chance to cancel the update.

Figure 8-4:
This alert box warns you that you're about to override text that you modified in PageMaker after you imported it from your word processor.

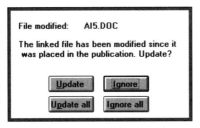

The Alert Before Updating option

The last option, Alert Before Updating, is available only if the other two options are selected. This option gives you a chance to override an automatic update as the PageMaker file is being opened. We all know how smart it is to let something go off on its own without someone paying attention — the IRS, the Congress, the high-school student. No, we insist that they check in with us before doing something that might affect us. That's what this option makes PageMaker do.

If you want automatic updating to catch any unplanned changes to your source files but you want to retain control over whether those updated files actually get used in PageMaker, check this option. If you are certain that you want elements to be updated automatically, with no notice to you, don't check the box.

Updating individual elements

After you establish your default link settings, you may want to change them for individual elements, as explained earlier. You can change the link settings for individual elements by selecting the elements and using the Link Options dialog box to set their behavior, as previously described. But you can do more than that, too.

PageMaker offers a separate dialog box to manage the links themselves. The Link Options dialog box controls the behavior of the linking feature; the Links dialog box controls which element is linked to which source file. Figure 8-5 shows the Links dialog box, which you access by choosing File⇨Links or pressing Ctrl+Shift+D).

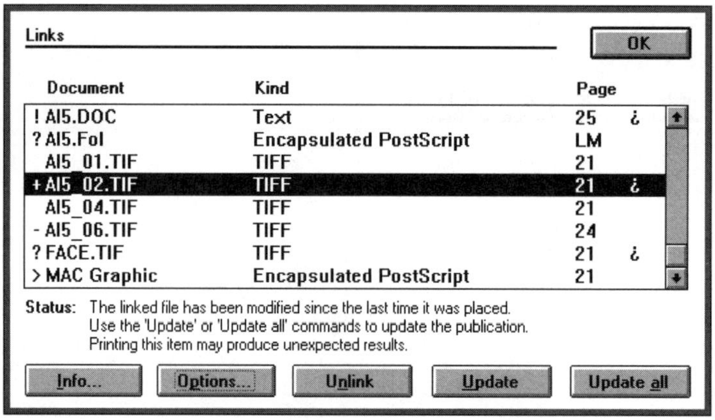

Figure 8-5:
Here's
where you
examine the
links made
to every
imported
element in
your
publication.

Links				OK
Document		**Kind**	**Page**	
! AI5.DOC		Text	25	¿
? AI5.Fol		Encapsulated PostScript	LM	
AI5_01.TIF		TIFF	21	
+ AI5_02.TIF		TIFF	21	¿
AI5_04.TIF		TIFF	21	
- AI5_06.TIF		TIFF	24	
? FACE.TIF		TIFF	21	¿
> MAC Graphic		Encapsulated PostScript	21	

Status: The linked file has been modified since the last time it was placed.
Use the 'Update' or 'Update all' commands to update the publication.
Printing this item may produce unexpected results.

[Info...] [Options...] [Unlink] [Update] [Update all]

From this dialog box, you can do several things:

✔ Click on the Info button to get information on a current link, including the file's physical location, the date it was placed in PageMaker, its size, and the date it was created. Figure 8-6 shows the dialog box with information about an imported graphic.

✔ Via the Info button, you also can change the source file for an element. Suppose that you're doing a story on Jane Fonda. But the only picture you have of her is an old movie still from *Barbarella*. For lack of a better image, you go ahead and use it. The next day, a coworker comes in with a copy of "Jane Fonda's Best-Selling Workout for the Dead." You rip it from said coworkers hands, throw it on the scanner — completely ignoring copyright laws — and use the Info button to link the imported Barbarella graphic to the new image. The old image is then replaced.

Notice that the file selected in the file list is not the one named at the top of the Link Info dialog box. By selecting a new file and clicking on Link, you can substitute files. Note that files display only if they are of the same type (such as a text file). Also, note that if you're linking to a new graphic, there's an option called Retain Cropping Data. Checking this option ensures that the cropping you did in PageMaker on the original is applied to the new graphic. If the new graphic is basically the same as the original, leave this option checked. If it is so different that you will need to recrop it, uncheck the option.

✔ Via the Options button, you can change the link behavior — this button invokes the same Link Options dialog box described earlier.

✔ Use the Unlink button to break the link to a selected element. This makes the internal PageMaker copy the only copy PageMaker uses or tracks. If there is no internal PageMaker copy, PageMaker creates one when you unlink the source file.

✔ You can update a link for an element whose source has been modified by clicking on the Update button. You only need to use this option when you turn off automatic updating for an element.

✔ If you click on Update All, PageMaker updates all links to source files that have been modified. Again, you only need to use this option if automatic updating is turned off.

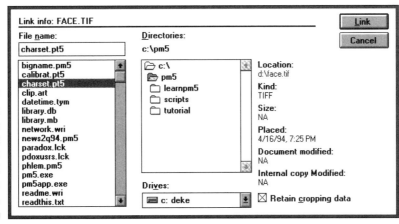

Figure 8-6:
Use this dialog box to link an imported element to a file on disk.

Symbol shorthand

You've probably noticed all the wacky symbols that accompany element names in the Links dialog box. (See Figure 8-5.) These symbols are shorthand for link problems; if you select a file name, you get a detailed description after the word *Status* at the bottom of the dialog box. Here's a rundown of what the symbols mean:

✔ The upside-down question mark (¿) means that the text or image may not print correctly.

✔ The greater-than sign (>) means that the file came from a Mac and did not have its name translated during import; that means that PageMaker can't check to see whether the file has been modified. (See Chapter 18 for details on dealing with Mac files.)

✔ An exclamation point (!) means that both the source file and the copy inside PageMaker have been modified (this applies just to text), and updating the source file will overwrite changes in the PageMaker copy.

✔ The minus (–) character means that a source file has changed but PageMaker has not updated the internal copy.

✔ The plus (+) character indicates an element whose source file has been changed and is marked for automatic updating the next time you open the PageMaker document.

✔ The right-side-up question mark (?) means that PageMaker can't find the source file.

✔ The code *NA* means that there is no source file — the file is an embedded OLE object (covered later in this chapter) or was pasted via the Clipboard.

Live links

PageMaker supports *live links,* which it calls *hotlinks.* When you have a live link, you can double-click on an element in PageMaker and have the source file and the program that created the source file launched for you. In some cases, if someone launches that program and edits the source file, your PageMaker layout updates itself automatically after the source file is modified.

Sometimes, you'll want to use hotlinks merely to have quick access to a source file and the program that created it. But one live-link option, OLE (described a few sections down the road), also comes in handy when you want to import data from a program that can't export to a PageMaker-compatible format. But be aware that in this last-hope import approach, you'll often get a medium-quality version because the data is translated to a text format (usually resulting in a loss of formatting) or to a graphics format (usually TIFF).

Edit Original

Say that you're working in a layout and you notice that a graphic needs a touch-up. You know how to use Photoshop for this kind of work, so why not just fix the flaw yourself? Why not indeed. You can switch to Photoshop and load the image, or find the image via the Windows File Manager and double-click on it to launch Photoshop.

Or, if you want to save some effort, press and hold the Alt key while double-clicking on the image in PageMaker; this action loads Photoshop and the source image. Another way to do the same thing is via Edit⇨Edit Original, which is the bottom-most item in the Edit menu. (Of course, you need to have enough RAM to have both PageMaker and Photoshop running at once — which requires about 16MB of system RAM. If you have less, you'll need to quit PageMaker, launch Photoshop and fix the graphic, and then quit Photoshop and relaunch PageMaker.)

If you want to edit the element in a program other than the one that created it — for example, if you want to use Fractal Design Painter to alter a TIFF image that was created in Photoshop — hold the Shift key when selecting Edit⇨Edit Original or press Alt+Shift when double-clicking on the image. You can then choose which program you want to launch for your editing work.

Using the Edit Original feature can get a little tricky at times:

✔ You may still have to update the link to the modified graphic (via the Links dialog box, accessed by File⇨Links) even if you use Edit Original. PageMaker updates the graphic automatically only if Update Automatically is checked and Store Copy in Publication is *un*checked in the Link Options dialog box (Element⇨Link Options). Got that? If these options aren't exactly right, the graphic won't get updated.

✔ Text will not update automatically — you'll have to update the link manually or wait until the next time you open the publication (assuming Update Automatically is checked). This is why the best place to edit text in PageMaker is in the Story Editor (see Chapter 10). Editing in a word processor runs the risk of wiping out changes made in PageMaker — even if you don't change the words, you've likely applied formatting. So don't use Edit Original with text.

OLE

Some programs use a live-link method called OLE, which stands for *Object Linking and Embedding.* (It's pronounced like the Spanish word *olé.*) OLE is complicated, and chances are you won't use it much. You may use it to link to a spreadsheet or equation editor or other such specialized program. Because OLE is a Microsoft invention, you'll find it implemented in Microsoft products such as Word and Excel. A nice thing about OLE is that it works between PCs and Macs, as well as within each platform. (OLE requires Windows 3.1 on the PC and System 7 on the Mac.)

To insert OLE objects, you have a choice of several methods:

✔ Use Edit⇨Insert Object. You'll then get a list of *server* types — programs that OLE links can come from. Examples include a Word document, Excel chart, Excel Worksheet, and Equation (a utility that comes with Microsoft programs). Select the type you want, and OLE launches the appropriate program. Create the object — chart, equation, spreadsheet, or whatever — and when you're done, select File⇨Update and then quit the OLE server program. (If you forget to update the object and quit, the program prompts you to update. Also, you don't have to quit after updating, but doing so frees up the memory the OLE server program consumes.) The file will be placed in PageMaker. This sort of OLE link is an *embedded object*. It's called that because the actual object is stored (embedded) in PageMaker, and the link is just to the program that created it.

✔ Use Edit⇨Copy (or Ctrl+C) or Edit⇨Cut (or Ctrl+X) in a source (*server*) program to place an object on the Windows Clipboard. Then, in PageMaker, use Edit⇨Paste Special to paste it. You will often get multiple choices for the format to use for the pasted object — typically as the original file type (chart or equation, for example) and as a graphic (such as WMF). If you choose the original file type, you'll be able to link back to the program that created the object. The object itself is embedded in PageMaker, and so it too is an embedded object. Note that if you choose a graphic format for an object that was originally not a graphic, you are essentially pasting in a *copy* of the object, and you'll be unable to link back to the original object — it's like doing a normal paste.

✔ Use Edit⇨Copy (or Ctrl+C) or Edit⇨Cut (or Ctrl+X) in a source program to place an object in the Windows Clipboard. Then, in PageMaker, use Edit⇨Paste Link. This sort of OLE link is a *linked object*. The link is to an object stored elsewhere, and the link references both that object file and the program that created it.

To edit OLE objects (whether linked or embedded), you have two choices:

✔ Double-click on the element in PageMaker, and OLE launches the source program and the object file.

✔ Choose Edit⇨*Type* Object, where *Type* is the name of the object type, such as *Excel Worksheet* or *Equation*. This is the bottom-most item in the Edit menu. (No, you're not crazy; we did say earlier that Edit⇨Edit Original was the bottom-most item in the Edit menu. PageMaker changes the item depending on what type of element you select.)

If you embed the same object multiple places in your layout, and you want to update it, you must update each instance of that object separately.

Text turns graphic

Some text objects become graphics when created or linked via OLE. For example, if you link an equation generated in Microsoft Equation, the equation becomes a graphic object because the equation formatting is not supported outside the Equation utility. Similarly, if you highlight several cells in Excel, the group of cells is translated into a graphic. You cannot edit such text-based graphics in PageMaker, although if you go back to the original OLE program, the object will be in its original format (as text or graphics). Of course, if you selected text in a word processor, or text within an Excel cell, the text remains as text even when linked via OLE, as long as there are no nontext elements in the selection.

To make matters more confusing, PageMaker establishes OLE links to graphics, so if you use Edit⇨Paste Special and select a text format (like PageMaker 5.0 Format or Rich Text Format), you get a standard paste (no link). Of course, PageMaker gives you no clue that it's doing just standard paste. Still confused? Try this: To be preserved as OLE objects in PageMaker, OLE objects must be pasted in as a graphical format or in the original program's format. If you choose a text format, the object is converted to plain text and treated like text you enter directly in PageMaker or paste in through normal copy and paste. Still confused? Try this: Don't use a text format when pasting in an OLE object.

One way of distinguishing object links from embedded links is to check the Link Options dialog box for the item. If the Link Options menu item is grayed out in the Element menu, the object is embedded. If it's available, the object is linked. (The other way is to double-click on the element and see whether its source program launches, but that takes time and precious RAM.)

Combining Publications

Another way to keep track of files is to create *books*. A book is a collection of PageMaker documents — think of it as a collection of chapters. You use the book feature to do page numbering, indexing, table-of-contents generation, and printing across a series of documents. For example, you might use this feature if each chapter in a manual is kept in a separate PageMaker file, but you want a common index or want PageMaker to number the pages after all the chapters are done.

Actually, books aren't *really* collections of chapters. They are instructions for handling page numbers. A book lists all the chapters — documents — that you want to have numbered, indexed, included in a table of contents, or printed as one batch. It doesn't actually combine the files or anything — in fact, a document can be part of more than one book. A book is actually a list of all documents that are to be processed together.

Although books are collections of documents, PageMaker creates no book files on your disk. Instead, it puts the list of book documents in the document you're working on when you choose the File⇨Book command. You should thus create the list in the table-of-contents document or the index document.

Making book

Let's skip the theory and get into the reality. Figure 8-7 shows the Book Publication List dialog box (File⇨Book). On the right side of the dialog box are the PageMaker documents in the book list. On the left is the Files/Directories scrolling list, from which you add documents — it works like any Open dialog box. The buttons in the middle let you manage what's in the book list. Buttons are grayed out if they don't apply (for example, you can't click on Insert if no document is selected to be inserted).

Figure 8-7:
PageMaker's
Book
command
allows you
to create
collections
of publica-
tions to
facilitate
indexing and
page
numbering.

Book publication list

Path: c:\pm5

Files/Directories:		Book list:
BIGNAME.PM5	**Insert**	BIGNAME.PM5
CALIBRAT.PT5		PHLEGM.PM5
CHARSET.PT5	**Remove**	NEWS2Q94.PM5
NEWS2Q94.PM5		CHX@.PM5
PHLEGM.PM5	**Move up**	AI5.PM5
[..]		
[learnpm5]	**Move down**	
[scripts]		

OK **Cancel**

Auto renumbering: ⦿ None   ◯ Next odd page
                   ◯ Next page   ◯ Next even page

- ✔ Clicking on the Insert button inserts the document selected in the left window into the location above the document selected in the right window (the book list).

- ✔ Clicking on the Remove button deletes the document selected in the book list. It does *not* delete the file from your hard disk.

- ✔ Clicking on the Move Up button moves the document selected in the book list up one position. Use this button or the Move Down button to reorder elements in the book list.

- ✔ Clicking on the Move Down button moves the document selected in the book list down one position.

That takes care of getting documents in the book list. Now for the page numbering. You use the four options at the bottom of the dialog box to tell PageMaker how to number the pages.

✔ **None:** This option turns off the book page-numbering feature. Your documents use whatever page numbers you establish in the Page Setup dialog box. This option is handy for documents such as manuals, where each chapter tends to have its own prefix, and the page numbering restarts in each chapter. For example, Chapter 1's page numbers might be A-1 through A-49, Chapter 2's might be B-1 through B-193, and so on.

✔ **Next Page:** If you choose this option, the page numbers go consecutively from number 1 (or from whatever page number you defined as the starting page number in the Page Setup dialog box (File⇨Page Setup) for that document. For example, say that Chapter 1 is 24 pages long, Chapter 2 is 67 pages long, Chapter 3 is 41 pages long, and Chapter 4 (a supplement) is 34 pages long. In the Page Setup dialog box for Chapter 4, the Restart Page Numbering box is checked, and the Start Page # value is set at 1. With this option, Chapter 2's numbering begins at 25, Chapter 3's numbering begins at 92, and Chapter 4's numbering begins at 1.

✔ **Next Odd Page:** Each chapter (document) is forced to start on a right-hand page (and a blank left page is added at the end of the previous chapter if needed to ensure this). Using the same example as above, then, Chapter 2's numbering begins at 25 and Chapter 3's begins at 93 — a blank page is inserted at the end of Chapter 2 so that Chapter 3 begins on a right-hand (odd-numbered) page.

✔ **Next Even Page:** This works like Next Odd Page except that each chapter is forced to start on a left page. In the example, then, Chapter 2's page numbering begins at 26 (a blank page is inserted before it so the chapter starts on a left page) and Chapter 3's page numbering starts at 94 (another blank page is inserted here).

If you didn't insert page number markers in your chapters, PageMaker still renumbers your pages. (The page numbers in the page icons at the bottom of the PageMaker screen reflect the new page numbering.) But when you print, you won't see page numbers. The book feature does not add page markers — it just renumbers them. Chapter 9 covers how to insert page numbers, but here's a quick preview: In your master pages, enter Ctrl+Shift+3 in a text block where you want the page numbers to appear. Keep in mind that the book feature actually renumbers the pages in each document.

Handling changes

When you click on OK to leave the Book Publication List dialog box, PageMaker asks you whether you want it to do the renumbering. Figure 8-8 shows this dialog box. If you select No, PageMaker waits to do the renumbering until you do something with the book feature, such as print all documents in a book list or index across a book's documents.

Figure 8-8:
PageMaker
lets you
defer page
renumbering
until you
print or
index a
book's
documents.

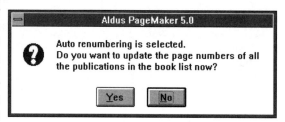

If you change the number of pages in a document, PageMaker won't update the other documents in the book list automatically. And there's no command to make it renumber the documents in the book list. To renumber them, you must either re-create the book list (by removing the current list's documents and inserting them back) or use a feature such as book printing, book indexing, or generating a table of contents to force PageMaker to renumber the documents. Otherwise, you'll have misnumbered pages — either gaps between chapters if you deleted pages in one document or duplicate page numbers if you added pages.

Print considerations

When you print from a document that has a book list defined, you can tell PageMaker to print all documents in the list. Figure 8-9 shows the Print Document dialog box with book printing checked. (Chapter 17 covers printing in detail.)

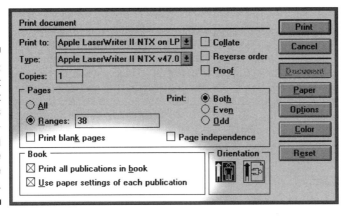

Indexing and table-of-contents considerations

When generating a comprehensive index with lots of cross-references, you need to take an extra step if you want PageMaker to work across all documents in a book list. (Chapter 12 covers indexing and tables of contents in depth.) That extra step is copying the book list to every document in the list. It sounds worse than it is.

The process is straightforward: Press the Ctrl key as you open the File menu and choose the Book command. This tells PageMaker to copy the book list to each document in the book list. You'll see the status box shown in Figure 8-10. (If you don't see this status box before the Book Publication List dialog box opens, click on Cancel and try again.)

Figure 8-10:
This status
box lets you
know that
PageMaker
is copying
the contents
of a book list
into all
documents
in the list.

Copying book publication list.

Publication: C:\PM5\NEWS2Q94.PM5

As you can see, the book feature can be a really powerful way to work with multidocument projects — books, manuals, reports, proposals, magazines. Armed with this detail, you could delve more into indexing and table-of-contents generation (see Chapter 12) or printing (see Chapter 17), but we suspect that you're yearning to get back to layout (the next chapter). OK, pick a chapter, and if you lose track, there's always the table of contents to find your way back.

Part III
That's Nice, But I Want It to Be Different

In this part . . .

So now you know how to put elements on your page. But what if you didn't place them perfectly the first time? Or you want to make an element run across several pages? What do you do? You read the chapters in this part, that's what. In these three chapters, you learn to change your layout to meet your evolving needs, to edit your text in the miniature word processor built into PageMaker, and to automate some of the work you've been doing. After you have these techniques under your belt, the sky's the limit!

Chapter 9
The Layout Shuffle

. . . .

In This Chapter

▶ Constructing a layout

▶ Placing text across multiple pages

▶ Adding cross-references

▶ Changing the number and positions of columns

. . . .

Layout is not something that happens right the first time. After all, you're working with a whole bunch of pieces, and you're trying to make them fit together as well as look nice. It's like doing a jigsaw puzzle while also figuring out what you want the end result to look like. Even if you have a basic design in mind — like a three-column format — you'll end up placing text and graphics, moving them, moving them again, and modifying some of their settings as you work with other elements and begin to see how the various pieces interact.

In Chapter 4, you learned how to place text into PageMaker, but clearly there's a lot more to doing layout than randomly placing text. You probably noticed right off that placing a text file didn't lay it out for you — or even put text in the next column. Why not? PageMaker is not a mind-reader, and it has no idea what layout you have in mind. You wouldn't want PageMaker to automate your job out of existence, would you? You would? Well, give it time. Machines will take over all our jobs one day, and then they'll round us up and put us in zoos, and our pain and suffering will be over. But in the meantime, you still have to tell PageMaker what to do with your text and graphics.

Starting a Layout

The best way to explain the layout process is to provide you with an example. Suppose that you're creating a simple black-and-white newsletter. It's a three-column newsletter, and its master pages include the page numbers and some decorative lines at the top and bottom of the page. Prior to laying out the newsletter, you created a blank copy of the newsletter — called a *template* —

that has only the regular stuff placed: the title, contents box, and the like, plus styles. (Chapter 11 shows how to create a template — it even uses the one shown in this chapter as the example.) Figure 9-1 shows page 1 of the template.

Don't worry that you don't have access to this specific template. It's not important that you learn how to create a Computer Press Association newsletter. What is important is that you learn how to approach such a newsletter and how to use PageMaker's tools. Also, because you don't learn the steps involved in creating a template until Chapter 11, some of the information being presented here may be a little fuzzy to you. Rest assured that everything will fall into place later. The steps in this chapter are just to give you an idea of the overall process of laying out your pages.

Before randomly placing text, you first need to make a list of all your stories and all your graphics. Prioritize those elements — which should get prominent attention and appear on the front page or early in the document? Which can be cut or shortened if space is a problem? Which stories include graphics — a chart, scanned photo, or maybe illustration?

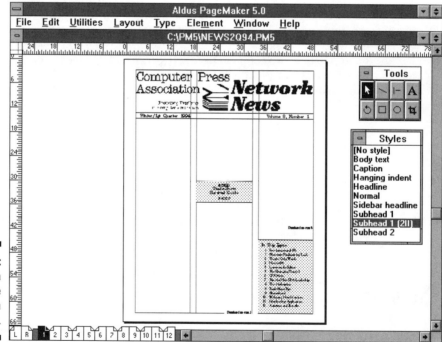

Figure 9-1:
Page 1 of a template for a newsletter.

It's a good idea to sketch out your layout placement ideas before you start the layout. It's really easy to do a rough sketch via paper and pencil — less work than doing it on a computer, even with PageMaker. Figure 9-2 shows such a sketch for the example newsletter's front page. (By the way, the # symbol is a layout convention for "end of story," while the down arrow is a convention for "text continues.")

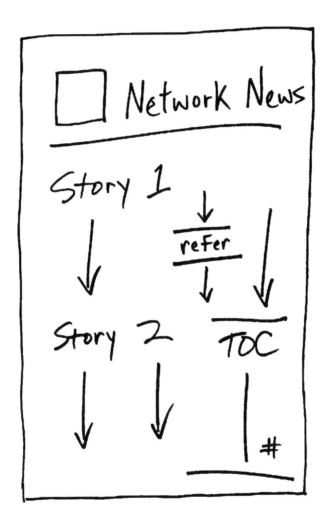

Figure 9-2:
Sketching
out a layout
before
implementing
it in
PageMaker
can be a
real time-
saver.

Page 1: Placing stories

Assume that you have your list of stories and graphics and have decided which ones should appear where. The next thing to do is place the lead story, as in Figure 9-3. Notice a few things:

✔ The story starts about a half inch below the issue date and volume number text. That's no accident — there's a rectangle there with no fill and no line but with text wrap turned on (see Chapter 7). The rectangle ensures that no matter where you click the mouse underneath that text, the story always appears the correct distance away. (Normally, the text block begins wherever you click the paragraph icon when placing text.) Without such a device, you'd have to place the text accurately by eye or place it and then modify its location, either by hand or by using the Control palette's X and Y fields to specify its starting points.

You can also accurately place text and graphics by dragging a ruler guide to the point at which you would like your text blocks to originate. If you turn on Snap to Rulers, the loaded text placement icon snaps to the guides you have set up.

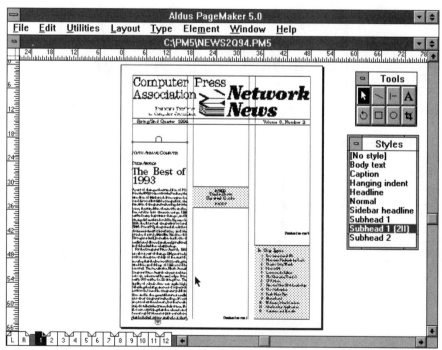

Figure 9-3:
Placing the
first story on
page 1.

✔ The story falls within the column guides. By turning on <u>S</u>nap to Guides in the <u>L</u>ayout⇨Guides <u>a</u>nd Rulers submenu, you can be assured that even if you don't position your story's paragraph cursor precisely on the column's left boundary, it will be positioned there. Otherwise, the text's left boundary will be wherever you click, even though PageMaker still makes the right boundary the nearest column guide.

✔ PageMaker doesn't always place text inside your column guides. If you click too far away from the column boundary, it doesn't realize that you want the text to be in the column and it makes the text as wide as it can — either to the page's right margin or to the boundary of a graphic with text wrap turned on. This can be a real nuisance because you then have to resize the column by hand. The only real way to reduce the chance of this happening is to work in a close-up view so that you can make sure that your cursor is near or on the correct column location to begin with.

✔ The story does not continue on the next column because the Autof<u>l</u>ow option in the <u>L</u>ayout menu is turned off. (If the option is turned on, PageMaker places the entire story, one column at a time page by page, automatically.) Why turn off the option? Because at this point, you probably don't know where you want your text to flow throughout the newsletter, and there's no point in having PageMaker do a lot of work that you'll likely undo later. So when would you use Autoflow? Any time your layout is less modular, as when laying out a report or book that flows one story at a time.

✔ That down-pointing triangle at the bottom of the text block (it's red if you have a color monitor) means that there's more text in the story that hasn't been placed.

✔ The headline and kicker (the text above the headline) break awkwardly — they clearly should be wider than the column.

Now you have to decide what to do next. You could place another story on the first page, or you could fine-tune this story. Neither option is wrong — it just depends on how certain you are of what you want to do.

For this example, suppose that you know that you want the first story to consume the top half of the page, as in the upcoming Figure 9-7 (go ahead, take a peek now). You decide to tackle that text placement before worrying about the second story. The first thing to do is make the headline go across the three columns. This story is the lead story, after all, and its headline should be really hard to miss. To make the change, you just select the bottom right handle on the text block and resize the block so that only the kicker and the headline appear, as shown in Figure 9-4.

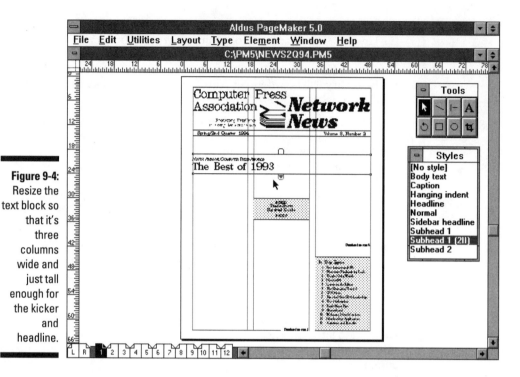

Figure 9-4:
Resize the
text block so
that it's
three
columns
wide and
just tall
enough for
the kicker
and
headline.

Now, to lay out the rest of the story within the right column sizes, you need to create a new text block. Pay attention — this is something you'll need to do time and time again. You click just once on the red down-pointing triangle in the text block containing the headline. You'll get the [▤] cursor, which we some-times call the *paragraph icon.* Click near the left margin of the first column, just below the headline. That places the text back below the headline, as Figure 9-5 shows.

Because you don't want the text in the first column to go all the way down the column, you have to resize it. The way to do that is to select the text block with the Arrow tool and drag up on the text placement handle or the resize handle (see Figure 9-6). The text placement handle always has one of three symbols in it.

Now let's make another assumption about this layout: You decide that you want the second story's headline to align with the top of the contents box at the lower right of the page. (Take another peek at Figure 9-7 for a preview.) So you have to roll the first story's text up to just above that location. (You need to raise it slightly higher so that there is some space between the two stories — so that people can easily recognize that there *are* two stories.)

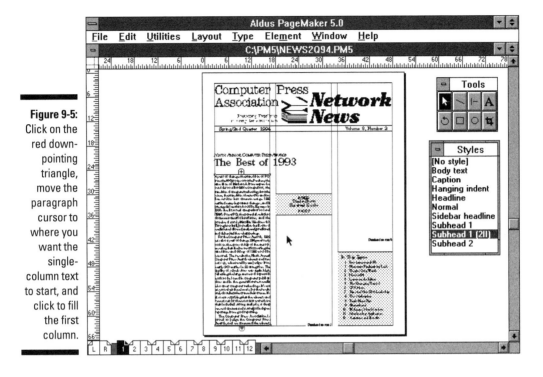

Figure 9-5:
Click on the red down-pointing triangle, move the paragraph cursor to where you want the single-column text to start, and click to fill the first column.

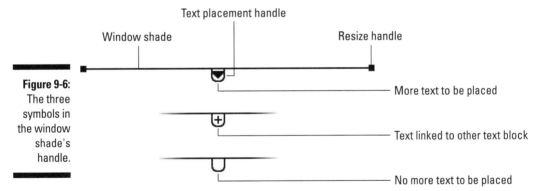

Figure 9-6:
The three symbols in the window shade's handle.

A better way to approach this is to create the right size text block in the first place. You can drag the 🗒 cursor to create a newly sized text block. For example, after creating the headline text block, you would click on the red down-pointing triangle and then drag to create a new text block that is as wide as the first one but only half as tall. PageMaker reflows the text into your text block.

If you see a dashed box below a window shade, it means that the depth of the window shade is not deep enough to accommodate the current line of text. The bottom of the dashed box indicates the text's depth. If you make the window shade as deep as that dashed box, the line of text will fit.

Continue placing each column the same way: Click on the red down-pointing triangle, move the paragraph cursor to the location where you want to put the text, and click. You can move to other pages — click on the page numbers at the bottom of the screen — and continue the placement of the story, if you know where you want the text to go. For now, assume that you've placed the rest of this story's text on page 1 and have also placed the second story. Figure 9-7 shows the result.

Clicking on that down-pointing red triangle, moving the paragraph icon to the new column, going back to the down-pointing red triangle, and so on, and so on, is a real pain. PageMaker's creators aren't sadists, so they added a little something to ease the work. If you are going to place text into several columns, hold the Shift key when you click the paragraph cursor. PageMaker flows the text into the column and then displays another paragraph cursor — no need to click on that down-pointing red triangle. (The difference between this and Autoflow is that *you* get to decide which columns the text is placed in, and at what locations in those columns. With Autoflow, PageMaker places the text in every subsequent column, and it always places text at the top of each column.)

Figure 9-7:
The completed placement of the first page's two stories.

What if you selected that triangle accidentally? You really don't want to create a new column. Just click on any other tool in the Tool palette and then click on the Arrow tool again. The paragraph icon is gone.

That red down-pointing triangle is called, officially, the *down arrow in the window shade handle*, which is worse than *that down-pointing red triangle*. So, from here on out, it shall be christened the *more-text handle*.

Page 1: Fine-tuning placement

Take a look at Figure 9-8: Notice how the columns don't align? That's an inevitable problem when you're creating a PageMaker layout. Fortunately, you can use the Control palette to fix these off-balance columns by giving them the same upper coordinate. Here's how.

1. **Select the text block in the first column.**

2. **Select an upper handle in the Control palette.**

   The handles are in that little square on the left of the palette; the handle that is thicker than the others is the selected one. Note that the handle selected in the palette has nothing to do with which window shade handle was last selected. As far as we can tell, it's random. But the handle selected stays selected as you select other text blocks.

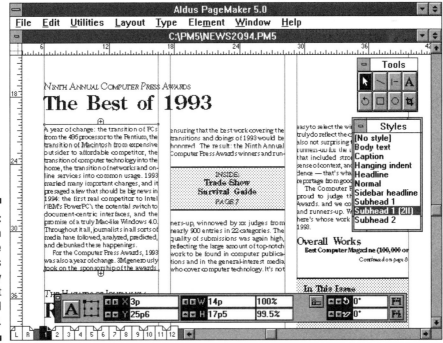

Figure 9-8:
The problem
with these
text blocks
is they
aren't
aligned
correctly.

3. Jot down the Y value.

The Y value in the Control palette reflects the vertical position of the text block. In the text block selected in Figure 9-8, it's 25p6 (25 picas, 6 points, or 4.25 inches). The measurement system doesn't matter, by the way — just write the Y coordinate down.

4. Select the next text block and look at its Y coordinate.

If you want the second text block's Y coordinate to match the first text block's, enter the first text block's Y coordinate (25p6, in this case) in the Control palette and press Return or click on the big *A* icon at the far left of the Control palette.

5. Do this for every column you want to align.

Figure 9-9 shows the columns in the first story aligned.

Another way to align text blocks is by using the Balance Columns addition. It's a lot faster to use this addition than to change each column's coordinates in the Control palette. To use this addition, select all the columns you want aligned (click on the first text block and Shift+click on the others). Then choose Utilities⇨Aldus Additions⇨Balance Columns to get the Balance Columns dialog box (shown in Figure 9-10). Select the alignment you want (you'll almost always want to align text by the top) and click on OK.

Figure 9-9: The text blocks are now aligned.

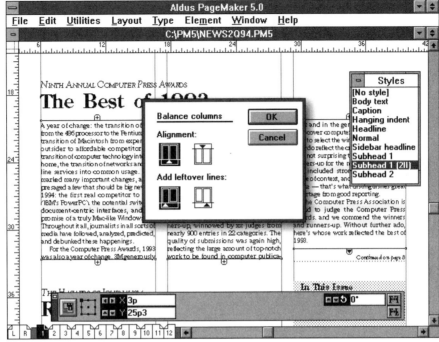

Continued on page 8

Figure 9-10:
The Balance
Columns
addition can
align
multiple text
blocks
simul-
taneously.

So why would you ever align columns the long way described earlier? Because Balance Columns makes an assumption that may not be true: It aligns the columns based on the position of the highest text block (or the lowest, if you're aligning the bottoms). Of course, you can still use this addition and then use the Control palette to change the Y coordinate for all of the text blocks simultaneously. If multiple elements are selected, the icon at far left in the Control palette changes to the multi-element icon (as is shown in Figure 9-10), and any changes made to coordinates or other palette values are applied to all the selected elements. Any options that can't be applied to multiple elements don't appear in the Control palette.

By the way, while you're using the Control palette to align columns, you can also change the column width, height, and horizontal coordinate (via the settings in the W, H, and X option boxes, respectively).

With the text blocks aligned, creating the rest of the sample newsletter, shown in Figure 9-11, is related to a few embellishments:

✔ Adding a drop cap to the second story. (See Chapter 6 for details on drop caps.)

✔ Adding a graphic for the first story (instead of a drop cap, the example uses a logo related to that story's contents). (See Chapter 7 for details on wrapping text around graphics.)

✔ Adding a square box in front of the kicker text. (The square box is just a symbol from a symbols font. You could also use embedded graphics, which are covered in Chapter 14.)

✔ Rewriting the lead headline so that it fills up the three-column space. The original headline was too short for the space it occupied — generally, every column should have some headline text above it, although the last column doesn't need to have the headline extend all the way to its right margin.

Headlines often have to be rewritten to better fit the layout — they may be too long or too short. If you're just doing layout, have an editor rewrite the headline for you — just mark on the printout that the headline is too short or too long. If you're doing both the layout and the editing, be prepared to change the headlines as you lay out stories.

Except for putting in the correct page numbers for the cross-references, the contents box, and that "In This Issue" box, you're now done with page 1.

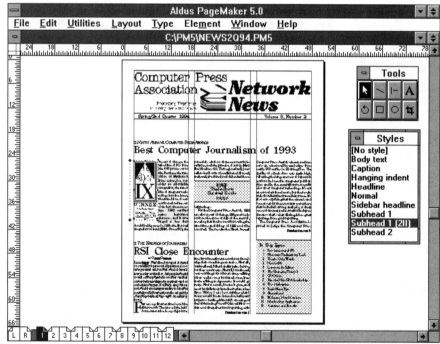

Figure 9-11:
The final page 1, with drop caps, graphics, and other typographic embellishments added.

Pages 2 and 3

At this point, you have a choice: Move on to page 2 or move to the page(s) that will contain the rest of the text from the stories on page 1. Again, the order of creating the pages and placing the stories is not important from a technical view — *you* decide what you want to work on when.

Let's assume though — we're making a lot of assumptions here, aren't we? — that you've decided to move on to page 2. In many cases, such as when working on a newsletter, it makes sense to place the start of each story first and then deal with the remainder of each story later. However, that may not be a good approach for other documents. You certainly wouldn't lay out a book that way — you'd place all the text and graphics for one chapter before moving on to the next.

At any rate, take a look now at the blank page 2 (and page 3, since they're on facing pages) in Figure 9-12. The text block with the gray box in the first column is the *masthead* — the text that contains the names of the staff, the address, and other such information. Most newsletters and magazines have something like this, and it's traditionally on the second page. (It could, of course, go any-where.) Because the masthead appears in every issue, it's an element that you would normally place in your template. (Again, creating and using templates is explained fully in Chapter 11.) Imagine that you did so and that the masthead — along with a few other elements, including page numbers and the newsletter

Figure 9-12: The template for pages 2 and 3.

title — are already present and accounted for when you turn to page 2 in your PageMaker layout.

That masthead leaves just two columns on page 2 for new material. It's a good idea to use such a regular space to hold regular elements, such as letters to the editor, or the president's message, or a column by a particular contributor to your publication. In this newsletter, a columnist's work gets this position. You place the column as you place any story.

But let's make this column a fancy one. Suppose that a caricature of the columnist is to appear within the story, with the text wrapping around the graphic. (See Chapter 7 for details on text wrap.) And suppose also that when you try to place the story and graphic, there's not enough text from the columnist to fit the available space, as in Figure 9-13.

No matter what you're laying out, you'll run into this kind of situation — text and space almost never match. Usually, you have too much text, but sometimes you have too little. (It's a conspiracy!) If you're dealing with reports and books, you can always add another page (or at least almost always) or go a page short — the length of the document is flexible. That's usually not true for newsletters. Most are printed on 11 × 17-inch sheets and folded — so a sheet contains four pages. If you run short, you have blank pages. If you run over, you have to add blank pages. Even if your elements fit in the number of pages required for printing, you may have some pages with gaps in them, as in Figure 9-13.

If you're responsible for producing newsletters, you'll need to deal with such gaps frequently. You can do several things to fix the problem. But first, there are some things you should *never* do:

- ✔ Never change the size of the text, the space between lines, or the width of the columns to "stretch" the text. Your text will look awful — amateurish. You get a ransom-note effect, with different-size text throughout. Embarrassing!

- ✔ Never leave the gaps. They look unprofessional — like you forgot something or were too lazy to handle the problem.

So what can you do? Try the following:

- ✔ Have extra elements available. Maybe a selection of small cartoons. Or some short stories (such as notes to your reader about upcoming events, or "For more information" announcements, or "Help wanted" notices, or "Did you know" trivia). This is the best option because it lets you add information for the reader while giving you layout flexibility. Figure 9-14 shows how to close a gap with such an element. It's a good bet that if you didn't know that the columnist's text was short and this element was added as filler, you would think that the designer planned the page to look this way.

Figure 9-13:
Whoops! Even with the graphic, the columnist's material is too short for the space.

Figure 9-14:
Adding a filler story takes care of the gap — and adds information for the reader. A two-for-one deal!

✔ Use *pull-quotes*. Pull-quotes are short excerpts from the text that are printed in larger type and set apart from the story — they may be in a box, or between lines, or on a background. (The right page in Figure 9-15 includes a pull-quote.) However, a pull-quote won't solve the problem in Figure 9-13 because there's no room for one — the graphic is too large and leaves insufficient space for another element in the story. It works in Figure 9-15 because there is plenty of space — in fact, adding a second pull-quote at the bottom left section of the page might make it look more attractive; now it's pretty dull and gray. Figure 9-16 shows examples of different pull-quotes. Remember, the idea is to call attention to the story's content (so pick interesting excerpts) *and* to offer a visual element on the page that makes it more attractive (so make sure that the pull-quote design isn't altogether ugly).

✔ Use a longer headline. Rewrite the headline so it takes two lines rather than one. This works only occasionally; a two-line headline can be overwhelming if the headline is wide or if its typeface is bold and/or size is large. That's the case in this example newsletter — two-line heads are just too intense.

Figure 9-15:
A pull-quote (right side of right page) can fill out a short story and add visual interest to an otherwise dull page.

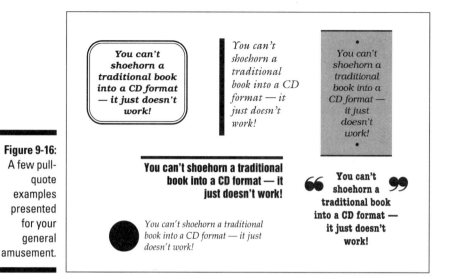

Figure 9-16:
A few pull-
quote
examples
presented
for your
general
amusement.

Look more closely at the filler element on page 2 (refer to Figure 9-15). Notice a couple of things about it:

- ✔ It's on a gray background, which helps differentiate it from the columnist's text. There is also a line above and a line below the background — this is just a variation on putting a box around a sidebar or small text element. (Why doesn't the text placed on top of the gray background wrap around the background, like the columnist's text does? Glad you asked. If you place a text block so that it falls wholly within a graphic's boundaries, it won't wrap — after all, there's no place for it to wrap to.)

- ✔ The text runs across the two columns, which also helps differentiate it from the other text. And because of the gray box, the text doesn't quite go all the way to the edge of the columns. To create this element, the text block was resized to leave about 0.2 inches of space on either side. But the work is worth it — the margin of gray around the text makes the text more readable. The first example in Figure 9-17 shows what happens when there's no margin. If you used a box instead of a gray background to separate the filler text from the columnist's text, you would have had a similar margin.

If you're eagle-eyed, you may have noticed a symbol at the very right of the last line in the columnist's text on page 2 in Figures 9-14 and 9-15. The use of a symbol, called a *dingbat*, to indicate the end of a story is a common technique in newsletters, magazines, and other multistory documents. The symbol lets the reader know definitively that a particular story is done. To create a dingbat, pick a character from a symbols font or use an embedded graphic (see Chapter 14). To position it at the end of the line, precede the dingbat character with a tab. In the style for your text, define a right-aligned tab that stops just shy of the column width. For example, if your column is 2 inches wide, place the tab at 1.9

inches. (You need to do this because PageMaker will position the dingbat at the beginning of the next line if it aligns completely against the right margin. Clearly, it *should* work if you make the tab stop the same as the margin location, but *should* doesn't mean *does*.) Chapter 6 covers special type techniques in more detail.

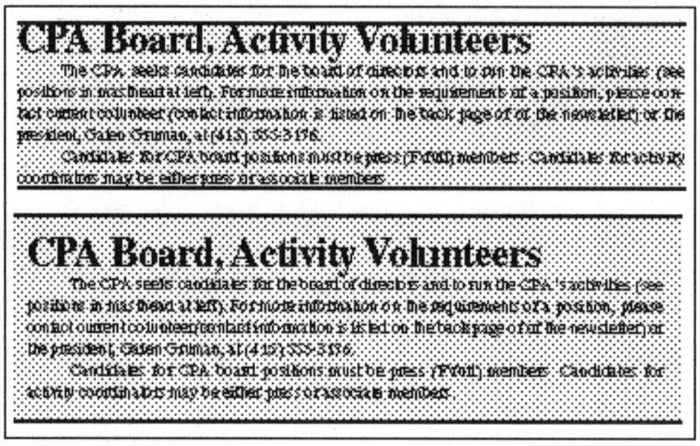

Figure 9-17:
Without any margin between text and graphic elements (top), your design looks cramped. A looser alternative appears at bottom.

By continuing the placement of stories on subsequent pages, using the same techniques, you'll soon have the main elements arranged. But there's still that pesky detail of the extra text that will go on "other" pages. How does it get there, and how does the reader know where it is? Read on.

Handling Jumped Text

Text that starts on one page and continues on another is called *jumped text* among layout *cognoscenti* (that's Latin for *know-it-alls*). You've probably figured out that placing the text on other pages is easy: you click on the more-text icon, move to the page you want to put the text on, click the paragraph icon at the desired location, and continue the layout.

But you need to do one other thing to properly jump text: add continued lines.

What's a *continued line*? It's a line of text that tells the reader where the rest of the story is — what page it came from or what page it continues on to. Take a look at Figure 9-18. It shows both kinds:

  ✔ At the bottom of the first column is a *continued-on line*. It's very simple — just a line in italics that aligns to the right of the column. No frills.

➤ The third column contains a *continued-from line,* which is more elaborate. It includes a headline (so that people can find the topic when they flip over to the new page) and a line saying what page the story continues from (for people who may be intrigued by the topic and want to find the beginning of the story). Because unrelated text appears above the continued story, it's a good idea to place a line between the two stories to help the reader distinguish the continued head from a subhead in the other story.

Figure 9-18: Two kinds of continued lines (both spotlighted).

When using devices such as headlines, continued lines, and the like, it's best to be consistent. Yes, walking on the wild side has its benefits — but not for bread-and-butter elements. Use common techniques for the common elements. For example, notice that both the continued-on and continued-from text in Figure 9-18 are in italics — it helps tie them together and reinforce to the reader that they serve the same function (identifying cross-references). And the line above the continued story means the same thing that it meant in Figure 9-15: It separates unrelated elements.

In constructing a continued line, don't just type it into the text block containing the story; put the continued line in its own text block, as in Figure 9-18. Otherwise, if you add a line to the story, your continued line will get bumped to a new page. Whoops!

You should know one more thing about creating continued lines: PageMaker can't manage the cross-referenced page numbers for you. You have to keep track of the page numbers yourself and then update the numbers when the layout is truly complete. (You may want to use *X* as a placeholder instead of an actual page number; that way, you know which page numbers need to be checked and updated.) Sounds like the kind of thing that PageMaker should do for you, doesn't it? Maybe one day. In the meantime, the program offers a tool that helps you find where a story continues to or came from, in case you lose track. The tool is called Traverse Textblocks, and you can find it in the Utilities⇨Aldus Additions submenu. (If you don't see the command in the submenu, choose the More option to display more commands.)

PageMaker also has an addition to create continued lines for you. It's not great, but it's serviceable for many people. One advantage is that it will figure out the right page number — but it won't update that page number if the story's page order is changed later. The addition, which is called Add Cont'd Line and is available via Utilities⇨Aldus Additions, automatically adds a *Continued from page x* or *Continued on page x* line above or below the current text block. It also creates a style called *Cont. On* if you choose the Bottom of Textblock option and a style called *Cont. From* if you choose the Top of Textblock column. (It's a good idea to define these styles first with the settings you want rather than let the addition create them. You'll likely want to change the settings of the styles it creates anyhow.) The addition rolls down the top of the text block by one line — or rolls up the bottom of the text block by one line — to make room for the continued line.

Because this addition shortens the text block for which you are adding a continued line, you may have text missing at the end of your document. The number of lines that end up being pushed into the final text block may not fit in that final text block. To avoid this, shorten text boxes that will have continued lines by one line *before* using the addition — in other words, make room for the continued line in advance. The addition will still shorten the text block by a line, but you can lengthen it when the addition is done.

Speaking of having text scroll off into oblivion, an addition called Find Overset Text shows you which stories have text that hasn't been placed in your document — that is, any story whose final text block has the more-text icon rather than the no-text icon on the window shade handle.

Altering Columns and Text Blocks

After you've laid out text in columns, you may decide that you want to change the number of columns or maybe move a column somewhere else. Be careful. This part of doing a PageMaker layout can really get you in trouble. It's not your fault — the blame is in how PageMaker handles text blocks. If you're not careful, you can delete text accidentally, and perhaps permanently. Here's an example of how it works.

Changing the number of columns

Take a look at Figure 9-19. It shows a three-column sidebar in a three-column page. After looking at it, you decide that you want the sidebar to be a two-column sidebar to make it more visually distinct from the rest of the text on the page and its facing page. So all you have to do is select the three columns and change the number of columns to two, right? Wrong — just try to find a command or option to do this. There isn't any. No, what PageMaker makes you do is delete one column and resize the remaining ones. It's in the deletion of a column where you can lose text. (If you want to *add* a column, all you have to do is resize the existing ones, click on the more-text icon on the last column's window shade handle, and place the new column.)

Let's say that you delete the middle column (using Edit⇨Cut or Ctrl+X) and resize the other two columns so that they're wider. That deleted text block is removed from the chain, or thread, of text blocks making up the story. Even if you paste the deleted text block back in, it remains apart from the original story — when you select the block, you'll notice that the linked-text icon is replaced by the no-text icon on its window shade handles. To reinstate the text from that cut block back into the story, you'd have to switch to the Text tool, select all text in that block (via Edit⇨Select All or Ctrl+A), place your text cursor at the end of the previous block or the beginning of the next block, and paste that text into the block. A royal pain. (And if you used Edit⇨Clear or pressed the Delete key to delete the text block, you can't paste it back in — it's gone for good.)

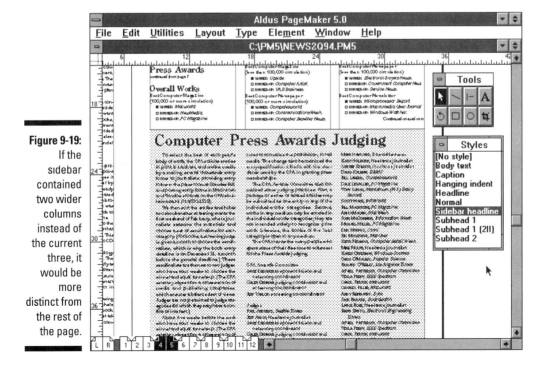

Figure 9-19:
If the sidebar contained two wider columns instead of the current three, it would be more distinct from the rest of the page.

There's another possible way to recover deleted text and relink it to the rest of the story: re-import the text via File⇨Place or Ctrl+D. When doing so, you would click on a text block containing the story, open the Place Document dialog box, select the text file, and — this is crucial — click on the Replacing Entire Story button before clicking on OK. However, this approach has several potential problems:

- ✔ If the text was created in PageMaker, there is no text file to reimport.

- ✔ If the text was changed in PageMaker, those changes will be lost. Even if you exported the changed text from PageMaker to the text file (via File⇨Export), much of the formatting done in PageMaker can be lost because this information is not compatible with the text file's word processor format.

- ✔ If the source text file was modified in the word processor after you imported it the first time, you'll be importing the new version, and it may have changed significantly.

What to do? Instead of deleting the unwanted column, select one of the window shade handles and roll it up (or down) until it touches the other handle. Figure 9-20 shows what this looks like. You don't even have to delete the empty window shade — if you select any other element and then try to reselect it, you'll find that it's gone — kaput, dead.

Figure 9-20:
Roll up a window shade until there's nothing left of it to get rid of a column or text block and flow its contents into a linked text block.

Moving columns or text blocks

The same potential problems exist if you decide you want to move a column of text from one page to another. *Don't cut and paste linked text blocks.*

Instead, use the empty window shade technique just described to remove the text block from one page. Then click on the linked-text or more-text icon on the bottom of the last remaining text block on the page to get the paragraph icon, move to the new desired page, and click where you want the column to continue. (You get the linked-text icon if the text block you're deleting and adding somewhere else falls within a series of linked text blocks; you get the more-text icon if the text block to be deleted and added elsewhere is the last text block in the series.)

If you want to move a text block within the current page or within the current facing pages, just drag it to its new location.

Inserting columns or text blocks

Let's say that you have a story on page 6 that continues on page 29, and you discover there's enough free space on page 15 for some of that story. How do you add a text block between two linked text boxes so that the text flows through the new, middle block? You click on the linked-text icon on the bottom window shade handle of the text block on page 6 or click on the linked-text icon on the top window shade handle of the text block on page 29. Either way, you get the paragraph icon. Move to page 15, position the paragraph icon where you want to place the new text block linked to those on pages 6 and 29, and click the mouse button. A text block appears, and if you check, you'll see that the text is flowing properly through it from the previous text block and to the next one.

You can use this same technique to start a story earlier in the layout — just click on the no-text icon on the top window shade handle for the first text block in the story. You can also use it to add columns or other text blocks on the same page, not just on different pages.

Chapter 10

I Didn't Mean to Say That

*Y*ou may not know this about PageMaker, but hidden within the labyrinths of this page-layout program is a fully functioning word processor. No kidding. It can check your text for spelling errors, search and replace text, and view hidden characters such as tabs, spaces, and carriage returns. But the biggest benefit to the *Story Editor*, as it's called, is that it's fast. If you've ever tried to edit text inside PageMaker on a 386SX or some other moderately capable machine, you know that PageMaker can be fiendishly slow, often refusing to so much as keep up with your keystrokes. But this is not a problem in the Story Editor. Thanks to its simplified interface and straightforward options, the Story Editor is always fast.

How Do I Get There?

Well, there is one slow part to using the Story Editor, and that's opening it. To accomplish this, click anywhere inside the story you want to edit with the Text tool or the Arrow tool and then choose Edit⇨Edit Story or press Ctrl+E. Another method is to triple-click on the text block with the Arrow tool selected. The Story Editor appears on-screen, as shown in Figure 10-1.

To create a new story, make sure that your cursor is outside of all text blocks and press Ctrl+E.

Style sheet Tab

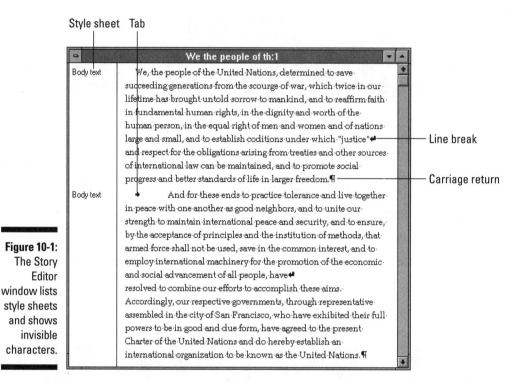

Line break

Carriage return

Figure 10-1:
The Story
Editor
window lists
style sheets
and shows
invisible
characters.

Before we go any farther, you should know a few things about the Story Editor window:

✔ The Story Editor displays all text in the selected story. Whether the story continues across 70 pages or is only a single word long, all text in the story is available in the window. Just use the arrow keys and scroll bar to scroll to the portion of the story that you want to edit.

✔ Several menus change in the Story Editor. The Layout menu is replaced by the Story menu, the Element menu disappears (because you can't edit graphics), and a few commands that were previously dimmed in the Utilities menu become available.

✔ You can't access any of the tools inside the Story Editor. It's as if the Text tool is perpetually selected.

✔ You can apply formatting commands, including fonts, type sizes, style sheets, and all the others, to text inside the Story Editor, but you won't see the results of your changes. The Story Editor shows all text in a single typeface and type size, regardless of its real formatting. (You can still see type styles such as bold and italic.) This may seem weird but it's actually good news. The Story Editor is designed especially for text editing; showing only one font and type size helps the editor run faster.

✔ If you don't like the way the text looks on-screen, you can change it. Choose File⇨Preferences and click on the Other button to display the Other Preferences dialog box. The options toward the bottom of the dialog box, spotlighted in Figure 10-2, allow you to change the appearance of Story Editor elements on-screen. To change the typeface and size, select new options from the Font pop-up menu and enter a value into the Size option box. Keep in mind that your changes have no impact on the font and size of the actual text; the only purpose of these options is to make your text more legible on-screen.

✔ The style sheet applied to each paragraph is listed in the left column of the window. If no style sheet name appears in the column, no style sheet is applied to the text. If you don't want to see the style name column, deselect the Display Style Names option in the Other Preferences dialog box (see Figure 10-2). You can also choose Story⇨Display Style Names.

✔ In the Story Editor, you can view invisible characters such as tabs, line breaks, and carriage returns, as labeled in Figure 10-1. Spaces appear as small dots. Being able to see these characters can be very useful; they're normally invisible, so it's easy to lose track of them. But if you want your invisible characters to stay invisible, you can choose Story⇨Display ¶ to hide them. (You can also deselect the Display ¶ checkbox in the Other Preferences dialog box.)

✔ All selection techniques work the same way in the Story Editor as they do in the standard layout view. Double-click on a word to select it, triple-click to select an entire paragraph, and so on.

✔ Changes made inside the story window are automatically applied to your document, just as if you had edited the text in the standard layout view.

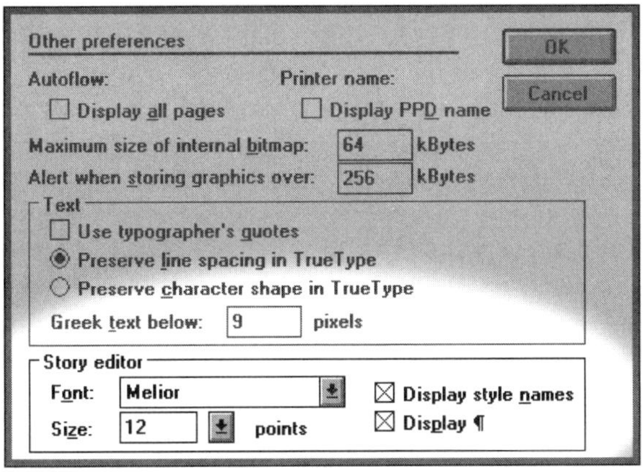

Figure 10-2:
Use the options at the bottom of this dialog box to control the appearance of text and other elements inside the Story Editor.

✔ To return to the layout view at any time, double-click on the close box of the Story Editor window, press Ctrl+Shift+E, or choose Story⇨Close Story.

✔ You can also return to the layout view without closing the Story Editor, which makes it faster to access the editor next time around. Either press Ctrl+E (Edit⇨Edit Layout) or click in the layout window in the background. When not in use, the Story Editor remains on-screen but appears gray.

Checking Your Spelling

The Story Editor is fast — you can scroll through text on multiple pages in a matter of seconds — but editing text inside the Story Editor is not much different than it is in the standard layout view. You apply commands from the Type menu to change formatting and apply style sheets, you use commands in the Edit menu to cut and copy text, and you select and replace text just as described in the previous chapters.

The big difference between the Story Editor and the layout view is the addition of a few commands under the Utilities menu. The most important of these, Spelling, lets you check the spelling of words in your document.

Choose Utilities⇨Spelling or press Ctrl+L to display the Spelling dialog box. Click on the Start button to instruct PageMaker to begin looking for misspelled words. When it finds a word that doesn't match any of the spellings in its dictionary, it displays the word at the top of the dialog box, as in the case of *coditions* in Figure 10-3. Provided that the Alternate Spellings checkbox is checked, PageMaker also offers a list of alternates below the Change To option box.

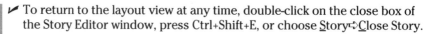

Figure 10-3:
The Spelling dialog box lists misspelled words and offers alternate spellings.

Spelling	
Unknown word : coditions	Ignore
Change to: coditions	Replace
conditions	Add...
coactions	
collections	

Options: ☒ Alternate spellings   ☒ Show duplicates

Search document: ⦿ Current publication   ○ All publications
Search story: ○ Selected text   ⦿ Current story   ○ All stories

At this point, you have three options:

✔ **Select an alternate:** Click on one of the alternate spellings in the list to make it appear in the Change To option box. Then click on the Replace button to change the word in your document and search for the next misspelling. Or just double-click on the correct word in the list to do the same thing in a single action.

✔ **Correct the word manually:** If no correct alternates appear, you have to locate the correct spelling the old-fashioned way: by looking it up in the dictionary. So much for progress, eh? When you find the right spelling — it won't be obvious, otherwise PageMaker would probably have figured it out — enter it into the Change To option box and click on the Replace button.

✔ **Ignore the word or add it to the dictionary:** If the word is spelled correctly — not even PageMaker knows every word on the planet — you can follow one of two courses of action. Either continue on to the next misspelling by clicking on the Ignore button or take a moment to teach PageMaker this new word by clicking on the Add button, which is the subject of the next section.

Teaching PageMaker to spell

PageMaker can be a little irritating in its zeal to find misspelled words. You can't tell the program to ignore words that contain only a single letter, abbreviations composed entirely of capital letters, or words with special punctuation (as in *PageMaker's* vs. *PageMaker*). To get PageMaker to stop bugging you about a specific spelling, you have to add the spelling to the dictionary. To do this, click on the Add button in the Spelling dialog box. The dialog box shown in Figure 10-4 appears.

The Word option box contains the word as it's spelled in your document. Tilde (~) symbols divide the word into syllables. Each tilde represents the location of a possible hyphen. The number of tildes indicates precedent. In other words, PageMaker is more likely to break the word at a two-tilde point than a one-tilde point.

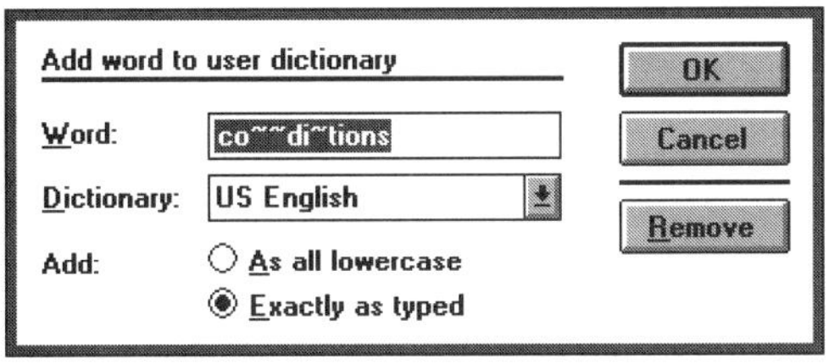

Figure 10-4:
Use this dialog box to add a word to PageMaker's spelling dictionary.

Add word to user dictionary

Word: co~~di~tions

Dictionary: US English

Add: ○ As all lowercase
● Exactly as typed

OK   Cancel   Remove

The original tildes represent PageMaker's best guess. If you don't like the location of a tilde or the precedent applied to a specific hyphenation point, delete a few tildes, add a few more elsewhere, and so on. For example, if you prefer that PageMaker hyphenate *coditions* as *codi-tions*, rather than *co-ditions*, position more tildes between the *i* and *t*, as in *co~di~~tions*.

You can enter up to three tildes in a row to represent a very high level of preference. If you never want the word to hyphenate, delete all tildes from the word.

If the misspelled word begins with an uppercase character because it appears at the beginning of a sentence, but you want PageMaker to save the word using only lowercase characters, select the <u>A</u>s All Lowercase radio button near the bottom of the dialog box. If the word is a special term that should always be capitalized exactly as it appears in the <u>W</u>ord option box, leave the <u>E</u>xactly as Typed radio button selected.

Finally, click on the OK button to add the word to PageMaker's dictionary. After the program adds the word, you'll be returned to the Spelling dialog box.

In case you're wondering about the <u>R</u>emove button, this allows you to remove words from the dictionary. Say you accidentally add the word *coditions*, even though it's not a real word in any one's book. To get rid of it, you click on the Add button in the Spelling dialog box (it doesn't matter what word appears in the Change To option box). Then you enter *coditions* into the <u>W</u>ord option box — with or without tildes, again it doesn't matter — and click on the <u>R</u>emove button. The word is out of there.

Other spelling options

Just to make sure that you understand everything, the following list explains the remaining options in the Spelling dialog box:

- ✔ **Show Duplicates:** Selected by default, this checkbox instructs PageMaker to search for any repeated words. The makers of the B-movie "Attack of the the Eye People" — that's how the title read on-screen — could have used this option. Unfortunately, they didn't have spell checkers back then. Leave this option turned on.

- ✔ **Search Document:** You can check the spelling of words in more than one PageMaker document at a time. If you select the All Publications radio button, PageMaker checks all documents belonging to the same book as the current document. (As discussed in Chapter 8, you establish a book using <u>F</u>ile⇨<u>B</u>ook.) Keep in mind that checking multiple documents at once may take a lot of time.

✔ **Search Story:** These radio buttons let you check only the selected text in the Story Editor; all text in the story, whether selected or not; or all stories throughout the entire PageMaker document. Select the All Stories option at least once before saving the final version of your document so that no text block is left unchecked.

Finding that Special Word

The Spelling command searches your text for spelling errors. But what if you have something more specific in mind? Suppose, for example, that you're pretty sure you mentioned Vice President Muckimuck of Company X in your document, but you're not totally sure. No one wants to anger a VP — particularly the Muckmeister — so you decide that you'd better double check. The question is, how?

The answer is, Utilities⇨Change. When you choose this command (or press Ctrl+9), PageMaker displays the Change dialog box, found at the bottom of Figure 10-5.

PageMaker actually offers two commands for finding text, Utilities⇨Change and Utilities⇨Find. The Find command is specifically designed for finding text that you don't want to change. But what's the point? As Figure 10-5 demonstrates, the Find dialog box merely offers fewer options than the Change dialog box; there is nothing unique about it, so there's no point in using it. Furthermore, by sticking with Utilities⇨Change for all you searching needs, you have to memorize only one keyboard equivalent, Ctrl+9.

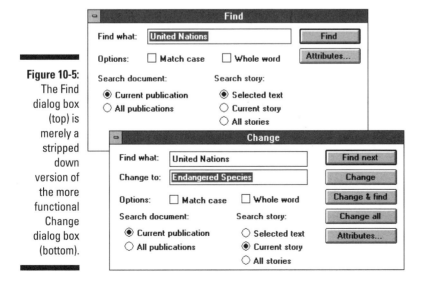

Figure 10-5:
The Find dialog box (top) is merely a stripped down version of the more functional Change dialog box (bottom).

Hunting down some text

After you display the Change dialog box, enter the characters that you want to find in the Find What option box. Then press the Return key (or click on the Find button). If the first instance of the text isn't the one you were looking for, press Return again (or click on the Find Next button). If PageMaker arrives at the end of the story, it asks you whether you want to continue your search from the beginning. That's all there is to it.

You can modify your search by selecting either of the two checkboxes below the Change To option box. Here's how they work:

> ✔ **Match Case:** If you select this option, PageMaker finds only those instances of a word that match the capitalization of the text entered into the Find What option box. For example, when searching for *Muckimuck*, PageMaker would ignore the colloquial use of *muckimuck* and search for the word exclusively in its proper noun form.

> ✔ **Whole Word:** When selected, this option searches for whole words and not just partial words. For example, if you search for *hang*, you might also find *hang*er, *chang*e, and *shang*hai. To eliminate all words but *hang* from your search, you must select the Whole Word option.

You also have access to the same Search Document and Search Story options that were present in the Spelling dialog box. To find out how these work, back up a page or two and read the earlier descriptions.

Searching by format

You can also modify your search according to formatting attributes. For example, you may want to find only italicized references to Muckimuck. To limit your search using formatting attributes, click on the Attributes button. The Change Attributes dialog box appears (see Figure 10-6).

Figure 10-6:
Click on the
Attributes
button in the
Change
dialog box
to search
text
according to
formatting
attributes.

Change attributes		OK

Find: Change :

Para style: Any   Para style: Any

Font: Any   Font: Any

Size: Any   Size: Any

Type style: Type style:

☒ Any   ☐ Underline   ☐ All caps   ☒ Any   ☐ Underline   ☐ All caps
☐ Normal ☐ Strikethru ☐ Small caps   ☐ Normal ☐ Strikethru ☐ Small caps
☐ Bold   ☐ Reverse   ☐ Superscript   ☐ Bold   ☐ Reverse   ☐ Superscript
☐ Italic   ☐ Subscript   ☐ Italic   ☐ Subscript

Cancel

Select options on the left half of the dialog box — those under the Find section (Para Style, Font, Size, and Type Style) — to affect the searched text. (The second set of four options controls the formatting of the replacement text, a subject discussed later in this chapter.) In addition to typeface, size, and type style, you can limit your search to a style sheet by selecting an option from the Para Style pop-up menu.

Press the Return key to exit the Change Attributes dialog box and return to the Change dialog box.

Searching for special characters

In addition to checking for plain old everyday text, you can search for PageMaker's special characters (em spaces, discretionary hyphens) and even invisible characters (carriage returns, tabs) by entering special codes into the Find What option box. All codes include the caret (^) character, which you create by pressing Shift+6. Most of these codes are the same as they are in Microsoft Word. Table 10-1 lists the most common codes.

Table 10-1	Character Search Codes	
Character	*Search Code*	*Note*
Tab	^t	
Carriage return	^p	*p* for paragraph
Line break (Shift+Enter)	^n	*n* as in line, possibly
Discretionary hyphen	^-	
Automatic hyphen	^c	*c* for computer-inserted
Nonbreaking hyphen	^~	
En dash	^=	
Em dash	^_	
Standard space	^w	*w* for white space
Nonbreaking space	^s	
Thin space	^<	< because it's so thin
En space	^>	> because it's thicker
Em space	^m	
Nonbreaking slash	^/	
Automatic page number	^#	

Capitalization of code characters doesn't matter. For example, both ^t and ^T will find tabs.

PageMaker provides one other special character code, ^?. This so-called *wildcard character* searches for absolutely any character of text. So if you enter *spr^?ng*, you'll find *spring, sprang,* and *sprung.* You can even use more than one wildcard character in a row. If you enter *spr^?^?^?*, you'll also find *sprint, sprite, sprout,* and *spruce.*

But wait. With all these caret codes, how do you manage to find a regular old caret? The answer is to enter two carets in a row (^^).

Replacing found text with new text

Now suppose that VP Muckimuck got the ax and that former mail-room worker Upstart has risen to the job. The company newsletter is going to press tomorrow and you need to replace every instance of *Muckimuck* with *Upstart.*

Again, the Change dialog box is your key to success. Enter *Muckimuck* in the Find What dialog box and *Upstart* in the Change To option box. Then use one of the following combinations of buttons:

- ✔ To change every instance of *Muckimuck* to *Upstart,* click on the Change All button. PageMaker automatically changes every occurrence of the text.

- ✔ To check each occurrence of *Muckimuck* before changing it — perhaps a couple of Muckimuck's duties are being transferred to Department L's VP Rapier — click on the Find button. When PageMaker finds an occurrence of *Muckimuck,* you have the option of changing it to Upstart by clicking on the Change & Find button, which changes the text and searches for the next occurrence. Alternatively, you can enter *Rapier* into the Change To option box and then click on Change & Find. Or finally, you can click on the Find Next button to leave this occurrence of *Muckimuck* intact and search for the next one.

- ✔ The Change button just changes the selected text without searching for the next occurrence. Most likely, the only time you'll want to use this button is when searching for a single occurrence of a word.

To this day, PageMaker doesn't offer an option to undo changes made from the Change dialog box, as do Microsoft Word and other word processors. So make sure that you really want to change your text — and that you've entered the correct characters in the Find What and Change To option boxes — before you initiate this command.

If you really need to undo changes you've made in the Find and Change dialog box, you may be able to use the following process. Press and hold the Shift key while choosing File➪Revert. PageMaker displays a dialog box asking you whether you want to revert to the last mini-saved version of your document. (A mini-save is something PageMaker does in the background when you use certain commands, such as opening and closing the Story Editor, turning pages, and so forth.)

Chapter 11
Doing Less Work Next Time

· ·

· ·

*L*ayout is like cooking: When you're tired after a long day of work, you want to get something already made or make something from a straightforward and proven recipe. When a boss or client comes over, you pull out the stops and prepare something that's guaranteed to delight. And when your friends come over, you may feel like experimenting with something you have in your pantry.

For layout, you want predefined, straightforward templates for the routine work, highly detailed templates for the big, high-profile projects, and the ability to work off the top of your head for the more creative, experimental projects.

In Chapter 9, you learned the basics of layout. That chapter referred to a predefined template for the example newsletter, and suggested that you should create it before you begin your layout. That may have seemed backwards to you at the time — to talk about doing layout before telling you how to create a template on which to base the layout — but there really is a method to this madness. Before you can create a good template, you first need a general idea about what good layout involves: what elements are included, how you arrange them, and so forth. But now that you know those things, it makes sense to learn how to do templates like the one discussed in Chapter 9. It's sort of a chicken vs. the egg thing — which is appropriate, given the cooking analogies used so eloquently to this point.

By the way, you don't always need a template. Templates are for standard documents — a newsletter, for example. If it looked totally different each issue, people would get confused and might not even realize that it is the same newsletter. The same goes for your corporate reports and even your letters (that's why companies have stationery). But if you're producing ads or flyers, you'll want each one to be customized instead of based on a standard template.

Understand, too, that templates don't have to be rigid — it's not boot camp for your documents. Templates just provide the basic assumptions, the starting point. When implementing the actual layout, you can modify the template to handle the specific needs you encounter for the particular layout. It's just like cooking: Your recipe may call for sage, but you know that you can just as easily substitute coriander to add a distinct flavor for guests who prefer coriander to sage.

Actually, you've already learned a fair amount about templates. Chapter 4 covered master pages and style sheets — the two fundamental building blocks of templates — and Chapter 9 showed a template in use. PageMaker also has another technique to save you from doing work over and over again — the library feature.

So you can skip this chapter, right? — you already know everything from earlier chapters. Sorry. You know the building blocks, but that's just the first step in understanding the process.

This book uses the term *template* to mean a PageMaker document you use as the basis for a series of documents. PageMaker uses the term to mean a PageMaker file saved with the Template option selected in the Save Publication As dialog box (File⇨Save As). The two are not contradictory — you can save what this book calls a template as a template file or as a regular publication file. All that the word *template* means in PageMaker terminology is that when someone opens a file, a copy is opened, rather than the original. This helps prevent you from accidentally overwriting the template with a layout based on that template — if you try, PageMaker prompts you for a new name. (You can save the new version as a regular publication by selecting the Publication option in the Save Publication As dialog box.)

Building a Template

There are two ways to build a template: the hard way and the easy way. Interestingly, sometimes the hard way is the best way. What are the two ways?

- ✔ Construct a template from scratch. This is the easy way, but it assumes that you know in advance what the template should contain, and therefore know the requirements and look of the layouts that will be based on it.

- ✔ Convert a layout into a template. This is the hard way because you have to remove many elements from the layout and leave just those that are used in all or most layouts that are to be based on the template. But this can be the best way because it lets you figure out what the layout should look like using a real example before finalizing the template.

For a brand-new template, let's use the first method. Because you already know how to place and edit text and place graphics, we won't spend a lot of time going over those techniques when explaining how to create a template. A template can use some elements covered later in the book — such as lines and graphic effects, covered in Chapter 14, and colors, covered in Chapter 15. If the template you want to build contains such elements, you can read this chapter now and then read those chapters for more details, or you can skip ahead now to those chapters and come back here when done. The order in which you read the chapters doesn't make much difference — and because the following example doesn't incorporate any special graphics effects or colors, it may be easiest just to keep reading.

What should a template contain?

No matter what kind of document you're creating, some elements are near-universal:

- Style sheets
- Page numbers
- Margins and columns
- Logos that appear repeatedly

Other elements are common for specific types of documents:

- A table of contents (magazines, reports, some newsletters, books)
- A masthead — a list of the staff and contact information (magazines and some newsletters)
- Continued lines — using dummy page numbers, of course (newsletters and magazines)
- Pull-quotes — using dummy text, of course (some magazines, some newsletters, some reports)
- Postal information and mailing label text (newsletters)
- Subscription and change-of-address forms (magazines, newsletters, some reports)
- Standing text — stories, such as *List of Benefits*, that appear in almost every issue (magazines, newsletters, some ads, and some reports)
- Highly formatted sidebars or tables — using dummy text, of course (magazines, newsletters, and some reports)

Not all of these elements should appear in the template file — you'd be lost in a jungle of elements. Instead, some should be placed in a library, which is a file that contains elements. Multiple users can access this file, which PageMaker displays as a scrolling palette from which you drag desired elements. (This option is covered last in this chapter.)

Okay, now that you know what kinds of elements to put in a template, let's see where best to put these various elements.

Setting up master pages

As Chapter 4 explained, whatever appears on a master page appears on all pages. If you have a document with facing pages, you have left and right master pages (the page icons are marked *L* and *R*, respectively); otherwise, you have just a right master page. As far as putting elements on a master page, a master page is no different than any other page — just place and edit the elements as usual.

When you create a master page, include only those elements that appear on every page, or at least on almost every page. The obvious candidates are page numbers — every page (except maybe a cover page) has them in almost every multipage document. If you use recurring artistic embellishments, such as a ruling line above the page numbers, add those here, too. Figure 11-1 shows an example set of master pages for a newsletter.

The most fundamental components in a master page are the margins and column guides. (You set those up via File⇨Page Setup and Layout⇨Column Guides, respectively.) They determine the basic text placement for your standard pages.

The master pages in Figure 11-1 also contain two basic elements on each page: a ruling line at the top and the page number and magazine name/issue date at the bottom. At the bottom, the Ruling Line Above feature was used to put the line above the text block, but you could just as easily draw the line with the Line tool.

You may ask yourself, "How do I work this?" Even if you're not a Talking Heads fan, you may ask, "How can I put page numbers in a master page if the number changes from page to page in the standard pages?" Ask no more — PageMaker has a special character that you place in your text block that basically means, "Hey! Fill in the correct page number!" You access this special character by pressing Ctrl+Shift+3.

Notice the icons at the bottom of Figure 11-1, next to the page numbers. Placing a graphic associated with your company in this spot is a nice way to reinforce your corporate identity. To put them into your master pages, just place them at the appropriate locations.

What else might be on a master page? If you're doing a corporate report, you

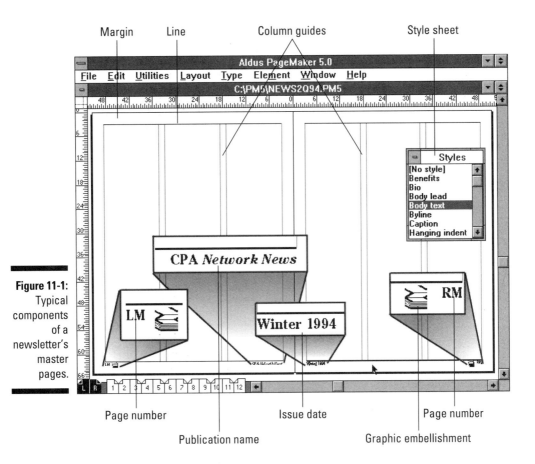

Figure 11-1:
Typical
components
of a
newsletter's
master
pages.

may want the company logo on each page. Or if the report is confidential, you may want the word *Confidential* to appear on each page. Or maybe you would want to include a copyright notice, if yours is a high-priced newsletter. You get the idea — include in your master pages anything that you'd otherwise have to place manually on every page.

Setting up standard pages

With the master pages set up, you now move into the rest of your template — into the standard pages that will actually contain your content.

First, deal with some basics, such as how many pages are there typically going to be? If it's a set number, such as 12, add that number of pages (via Layout⇨Insert Pages). If it's not a set amount, add enough pages to accommodate your regular nonstandard pages. (Regular nonstandard? What's that supposed to mean? It means pages that don't conform to your master page settings but appear regularly, such as the title page.)

It's a good idea to define your styles now, at least those for the basic text: body text, headlines, bylines, captions, and so on. (If you need a review of how to define styles, refer back to Chapter 4.)

After you set up your styles and the number of pages, you can begin working on those regular nonstandard pages. The sample newsletter in this chapter has four, as shown in Figure 11-2. The following sections explain the steps you would go through to create each of these pages. The steps labeled in Figure 11-2 correspond to the steps described for each page.

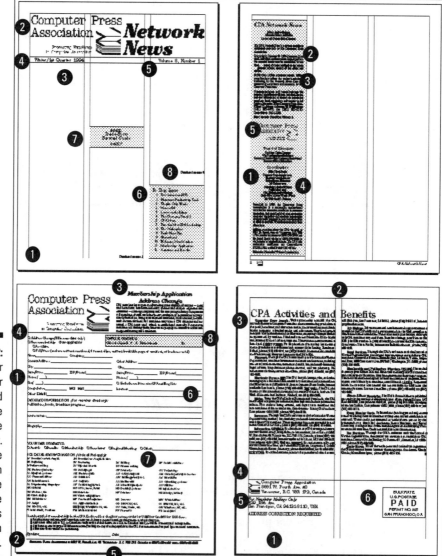

Figure 11-2:
The four regular nonstandard pages in the example newsletter. The numbers on each page refer to the steps outlined in this chapter.

Cover or title page

The first page is the cover page, but it could just as easily be a title page. This page, shown in Figure 11-3, doesn't need the page numbers, the issue date, or the ruling lines defined in the master page. But it does need the three-column format. The following steps explain how to create such a page:

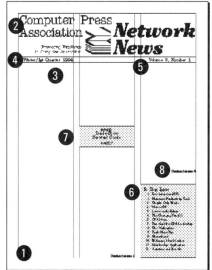

Figure 11-3:
The cover
page.

1. Cover up the unwanted master page elements.

You can do this by adding rectangles that have solid white (paper) fills and no lines (via Element⇨Fill and Line), as described in Chapter 14. Figure 11-5 shows the necessary settings. A nice fact about elements on a master page is that they always appear underneath something created on a standard page, so it's easy to cover them up using this technique.

Figure 11-4:
Use a solid,
line-less
rectangle to
cover up
master-
page
elements
you don't
want on a
particular
page.

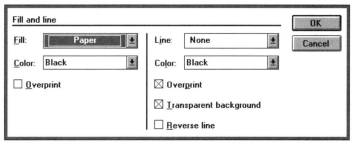

Be careful how you cover elements using "electronic whiteout." Sometimes, it's the best solution, but you can overdo it, adding unneeded complexity to your publications. Be particularly wary of covering up elements if you share files with others. They might uncover what you covered.

2. **Place the logo at the top, using the Place Document dialog box (File⇨Place or Ctrl+D).**

   The name of the newsletter is part of the graphic in this case. But it could just as easily be typed in and formatted in PageMaker.

3. **Enter the text for the issue date right below the logo.**

   You can use the Control palette's font options to set the font and size. This is the only text in the entire layout that uses these settings, so it doesn't make any sense to use styles.

4. **Add the lines above and below the text part of the text block.**

   You can use the Rules option in the Paragraph Specifications dialog box (Type⇨Paragraph or Ctrl+M) to make the lines. In this example, the line above is 1 point thick and is positioned 0.2 inches from the baseline (through the Options button in the Paragraph Rules dialog box); the line below is 1.5 points thick, which was set through a Custom line style. You may have noticed that the text is indented from the sides of the text block; to make sure that the lines aren't also indented, select the Width of Column option for both lines' Line Width setting in the Paragraph Rules dialog box. Figure 11-5 shows these settings. (You can also draw simple lines with the Line tool, but by making the rules part of the text, they automatically move with the text should the text block ever be moved.)

   The text itself is indented 0.2 inches on both the left and right in the Paragraph Specifications dialog box, via the Indents settings.

Figure 11-5: These settings tell PageMaker to put lines above and below a paragraph in a text block.

Paragraph specifications		OK
Indents:		
Left	1p3	picas
First	0	picas
Right	1p3	picas
Alignment:	Left	
Options:		
☒ Keep lines together		
☐ Column break before		
☐ Page break before		
☐ Include in table of c		

Paragraph rules		OK
☒ Rule above paragraph		Cancel
Line style:	1pt ———— ▼	Options...
Line color:	Black ▼	
Line width:	○ Width of text ● Width of column	
Indent: Left	0 picas Right 0 picas	
☒ Rule below paragraph		
Line style:	Custom... ▼	
Line color:	Black ▼	
Line width:	○ Width of text ● Width of column	
Indent: Left	0 picas Right 0 picas	

5. Add a tab and a tab stop.

Finally, set a right-aligned tab stop to be 0.2 inches away from the text block's right margin. Then place a tab in the text to align it to the tab stop. (Set up the tab via Type⇨Indents/Tabs or Ctrl+I.)

6. Add the *In This Issue* box at the bottom right of the page.

It consists of a gray rectangle with a 1-point line drawn above and below it. The gray rectangle has a text wrap of 0.167 inches — the default. Here, it's a good idea to define a style for the text because there are several entries in the contents box. The headline can be modified via the Control palette because its format is not used elsewhere. The text includes two tab stops, one to right-align the page numbers to a common margin, and one to left-align the text that follows to a common margin. Figure 11-6 shows the settings.

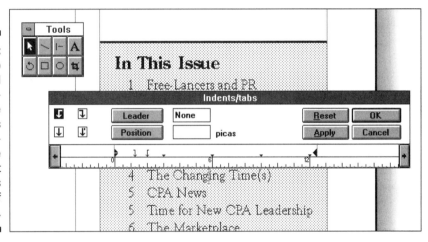

Figure 11-6:
The tab stops used to right-align page numbers and left-align the text descriptions for a table of contents.

7. Create a cross-reference box in the upper middle of the page.

This box calls attention to a major story that couldn't fit on the cover page. It uses the same visual style as the contents box: a gray rectangle with a line above and below. The text, though, is specially formatted using the Control palette, not a style.

8. Create a style for the continued-on lines and add dummy continued lines on the page.

Almost every story that starts on the cover page will continue inside the newsletter, so you may as well as have the continued lines ready in advance.

Imagine doing all that every time you create a new issue of the newsletter. No thank you!

Masthead page

Mastheads are usually easy to set up: They're basically just a text file with a logo or two. That's the case in the example newsletter as well. In the case of this page, shown in Figure 11-7, everything set up in the master pages is retained because the page is supposed to look like any other standard page, with the exception of the masthead. The masthead, which is styled like any other sidebar, is always in the first column.

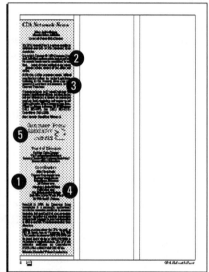

Figure 11-7:
The masthead page.

To create this page, you do the following:

1. **Create the gray rectangle used as the background and add the two lines, one below and one above.**

   As you can see, this style is a fundamental part of the newsletter's look. Don't bother turning text wrap on for this background because no text will wrap around it — the masthead takes up the entire column.

2. **Place the text for the masthead.**

   The text for the example masthead was created in a word processor.

3. **Create the styles for the masthead text.**

   The example uses one style for the basic text: whom to write for more information, the copyright notice, and so on. There's another style for the list of association officers (the centered text at the very top and at the bottom-center). And there's a third style for the labels that head up those lists.

4. **Adjust the text if necessary.**

In the text placed in the example, the column guides are the width of the background rectangle. So the text block had to be narrowed in order to allow margins on either side inside the background. The text was also centered horizontally within the rectangle.

It's easiest to use the Control palette to make such changes: Just make the W value smaller. Then add one-half of the difference between the old and new W values to the X coordinate. In the example, the width was reduced by 0.2 inches, and 0.1 inches was added to the X coordinate.

5. **Add the association's logo.**

The example uses an embedded graphic (see Chapter 14).

Application or subscription page

It's very typical to include membership or subscription information in a newsletter, as well as in some magazines and reports. However, these elements often look very different from the rest of the document — they're basically advertisements.

Before you see how the page in Figure 11-8 was created, understand that you don't have to put ads in the same file as the rest of the publication. One reason to do so is to keep the page numbers in order — but you can just as easily leave a blank page where the ad would go and uncheck the Print Blank Pages option in the Print Document dialog box (File⇨Print or Ctrl+P). PageMaker retains the page numbering throughout the document without printing blank pages. For the example, however, the membership form goes in the newsletter template.

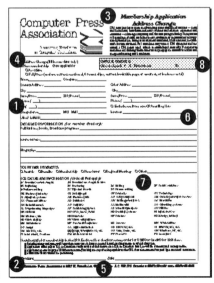

Figure 11-8:
The
application
page.

Here's how to create a page like this one:

1. **Change the column settings.**

   The application doesn't use the three-column format specified by the master pages. To override the number of columns set up in the master pages, open the Column Guides dialog box (Layout⇨Column Guides), as shown in Figure 11-9. It's in situations like this when the ability to set columns separately for left and right pages comes in handy, because you don't want to affect the page facing the application page.

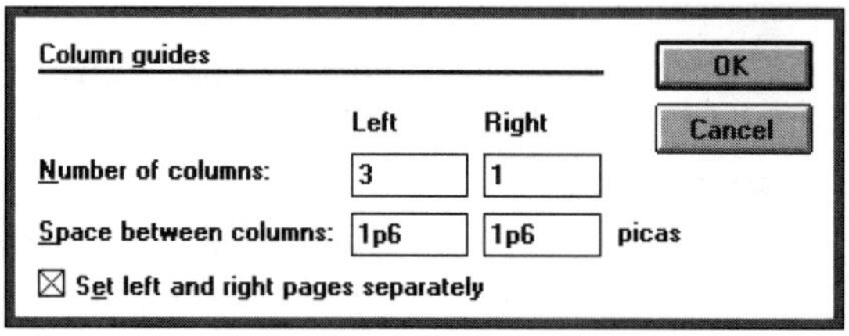

Figure 11-9:
The Column guides dialog box.

Column guides			OK
	Left	Right	Cancel
Number of columns:	3	1	
Space between columns:	1p6	1p6	picas
☒ Set left and right pages separately			

2. **Cover up unwanted master page elements.**

   As you did on the cover page, cover up the line at the top of the page and the page numbering information at the bottom by using solid rectangles.

3. **Place the logo and create a text block for the text at the upper right.**

   You can use the Story Editor (Edit⇨Edit Story, or Ctrl+E) to enter the text.

4. **Add a line below the logo and the text block at upper right.**

5. **Add the text block at the bottom of the page, which is the mailing address for the application.**

   The line above it is part of the text block — which you create using the Line tool or the Rules option.

6. **Add the text for the application itself — the block of text with the ruling lines in the upper center area.**

   The application in the example requires three styles: one for the text with checkboxes, one for the multicolumn text with underlines, and one for the single-column text with underlines. The underlines can be created via tab stops: Use right-aligned tabs that have an underline leader character. The tab stops for the multicolumn text are tricky. The text block is the width of the page, and the "columns" are actually a series of tab stops. The "gutters" between text are simply tab stops with no leaders. Figure 11-10 shows the tab settings.

7. **Create the four-column text at the bottom.**

   Create the four-column text by manually sizing four text blocks all linked together (as described in Chapter 9).

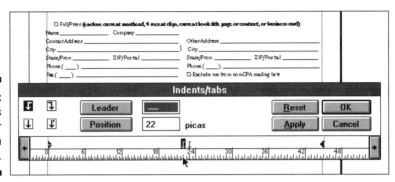

Figure 11-10:
Tab settings
for
multicolumn
text.

Another option would be to use tab stops — which option is best depends on whether the items would change. If they did, tab stops would be a bad idea, because to shift text up or down would mean cutting and pasting text among various tab stops and lines, and that's a *lot* of work.

8. **Last, create the gray "For official use only" box by adding a gray rectangle with a line around it and text wrap turned on.**

You can then create the text and format it with the Control palette.

Back cover page

The back cover can look like a regular page, like a regular page with space reserved for mailing labels (for newsletters), or like its own type of page. For the newsletter shown in Figure 11-11, it's basically its own type of page, for two reasons:

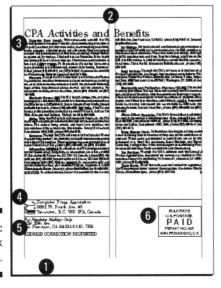

Figure 11-11:
The back
cover page.

✔ Room is needed for the postal information (the postage-paid text and the return address), because this newsletter is mailed with no wrapper, and for the mailing labels themselves. (Check with your local post office for the minimum size and type requirements for this kind of material. Although they don't change often, they do change, and your local post office can tell you the latest.)

✔ It was a convenient place to put the list of membership benefits because people were likely to find it easily.

Here are the steps involved in creating this page:

1. **Cover up unwanted master page elements.**

   As on the front cover and membership application pages, cover up the page numbering information at the bottom with a solid rectangle. You don't need to do so on the top because the layout retains that element of a standard page.

2. **Changed the layout to a two-column layout.**

   Use Layout⇨Column Guides, as for the membership application.

3. **Place the text in the upper part of the page and then define a style for it.**

4. **Add a line to separate the text from the postal portion of the page.**

5. **Add the return address text and place the logo next to it. Place other postal-oriented text below it.**

   Also draw a line between the return address and that other text.

6. **Add a rectangle with a line around it for the postage-paid notice, and then add the text into it, reshaping the text block to fit inside the rectangle.**

   Format the text with the Control palette, rather than with a style, because nothing else in the newsletter uses this formatting.

Odds and ends

Now, save the newsletter as a template, and your template is basically complete. What's left? The master pages contain elements that will appear on virtually every page. And the regular nonstandard pages contain elements that appear in virtually every issue. That leaves those elements that may or may not be used in a particular issue but that you want to keep handy: continued lines, pull-quotes, logos, and the like. You could place these on the pasteboard — the portion of the PageMaker screen outside the page boundaries — but that can get real cluttered real fast, and it doesn't let someone else easily access those elements for another layout, either. The answer is to put these common but irregularly used elements in a *library*. Aren't you lucky that PageMaker has a library feature?

Setting Up Libraries

A library looks like any other PageMaker palette, even though it is technically an addition. In fact, it's one of the only additions not accessed via the Utilities⇨Aldus Additions menu.

If no library is open, you use Window⇨Library Palette to get the Open Library dialog box. If you previously opened a library in the current document, PageMaker reloads that library when you select Window⇨Library Palette unless the library has since been moved or deleted. If that previously opened library is not the one you want, select Open Library from the palette's Options pop-up menu. (Skip ahead to Figure 11-14 to see the pop-up menu.) Figure 11-12 shows the Open Library dialog box.

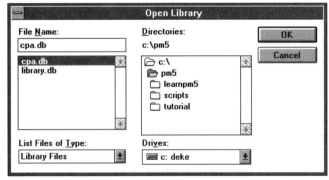

Figure 11-12:
The Open Library dialog box.

Note that you can have only one library open at a time; if a library is already open and you open another one, the previous library closes.

To create a new library, enter the name that you want to save the library document under in the File Name option box. Then press Enter. Using its vast reasoning skills, PageMaker detects that this document file does not exist and asks whether you want to create it. Respond in the affirmative.

When you have a library open, it will look something like the one in Figure 11-13. (If the library is new, it will have nothing in its main window.) Note that every library has a filename (which is displayed in the palette's title bar), and that library file is stored on disk like any other file, which is why it can be accessed by any PageMaker user who can access the disk or directory where it resides.

Figure 11-13:
The contents of a library appears as reduced "thumbnail" previews.

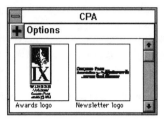

After a library is displayed, you can resize the palette to make it wider or deeper, which lets you see more of its contents. Use the scroll bar to move through the library. You can also select an option from the Options pop-up menu, shown in Figure 11-14. To display this menu, click on the word *Options* (not on the plus sign).

Figure 11-14:
The library palette's Options menu items.

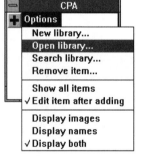

Adding to a library

To place an element — whether text or graphics — into a library, select the object and then click on that big plus sign in the palette's upper left corner. PageMaker copies the element into the library. Pretty easy, huh?

Note that if you copy a text block into a library, it retains its text formatting but not its style names. Thus, when you place the text in another layout, it will be formatted correctly but will have the No Style style. So if you planned on altering its appearance by changing the attributes of its style definition, you can't. Ditto if you wanted to import that text's style along with the text. But what you *can* do is click on the text and choose Type➪Define Styles (Ctrl+3) to define a new style based on that selected text. Then, in the first case, apply that style to all text from the text block copied from the library and then alter the style definition. Or, in the second case, use the new style on other text in your layout whose formatting you want to match the library text's formatting.

In truth, there's a little bit more to adding an element to a library than just copying it in — or there can be if you want there to be. When you paste an element into a library, PageMaker gives it the name *Untitled*. Because libraries are searchable — that is, you can enter the name of a library element and instruct PageMaker to hunt down that element for you — it's a good idea to give the element a name you can search, especially if you'll be creating fairly large libraries.

To give an element a name, scroll through the library palette until you find the one you want to name, and then double-click on it. PageMaker displays the dialog box shown in Figure 11-15. You can add keywords and a description into the dialog box to make it easier to find the element in the future.

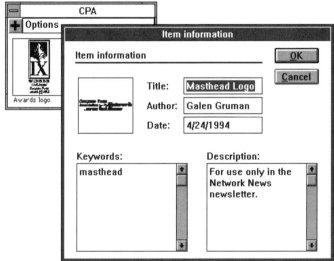

Figure 11-15: You can name a library element and add keywords and descriptions in the Item Information dialog box.

Finding library elements

As noted earlier, you can just scroll through the palette to find a particular element. But if the library has many elements, it's easier to search for an element by its keyword, author, or name (title). To do this, use the Search Library dialog box, shown in Figure 11-16. To access this dialog box, click on Options in the Library palette and select Search Library. When adding multiple keywords, separate them with spaces. The search option is smart enough that it doesn't require exact matches. For example, if the author's name is *Alexander* and you enter *Alex* as the name to search, PageMaker finds any author whose name includes the characters *a, l, e,* and *x,* in that order.

Figure 11-16:
Use this
dialog box to
search for
items in your
library
according to
keywords,
authors, or
titles.

Search library

Search library   [Search]
_____   [Cancel]

Search by keyword:

| masthead |

| And ▼ |

| logo |

Search by author:

| |

Search by title:

| |

Notice that there's a pop-up menu in the Search By Keyword section. The default setting is One Keyword Only. If you choose this option, PageMaker searches for the single word in the top option box. The other options are And (as shown in Figure 11-16), Or, and But Not. If you choose And, the element must use both keywords in order for PageMaker to find it. If you choose Or, the element must use at least one of the two keywords. If you choose But Not, the element must use the first keyword but not the second keyword.

If you search for a keyword, title, or author, and the search turns up no matches, the library palette becomes empty. That's supposed to tell you that PageMaker couldn't find what you wanted, but it could as easily scare you into thinking that the library was somehow deleted. Don't panic. And click on Options⇨Show All Items to get the library elements back.

Using library elements

This is the easiest part: To use a library element, just click on the element (the square border gets thicker) and drag it from the palette to anywhere in your PageMaker document. PageMaker places the element wherever you release the mouse button. Note also that it places the element at its original size, not the preview size shown in the palette. After you place the element, you can modify it just like any other element.

When you drag an element from the library into a document, the preview stays in the library — you're copying the element from the library, not actually removing it from the library. Figure 11-17 shows an item being dragged from a library.

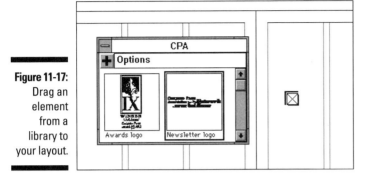

Figure 11-17:
Drag an
element
from a
library to
your layout.

Deleting library elements

To delete a library element, select it in the palette and select Options⇨Remove Item.

Note that you cannot use Ctrl+X or File⇨Cut to delete a library element. In fact, trying to do so deletes whatever is selected in your layout, not the element selected in the library. So be careful!

Setting library display

By default, the Library palette shows both a preview image and a name for each element in the open library. But you can change this display by clicking on the Options menu and selecting from the Display Images, Display Names, and Display Both options. The default option is probably the best because it provides two ways of identifying library elements. However, it can be easier to find something by viewing the contents according to their names, particularly when you're scrolling through a large list. Figure 11-18 shows what a library looks like with the Display Names option selected.

Figure 11-18:
A library
with the
Display
Names
option
selected.

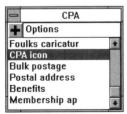

The usefulness of Display Images is less compelling: Why not just display the name along with the image? After all, it takes up basically no more space in the palette. Who knows what lurks in the minds of programmers?

Part IV

Documents for the Suit-and-Tie Set

"NOPE - I'D BETTER WAIT 'TIL ALL MY FONTS ARE WORKING. A HATE LETTER JUST DOESN'T WORK IN *Filigree Flowerbox Extended.*"

In this part...

Business users have special needs. For some, it's a day without wearing a chafing suit. For others, it's a day *with* a suit on. Whatever type of business you're in, you'll have some design needs. Funny enough, you've come to the right place. This section first explains how to add an index and table of contents to your PageMaker document, and then it shows you, step by step, how to create good-looking business documents. Here's your chance to prove that *business document* is not a synonym for *boring*. Who knows? Maybe you'll start a revolution at work, getting everyone (except maybe that guy who hides out in the corner cubicle under the fire extinguisher) to produce nice-looking documents. Just think: designer documents. Can Armani be far behind?

Chapter 12

How Would *I* Know What Page It's On?

In This Chapter

▶ Creating a table of contents automatically

▶ Creating index topic lists for easy reuse

▶ Formatting an index

▶ Indexing multiple documents at once

*H*ave you used the index in this book yet? Probably. It may be at the end of the book, but it's the one of the first things that people use in how-to books, manuals, and other documentation-oriented publications. If you've ever had to create an index by hand, you know the nirvana of having an automated indexing feature. You still have to do a fair amount of work to create your index, but at least it's doable.

Creating a table of contents manually isn't as bad as doing an index, but what the heck — it's great to automate that job, too. In fact, this chapter starts off with showing you how to produce a table of contents because it's the easier of the two tasks. Think of it as a warm-up exercise to the joy and agony of the Stairmaster.

Creating Tables of Contents

One way to create a table of contents in PageMaker is to print your document, write down the titles and headings and their page numbers, and then create a new document in PageMaker in which you enter this information. Of course, that's hardly the best way to do it, because PageMaker can do it for you — very easily.

Where the entries come from

When you define styles (as explained in Chapter 4), PageMaker gives you the option to include the style's contents in the table of contents. For example, if you specify that you want the style *Headline* to be included in the table of contents, the text of every paragraph marked with that style is included in the table of contents, including the page number of the text. You give PageMaker this instruction by checking the Include in Table of Contents option in the Paragraph Specifications dialog box, as shown in Figure 12-1.

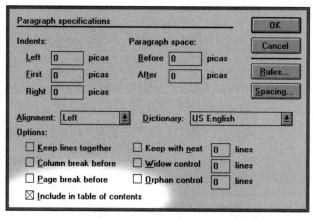

Figure 12-1: You tell PageMaker which paragraph styles to include as table-of-contents entries.

When you designate styles that PageMaker will use to find table-of-contents entries, don't use styles with really long text. Remember: PageMaker puts the entire contents of the paragraph into the table of contents. Imagine if your caption text, for example, were included in the table of contents — it'd be impossible to read. Of course, you can always edit long headlines if necessary after the table of contents is generated — it's not like you're carving the table of contents in stone.

Creating the table of contents

When you're completely done with your document, go ahead and generate the table of contents. Choose Utilities⇨Create TOC to get the Create Table of Contents dialog box shown in Figure 12-2. You can specify a title — *Contents* is the default. You can also tell PageMaker where to place the page numbers: nowhere, before the contents text, or after the contents text. Typically, the numbers go after the table of contents text.

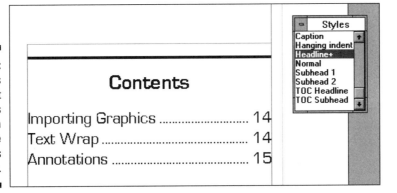

Create table of contents

Title: Contents

OK

Cancel

☐ Replace existing table of contents

☐ Include book publications

Format: ○ No page number
○ Page number before entry
◉ Page number after entry

Between entry and page number: ^t

You also have an option to put some text between the table text and the page numbers; you enter the text in the Between Entry and Page Number option box. The default is ^t, which is PageMaker's code for a tab character. (The ^ is the circumflex, which you get by holding the Shift key when pressing the keyboard's 6 character. It does not stand for the Ctrl key here, as it does in PageMaker's menus.) You'll probably want to keep this default because by using a tab, you can have the page numbers right-aligned and connected to the left-aligned contents text via a series of dots, as shown in Figure 12-3. In fact, this is the way that the automatic style sheet that PageMaker applies formats your text — how nice! (This style business is explained shortly, in case you're wondering.) But you may want to use something such as an em space (^m) or em dash (^_) between the numbers and text if, for example, you put the page numbers before the contents text. Note that you can put as many as seven characters between the text and numbers.

Figure 12-3:
PageMaker's
default
settings
generate a
typical table
of contents
format.

Styles

Caption
Hanging indent
Headline+
Normal
Subhead 1
Subhead 2
TOC Headline
TOC Subhead

Contents

Importing Graphics 14

Text Wrap 14

Annotations 15

Two other options in the Create Table of Contents dialog box may be available or may be grayed out — it all depends on whether the options are applicable to the current document. One is Replace Existing Table of Contents — if the current document or book doesn't have a table of contents, this option isn't available. The other option, Include Book Publications, is available if the current document defines a book list (which tells PageMaker to generate the contents from several related documents). See Chapter 8 for details on book lists.

If you are working with book lists — or, for that matter, with documents whose page numbers include a prefix, such as *A-* or *Antiques-* — make sure that you tell PageMaker to include that prefix as part of the page numbering *before* you generate the table of contents. (Assuming, of course, that you want those prefixes in the table of contents.) You'll find this setting not in the Create Table of Contents dialog box but in the Page Numbering dialog box, which you get via File⇨Page Setup⇨Numbers. (Figure 12-4 shows this dialog box.) Make sure that whatever you type here matches whatever you put in your master pages as a prefix to your page numbers — PageMaker doesn't check for you.

Figure 12-4: Make sure that you add any page-number prefixes to the Page Numbering dialog box before you generate your table of contents.

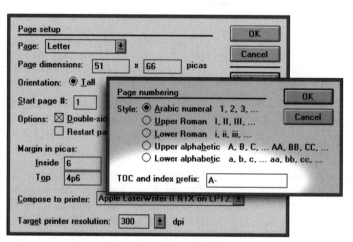

When you click on OK, PageMaker generates the table of contents. When it's done, you get the paragraph or autoflow icon with which you can place text. PageMaker also adds new styles to your style list. All begin with the word *TOC*. You get a style called *TOC Title,* which is always generated automatically. The others are *TOC* plus the names of the styles you designated for including in the table of contents. For example, if you had a style named *Headline* and you checked the Include in Table of Contents box in the Paragraph Specifications dialog box, you get a new style named *TOC Headline.*

Creating a stand-alone table of contents

After PageMaker generates the table of contents, you may be tempted to insert some pages at the beginning of your document, thinking that you can put the table of contents on those new pages. *Don't.* Doing so will change all the page numbers in your document, making the table of contents outdated. Plus, chances are that you want a different numbering scheme for your contents — such as lowercase roman numerals (i, ii, iii, iv, and so on) — and standard Arabic numbering (1, 2, 3, 4, and so on) in your main document. There's also a good chance that you'll want the page numbering in that main text to start over at 1 — you wouldn't want the contents section to end at page iv and number the first page of the text as page 5, right?

What to do? Use one of the following techniques:

✔ Add new pages to the end of the current document and place the table of contents there. (This way, you don't mess up the page numbering.) Use File⇨New (or Ctrl+N) to create a new document, and copy the text blocks containing the table of contents to that new document. (The TOC styles are copied along with the text blocks). Unfortunately, you can't just place the contents text directly in this new document as you're generating it — you must first place it in the document from which you generate the contents.

✔ *Before* generating the table of contents, create a new document and use the book list feature (via File⇨Book) to create a list of the documents from which you want the contents generated. Maybe the list includes just one document, but create it anyway. This technique puts the table of contents in its own document without affecting the page numbers of the other document(s).

Insert the new pages at the beginning of your current document *only* if you want the table of contents to be part of your current document — with its pages numbered along with the rest of the pages in the document. Then be sure to regenerate the table of contents via Utilities⇨Create TOC, this time selecting the Replace Existing Table of Contents checkbox so that the page numbers are updated to reflect the inserted pages.

OK, take a break. You're about to enter the woolly world of indexing. It's not a simple topic, so you should be rested before taking the plunge.

Creating Indexes

Why is creating indexes so hard? It's not PageMaker's fault. To create a good index means picking the right terms to track and then faithfully marking each such term, including variants. For example, if you index the word *weasel,* you wouldn't want to index the term *weaseling* (as in *weaseling out of*). And if you index *deoxyribonucleic acid*, you need to index *DNA* as well, and have the same index entry for both. Readers wouldn't expect to find some entries under one term and the other entries under another term. (In fact, they might expect to find a *See DNA* cross-reference from *deoxyribonucleic acid*, assuming that they had even the remotest interest in this topic.)

Here's another complication: You can index in a word processor (PageMaker can import the index entries from Word and WordPerfect, as well as those in RTF-formatted files, which several programs can create), or you can index in PageMaker. Where you do it depends on who's doing the indexing. If all the text editing is done in the word processor, the index entries should probably be done there, too. But if extensive editing work is to be done in PageMaker, it makes sense to do the indexing there. Of course, you can index in both places, starting in your word processor and finishing in PageMaker for the text that is added or changed.

Tips for better indexing

Few of us have any professional training in indexing. It's a job that requires familiarity with the topic being indexed — so that you know which topics are important and which text belongs in which topics. You also need to have the patience to go through an entire manuscript and correctly mark up all the index entries.

PageMaker takes some of the grunt work out of the job, but it can't do the thinking for you. Without stepping on the toes of the American Society of Indexers, whose members do this for a living and probably don't want their basic secrets revealed (not that any of us could do a better job than they can), here are some basic things to keep in mind when doing your own indexing:

✔ Build a basic topic list in advance. Fortunately, you can do that in PageMaker and then add to it as you uncover new topics or realize that some topics are too broad and need subtopics.

✔ Use multiple topics for some text. Readers may think of something with a different term than you do or perhaps from a different functional perspective. For example, in this book's index, *Place* and *Import* point to much of the same content because the terms are largely interchangeable in PageMaker parlance. Likewise, you'll find information on placing graphics under *Graphics, import* and *Importing, graphics* — some readers may consider importing to be a function of graphics, while others will do the opposite. A good index satisfies both points of view.

✔ Use cross-references such as *See also* for related topics or just plain *See* for synonymous topics. But don't be stingy — if there are several popular terms for the same thing, index it multiple ways — having to do the index runaround gets real annoying for the reader. The only thing more annoying is looking in the index for a particular term and not finding it there.

Creating index entries

In PageMaker, it's simple to add an index entry — Just use the Text tool to select the word or phrase you want to add to the index, and press Ctrl+; (semicolon). If you insist, you can insert an index entry the long way: via Utilities⇨Index Entry.

When you insert an index entry, you get the dialog box shown in Figure 12-5. This dialog box is an all-out indexing machine, the first of a series of dialog boxes that let you control almost every aspect of your index entry. If you're into power, you've come to the right place.

Let's go through this dialog box of power. First, make sure that the Page Reference option is selected — this tells PageMaker that you want your index entries to refer readers to a specific page in your publication. (The Cross-reference option is explained later.)

In the dialog box, you can enter up to three levels of index information in the three Topic fields. The top field is the top-level topic (the one that is first in the

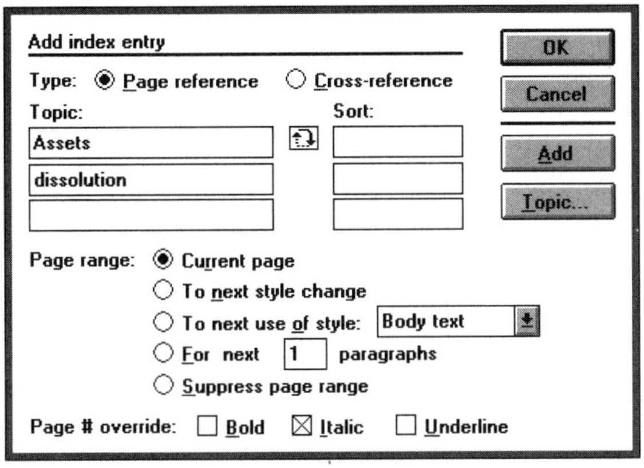

Figure 12-5:
Use this
dialog box
to create
index
entries.

index). In the figure, there are two levels: *Assets* is in the top level and *dissolution* is in the second level. In an index, this would usually look like:

Assets
   dissolution, *14*

The Sort boxes to the right are tied to the Topic entries. Use them if you want to sort the entries differently than their spelling in the levels option. "What does that mean?" you scratch your head. Let's say that one of the index topic entries is *S. Africa* but you want it alphabetized by its full name, *South Africa.* In the Sort field corresponding to the Topic field containing *S. Africa,* type **South Africa.** Thus, when the index is created, *S. Africa* appears after *South Acton* and before *South America,* not at the top (periods are alphabetized before letters by computers).

Now look at that funny-looking icon button in the middle of the dialog box. If you click on it, it moves topic entries around among levels. In all likelihood, you'll use this button only on rare occasions, but what the hey.

By selecting a Page Range option, you tell PageMaker how to select the page or pages that should appear with a particular index entry. Typically, you should use the default setting, Current Page. If you choose this setting, the index entry refers the reader to the page at which you clicked to add the word or phrase to the index, which is usually at the beginning of the relevant text. But you can pick any option that's appropriate to your text.

The final setting to establish is the page-number formatting, which you do by selecting from among the Page # Override checkboxes. You can use any combination (including none) of boldface, italics, and underline. Whatever you select is applied to the page numbers that go with the index entries, not to the index entry text.

When you're done, click on OK. The index entry code is now inserted in your text.

You won't see index entry codes in your text when you're working in layout view. But you can see them when in the Story Editor. Figure 12-6 shows the symbol that represents an index entry. To see or edit the entry, select the diamond character and press Ctrl+; or choose Utilities⇨Index Entry.

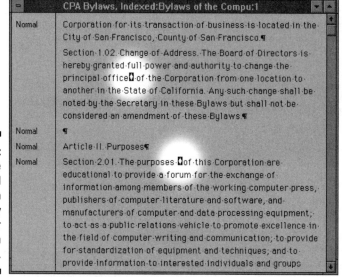

Figure 12-6:
The
diamond
symbol in
the Story
Editor
indicates an
index entry.

Using index topics

You don't have to keep typing in the same index entry topics over and over again. Just click on the Topic button and select from the existing topics. Figure 12-7 shows the Select Topic dialog box. Topics are arranged by section. The sections correspond to the letter of the alphabet; there's also a section called Symbols for index entries that begin with symbols or numerals. You can go directly to a section via the Topic Section pop-up menu, or you can click on the Next Section button to move to the next section. When you find the one you want, select it from the list and click on OK.

That's all well and good, but where do those index topics come from in the first place? When you enter an index entry, click on the Add button in the Add Index Entry dialog box before clicking on OK. That adds the entry to the topic list. Pretty easy, huh?

Here's the answer to a question that may have been bothering you since you read the last section: You probably thought that one of the Page Range options, Suppress Page Range, seemed a tad bit counterintuitive. Why would you have an index entry with no page range associated with it? If you're adding entries for use later, that's why — when you're building the topic list before actually applying the entry to a specific piece of text. Very likely, you won't need to use this option.

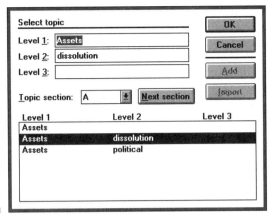

Figure 12-7:
The Select
Topic dialog
box lets you
use topics
defined
earlier.

And, yes, the Text tool cursor must be inserted somewhere before you can enter index topics. The only thing you can enter with no text selected is an index cross-reference.

Shortcuts for special entries

Some index entries are basic, and using the various dialog boxes for adding index entries or selecting index topics is overkill, plain and simple. So to simplify your life, PageMaker adds several shortcuts for common index entries:

- Shift+Ctrl+; creates an index entry for the selected word or phrase without bothering you with the dialog box.

- Shift+Ctrl+Z formats the index entry for a proper name. For example, if you select *Homer Simpson* and press Shift+Ctrl+Z, the name is indexed as *Simpson, Homer,* which is how names are usually indexed. If the name has more than two words in it, like *Mary Ellen Hickey* or *John F. Kennedy* or *Ingall Bull III,* use a nonbreaking space (Ctrl+Shift+spacebar) between all the words that would go on one side of the comma. In these examples, the nonbreaking spaces would go in *Mary Ellen, John F.,* and *Bull III.*

- In the Story Editor's Change dialog box (Utilities⇨Change or Ctrl+9), enter a word that you want indexed in the Find What field and enter ^; in the Change To field. PageMaker doesn't replace the word with ^; but instead marks those words as index entries throughout your document. You can also use this technique for proper names by using ^z instead of ^; as your Change To text. PageMaker formats the name specified in the Find What field like the Shift+Ctrl+Z keyboard shortcut described above.

In all three cases, the word or phrase is treated as a first-level topic, and the entry is *not* added to the topic list. However, for the Story Editor technique, you can search for each key word again, and as you find each occurrence, use Ctrl+; (or Utilities⇨Index Entry) to customize the index entry or add it to the topic list.

Cross-references within indexes

You'll often want to link index entries together so that readers know where to find related material or which index label is used for something that has several possible names (such as *place* and *import*).

If the Text tool cursor is not inserted in text, and you use Ctrl+; (or Utilities⇨ Index Entry), you get the now-familiar Add Index entry dialog box. But this time, the Page reference option is grayed out and only the Cross-reference option is available. (If your text cursor is inserted in text, you have to select the Cross-reference option to activate it.)

The dialog box looks very similar to the one you used for regular page references, as Figure 12-8 shows. The differences are twofold:

- ✔ One, it contains a new button labeled X-ref. If you click on it, PageMaker displays a dialog box identical in all but name to the Select Topics dialog box (see Figure 12-7). Use it to select a predefined cross-reference topic or add your own topic. If you enter your own text and click on the Add button, the cross-reference entry gets added to the index topic list. Frankly, it's not clear why PageMaker gives you both a Topic and an X-ref button — the Select Topics dialog box and the Select Cross-reference dialog box do exactly the same thing and use the same set of index topics. If you add a topic in one dialog box, it's available in the other. In other words, you can use X-ref and Topic interchangeably to select from index topics.

- ✔ Two, the bottom of the dialog box has a set of Denoted By options, in which you specify the kind of text you want to use to indicate the cross-reference as well as the formatting for that text.

Editing an Index

When you're all done indexing, you may want to review all the work you did. You may find some inconsistencies (was it *S. Africa* or *South Africa?*)or misspelled words. Use Utilities⇨Show Index to get the entire list of index topics and the page numbers they reference. Figure 12-9 shows the dialog box. From this dialog box, you can add cross-references, edit existing index topics, remove an index entry, and capitalize an entry by using the buttons at the bottom of the dialog box. The first two buttons — Add X-ref and Edit — open dialog boxes that you've already seen, and Remove is self-explanatory. So what's this Capitalize option? It brings up a tiny dialog box with just three choices. Choose This Selected Topic to capitalize the first letter in the highlighted index topic; select All Level 1 Entries to capitalize the first letter of every first-level entry; and All Entries to put an initial cap on all entries. Whichever option you choose, the capitalization won't change in the Show Index dialog box; the changes are made only when you generate the index.

If you want to look at index entries for a single chapter only and ignore the book list, press Ctrl and choose Sho_w_ Index.

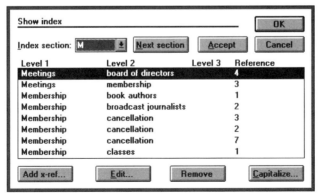

Figure 12-8:
The Add Index Entry dialog box when defining a cross-reference.

Figure 12-9:
Use the Show Index dialog box to edit your index entries.

Working with the book feature

When working with indexes, it's very likely that you'll have some documents that are composed of multiple PageMaker layouts, and you'll want to use the book feature to generate a common table of contents or index to this collection. You learned in Chapter 8 how to set up a book list. Basically, the document that contains the table of contents or index (and you can have a separate document for each) should include all relevant chapters in its book list, which you set up via File⇨Book.

After doing so, you'll find that a formerly grayed-out option in your Create Table of Contents dialog box (Include Book Publications) is now available. If you check it, any styles marked for inclusion in the table of contents in any of the documents in the book list are added to the table of contents.

Similarly, a couple of formerly grayed-out options in the indexing dialog boxes also become available. One is the Import button in the Select Topic and Select Cross-Reference Topic dialog boxes. Clicking on this button imports all index topics defined in all documents in the book list into the current book list.

In keeping with PageMaker's hidden treasure of keyboard commands, you can copy the contents of your index topic list into all other documents in your book list. To do so, press and hold the Ctrl key as you choose Book from the File menu. Just be sure that that the currently open document is not untitled — if it is, you need to save the document for this feature to work.

Generating Indexes

After your index is all set up and corrected, you're ready to generate the index. Use Utilities⇨Create Index to get the aptly named Create Index dialog box, which is shown in Figure 12-10.

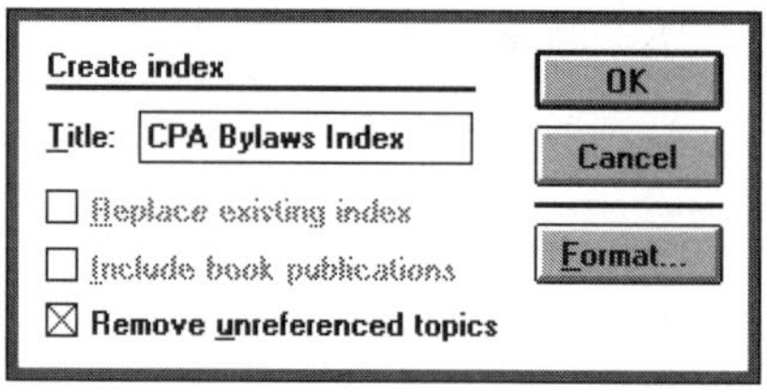

Figure 12-10:
This dialog box may be small, but it's instrumental in creating an index.

Create index

Title: CPA Bylaws Index

☐ Replace existing index
☐ Include book publications
☒ Remove unreferenced topics

OK
Cancel
Format...

In the dialog box, you have the option of specifying a title for the index. There are also three checkboxes, although the first two are often grayed out. The first is Replace Existing Index, which is available only if you previously generated an index for the current document. The second is Include Book Publications, which will index all documents in the current document's book list (see the sidebar "Working with the book feature").

The third option is Remove Unreferenced Topics, which you should almost always check. What does it do? It removes from the generated index all topics not actually referenced in the document. The index topics aren't removed from the topic list — don't worry about that. Checking this option just ensures that you don't have index entries listed with no page numbers (there are no page numbers because there is no text in the document that is indexed to these topics). Imagine having index entries pointing nowhere — avoiding that possibility is why you want to check this option.

Don't click on OK quite yet. First, check out the Index Format dialog box, which you get by clicking the Format button. Figure 12-11 shows the dialog box. These are the options:

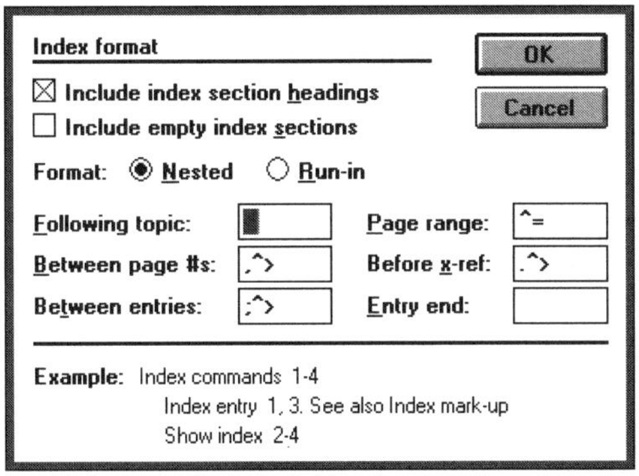

Figure 12-11:
Click on the Format button to control the appearance of the index.

☑ Selecting the Include Index Section Headings checkbox means that you want PageMaker to insert the letters for each set of index entries. For example, there'll be a big *A* above the index entries beginning with the letter *A*. PageMaker will create a style called Index section for these section headings, and you can redefine the formatting as you can for any style.

☑ Selecting the Include Empty Index Sections checkbox means that you want PageMaker to list all the letters of the alphabet, plus *Symbols*, even if there are no index entries that start with particular letters. You'd usually use this with the Include Index Section Headings option, and the result would be things like:

> C
> *no entries*

That's hardly useful. (If you don't check Include Index Section Headings, you just get the text *no entries* where each letter of the alphabet would be.) You may want to use this option, though, if you are constructing an index piecemeal and you want to see which areas are still missing entries.

✔ You have two choices of format: <u>N</u>ested and <u>R</u>un-in. The dialog box shows you what these options look like as you select each one in turn. Basically, <u>N</u>ested makes the entries look like an outline, with the entry for each level on its own line and indented in from the left, while <u>R</u>un-in puts all the page-reference text as one block, with text for each level separated by semicolons, then all the cross-referenced text as one block, again with text for each level separated by semicolons. The <u>N</u>ested option is easier to read, so unless you're really tight on space or trying to make the text hard to read (maybe for a legal brief), avoid <u>R</u>un-in.

✔ Finally, there are a bunch of fields for determining how the text is treated. You determine what characters follow the topic name via <u>F</u>ollowing Topic; what characters separate page numbers via <u>B</u>etween Page #s; what characters separate run-in entries via Be<u>t</u>ween Entries; what characters are used to show page ranges via <u>P</u>age Range; what characters precede a cross-reference (via Before <u>X</u>-ref); and what character is put at the end of each entry via <u>E</u>ntry End.

Here's where you get to have fun. Do you want hyphens to indicate page ranges (such as in *12-14*) or do you prefer en dashes (as in *12–14*)? Do you want a period and space before the *See also* text? Or how about a paragraph break? Do you want a comma or colon after the topic name? And maybe you want a tab as well (because you've defined a tab stop with a dot leader). The possibilities are almost endless. They're certainly mind-boggling. Table 12-1 lists the codes for the more common characters. You can also use standard characters, such as spaces, commas, and letters of the alphabet, plus symbols that you can access from the keyboard via Alt+key combinations. PageMaker doesn't care. But it does care that you put no more than seven characters in any field.

Table 12-1	Special Characters for Indexes	
Character	*Description*	*Code*
–	En dash	^=
—	Em dash	^_
/	Nonbreaking slash	^/
→	Tab	^t
	Nonbreaking space	^s
	Thin space	^<
	En space	^>
	Em space	^m
↵	Soft return (new line)	^n
¶	Return (paragraph break)	^p

After you finish specifying your formatting, click on OK to return to the Create Index dialog box, and click on OK to begin the index generation. Let 'er rip! When PageMaker is done processing, it gives you the place-text icon (either the paragraph or autoflow icon, depending on how your document is set up). Go to the appropriate page and place the index text like any other text. Figure 12-12 shows the result for one document. Note that the title was changed so that it spans the width of the full page; when PageMaker created the index, it placed the title in the first column.

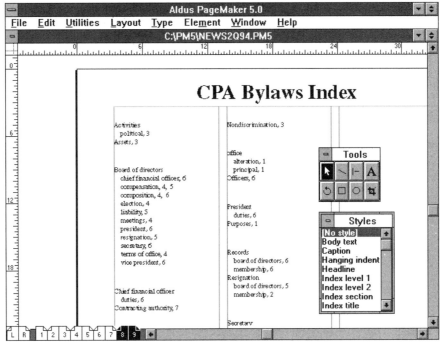

Figure 12-12: An example of a PageMaker-generated index.

You'll also find five new styles in your document: Index Level 1, Index Level 2, Index Level 3, Index Section, and Index Title. Like any styles, you can modify these to fit your design and layout needs.

Chapter 13

Tips for Making a Good Impression in the Corner Office

*E*isenhower was president, everyone wore white shirts, red ties, and gray slacks (well, the men did). They worked at gunmetal gray desks. Gray, long, hard-to-read documents spewed from their secretaries' typewriters. But wait! It's not 1953, it's the '90s! People wear power ties and purple shirts — even sneakers — to the office and live to tell about it. There's more information than ever, but there are also more fonts than ever. And clip art. And laser printers. And computers. Macs, even. Why, this portends something terrific: Business documents do *not* have to be ugly. Say it again: Business documents do *not* have to be ugly. Good, now try this: Business documents do *not* have to be boring. That's right!

Okay, okay. Point made. But it's a pervasive stereotype that "business" documents should be laid out as boringly as possible. The concept of "laying out a report" is probably a revelation to many people. But think about it: Layout is meant to enhance communication in two ways — attracting interest and clarifying the message. Whether a document goes to 120 million people or just to your boss or colleague, both goals are good ones. And with PageMaker, they're easy to achieve.

Take a look at the examples in this chapter — they show some nice-looking business documents, the kind that get attention and maybe even get you some praise. (But watch out: Give one of these documents to someone who's still using a 1939 Underwood typewriter, and you'll probably be accused of wasting valuable company time prettifying your documents. After mentioning the environmental damage caused by carbon papers and asking just how much time that particular someone spends taping hand-drawn charts to reports, you can dismiss such Neanderthal attitudes.)

A warning: This chapter is not like the preceding ones, or like most of the following ones (the exception is Chapter 16, which offers similar examples of newsletters, ads, and other such design-intensive documents). But you can handle it. Think of it as a break from the wonderful world of dialog boxes.

One last thought, before the fun begins: You can apply many of the techniques discussed here to documents you produce in your word processor as well as in PageMaker. After all, good design is good design.

Phone Lists

What's the point of a phone list? To help you find someone's phone number, of course. So design the phone list so that finding those numbers is easy. Look at the example in Figure 13-1. It shows a straightforward, no-nonsense approach that isn't boring. Let's check it out further. The numbers in the following list match those in the figure.

1. The layout is a simple, two-column one, which leaves enough room for many names on each page without crowding them. Notice that the left and right margins are different — the inside margins are wider than the outside margins — so that the document can be easily put in a ring binder. Because the document is set to be two-sided, PageMaker automatically adjusts the margins for left and right pages so that the inside margin remains larger. Also notice the fairly large margin between the columns (0.3 inches). This ensures that there is enough space between columns so that the names and numbers don't get confused from one column to another.

2. The title of the document is centered across the two columns so that it can't be confused with the phone listing information. The placement also lets readers quickly see what kind of information this document delivers.

3. The title of the document — *Employee Phone List* — is large and bold. It uses a bold, sans serif face that is easily readable, even on a cluttered desk. Notice that the headings for each general set of numbers, as well as

the headers for each letter of the alphabet, use the same font, although at a smaller size. This use of the same font for the same purpose (titles) lets the reader easily distinguish titles from other text and it also provides a visual continuity and identity. Even on later pages, you know what document you're looking at. The font used (Gill Sans) has some variations within its character shapes, so it's more visually refreshing than the usual sans-serif suspects, Helvetica and Arial. Be bold: Try a font that didn't come with Windows!

4. The secondary information (the name of the company and the date of update) is in the same font as the title, but the use of a smaller size, italics, and underlines readily differentiates this text from the title. The title gets the majority attention but the other text isn't lost. Because it's based on the same font as the title, the reader sees it as related information — which it is. The underlines also add a dash of graphics. The en dashes around the letter headings pick up on the underlines — the use of horizontal lines in both places gives a sense of visual continuity.

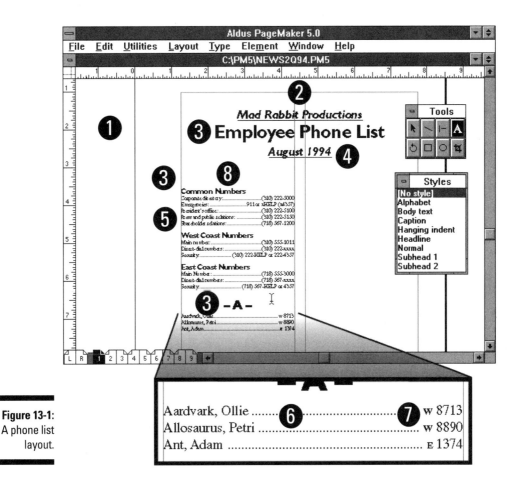

Figure 13-1:
A phone list
layout.

5. The phone listing text is in a very different font (Times, in this case). It's really easy to see which text is the basic phone information. The text size is also fairly large (12 points), which makes it easy to read. The use of a standard font coupled with the large size aids readability. You could use any of several fonts for this sort of text, as long as they aren't too stylized. New Century Schoolbook, Stone Serif, New York, Palatino, and Times New Roman all come to mind.

6. To help the reader line up the phone number with the names, there is a dot leader connecting the two elements. Why not just have the phone number right after the name? It would actually make it harder to find the number because people's brains work best when handling one chunk of information at a time: name, and then number.

7. The little codes in front of the phone extensions remind the reader what coast the person works on: *E* for East Coast and *W* for West Coast. This code serves two purposes. First, because the direct numbers for the different coasts have different prefixes (the first three numerals in a telephone number, not counting the area code, are called a *prefix* in telephone-speak), it helps a caller who might be outside the office remember to dial the right area code and prefix. Second, it reminds the caller to take into account any time difference before calling — it makes little sense to call a West Coast employee at 9 a.m. East Coast time. (Southern Californians tend to be early risers, but being at the office by 6 a.m. is early even for them.) To produce codes like these, you can use a combination of boldface and small caps — that way, the codes are visible and slightly different from the phone extension, but not distracting.

8. Because the goal of a phone list is to help people find phone numbers, it's a good idea to put commonly used numbers at the beginning. Remember, good layout anticipates how people will use the information, and then organizes the information in a way that is easy to find and easy to use.

Keep in mind that every document should be designed for its users. It may be important for a phone list to include other information, such as a person's title, mailing code, or e-mail address. Figure 13-2 shows an alternate formatting for the listings that provides space for such information. Note the use of boldface small caps for the name and italics for the title. In addition, the phone numbers extend to the left of the name and title text to readily differentiate each piece of information in a listing entry. The final touch is to use the Gill Sans font for the *W* and *E*, which sets them apart more forcefully but without introducing yet another new font or style. (The use of small caps for the names also adds a touch of elegance.)

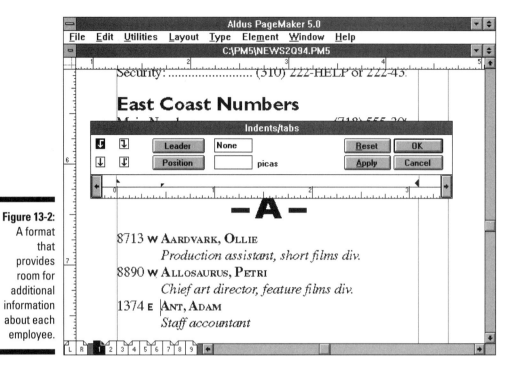

Figure 13-2:
A format
that
provides
room for
additional
information
about each
employee.

Price Sheets

A price sheet, like a phone list, is fairly functional. It's also the kind of document often formatted in tiny type that makes it so hard to read that you wonder how anybody manages to order anything. Imagine: A company goes out of business because of a poorly designed price sheet. Well, things may not get that bad, but bad enough.

The key again is formatting the layout so that elements are easy to find and easy to read. Look at Figure 13-3 for an example of such a price list. Here's the thinking that went behind it:

1. Because of the degree of detail for each item, the format of the price list calls for horizontal (wide) pages. That leaves room for fuller descriptions of the products so that people taking orders or wanting to place orders have sufficient information.

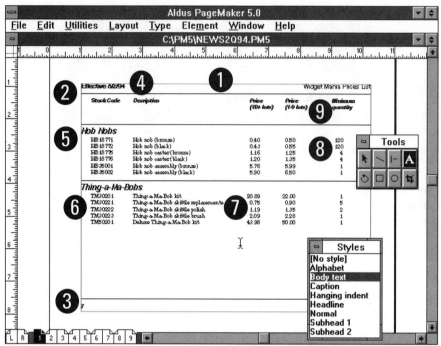

Figure 13-3:
An example
price list
layout.

2. Using master pages ensures that the basic information is repeated on every page. At the top, you see the effective date of the prices, the name of the price list, and a table key (the boldface italics text that lists the stock code, description, and so on). A ruling line separates the price sheet title and the table key. It both adds visual interest and separates the general information from the specific information — the table key is directly related to the tabbed text below it, while the title and effective date are not.

3. The master page also includes page numbers. A ruling line above the page numbers separates them from the product information.

4. The effective date of the prices is in boldface, making it hard for the reader to miss. Because prices change regularly, this is one piece of information you want to make easy to find.

5. The titles for each product category are in large, sans serif type. They happen to be in the same font (Helvetica) as the title and table key information from the master page. This keeps the number of fonts to a minimum, which avoids the ransom-note effect, and it reinforces that different fonts have different meanings: the Helvetica text is the title information, while the New Century Schoolbook text is the basic content. The Rules feature in the Type Specifications dialog box was used to add a

ruling line above each product category title to help the reader keep product categories separate. Such a rule is particularly useful when the text is so wide, as it is here, because the category titles aren't long enough to be really noticeable on the right side of the page if someone is scanning prices quickly.

6. The text is formatted in a serif typeface, New Century Schoolbook, known for its easy readability. The text is also fairly large for a price sheet — 12 points — because small type is hard to read, especially in tables. A lot of price tables are in tiny (8-point or smaller) text — take a look at the oil filter catalog at your neighborhood auto parts store, for example — and they're a pain to read. (Yes, smaller type means more products per page and thus fewer pages to print, which means lower cost. But who cares how much money you save if the end result is that you lose business because customers can't read your price sheet?) The indentation of the text (done by putting a left indent in the Body text style) helps the reader quickly find each product category; the category titles hang to the left of the text, acting as a visual speed bump.

7. Prices are aligned using decimal tabs — see how easily you can differentiate expensive items from cheap ones just by looking at the number of digits to the left of the decimal?

8. Numbers in the *Minimum quantity* column are right-aligned for the same reason prices are aligned with decimal tabs.

9. The table key was created in the master pages. And although its alignment appears to be the same as for the text, it's not. The tab stops for the two *Price* titles and the *Minimum quantity* title were modified. Why? Decimal alignment for straight text would align the beginning of the text to the right of where the decimal would be, which means that the *Price* titles would have appeared slightly to the right of the prices. The answer is to change the tab to a left-aligned tab and move the tab stop to the left so that the titles appear to align with the dollar digits of the text's prices.

Similarly, keeping a right-aligned tab for the *Minimum quantity* title would look weird — it would be the only item in the table key that is right-aligned — so a left-aligned tab was used. The tab stop was moved to the left so that the title would align better with the quantity numbers. You could also create a separate style for the table titles, but because they exist only in two places — the two master pages, it's easier to use the Body text style and then modify the text and tab formatting with the Control palette and Type⇨Indents/Tabs.

Proposals

When you're making a proposal, it's like going for a job interview: You want to make a great first impression. When you're interviewing for a job, you put on a nice suit to help create that positive impression. When you put together a proposal — for a potential customer or for your boss — you likewise should make a good impression by paying special attention to the presentation.

That's not to suggest that you should spend days twiddling with fonts and ignoring the core content of the proposal — that's like spending all day primping in front of the mirror and not taking the time to learn about the company that's interviewing you. But it's not an either/or situation. You *do* have time to make the presentation as good as your ideas. And when they look good, your ideas will come off even better.

Take a look at Figures 13-4 and 13-5. They show the cover and interior pages of a financial brochure. This example's a good one to consider because it's proposing that someone risk hard-earned money on the seller's product. The proposal had better look like the organization behind it is a top-class outfit. (Oh boy! Can't you just hear some consumer-protection agency spokesperson complaining that good design can be used to hoodwink poor, little old ladies out of their retirement savings. Sadly, it probably can, but you wouldn't do that, would you? Didn't think so.)

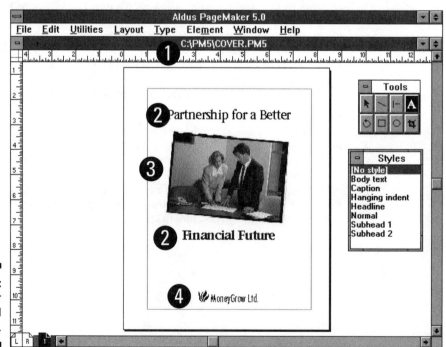

Figure 13-4:
A cover for
a financial
proposal.

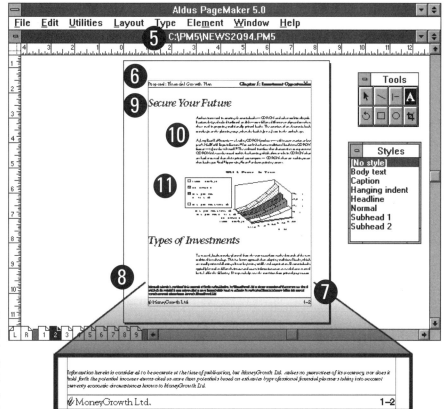

Figure 13-5:
An interior
page from
the financial
proposal.

Note that a proposal may have other elements, such as a table of contents or index, depending on its complexity. They're not shown here, but Chapter 12 shows you how to add such components.

Ready to dissect this proposal? Here goes:

1. The first thing to notice is that the proposal cover is its own PageMaker document. That's because the proposal is divided into multiple sections, each of which starts with a new page 1. The cover has to be in its own document so that each section can start with a new page number. Even if you have only a cover and one section, putting the cover in the document with the rest of the proposal would confuse the page numbering because the cover would be page 1, not the first real page in the document. PageMaker is unlike your word processor in that you can't have multiple sections and have each section's page numbering independent of the others.

2. The font is a conservative serif. Serifs in general have a feeling of substance and tradition behind them, while sans serifs have a modern, more artsy feel. This proposal is asking people to part with their money, so it needs to appear conservative. Notice how the title breaks around the image — this makes the title work better with the image. The first line stresses partnership, which is what the image below it conveys. The second line (it's even bolder than the first line) stresses the financial aspect. By separating them, the message of each line is more obvious.

3. The image is admittedly gratuitous. But imagine what the cover would look like without it — boring, that's what. Be sure that the images you use reinforce the message you're trying to convey. Here, the picture of two people working together reinforces the message of partnership, while the fact that they both look like yuppies reinforces the idea of making money. (You could really push this concept by having multiple images, each targeted to a different potential audience. It can be effective, if somewhat cynical.)

4. The company's logo appears at the bottom of the proposal. Logos bespeak *corporate*. Just using the name is not enough — if you can afford to have a logo, you must be a "real" company. Chances are that your company has a logo — it may even be available as an EPS file. Use it.

5. The interior page (see Figure 13-5) incorporates some familiar techniques from previous examples. (Hey, if it works, keep doing it!) As mentioned before, the interior section is in a separate document from the cover page because the proposal has multiple chapters, each of which has its own page numbering.

6. The master pages for the interior include the overall title (at left) and the chapter title (at right). The rule underneath this header separates it from the main text.

7. As mentioned, each chapter has its own numbering, which you can see in the footer. Notice several techniques here: First, there's a prefix in front of the page number to indicate the chapter (Chapter 2's prefix would be *2-*, for example). Second, notice the use of conservative fonts throughout (you can see them better in the close-up). Most of the document uses Goudy, which just oozes traditionalism (it's also a very nice-looking font). The page number is in Helvetica, though, which makes it very easy to find as you flip through the pages. This kind of slight departure from the main style can really call attention to something without being annoying. Finally, notice the use of the corporate logo in the footer, even though the company name is not in its logo font. The logo's in Goudy here, to blend with the rest of the text, although it could just have easily been in its standard font. Again, here's a subtle embellishment that bespeaks attention to detail.

8. The footer contains some boilerplate disclaimer text, placed in the master page, that satisfies legal concerns. (The disclaimer text is the fine print in all financial proposals that basically says, "Sure, we say we're the experts. But if we screw up and lose all your money, you take full responsibility for not having seen the risk.") The disclaimer here appears in the obligatory small print. It's also in italics, which serves several purposes: It makes the text look nicer, makes it more noticeably distinct from the standard text, and makes the text less likely to be read (long blocks of italics do that), taking some of the sting out of the warning. (Cynical, yes, but we are talking about what people really do, not what they *should* do.)

9. The headings within the proposal are large but classy. The use of italics helps, as does the use of a slightly different font. It's Stone Serif, one with fewer embellishments than Goudy. At larger sizes, some font embellishments that look nice in body copy start calling too much attention to themselves.

10. The body text is indented quite a bit from the left margin, which calls attention to both the headlines and the text. It also keeps the text width from being too overwhelming (the wider the paragraph, the more intimidating it looks). The use of slightly generous leading (12.5 points for this 10-point text rather than a more typical 12 or 11.5 points) also makes the text look less intimidating. (Remember, the proposal is asking people to risk their money, so it must be inviting and soothing). Last, instead of using indented paragraphs, the proposal uses extra space between paragraphs (it's built into the style, via the Before setting in the Paragraph Specification dialog box's Paragraph Space section.

11. The obligatory Excel chart was copied inside Excel and pasted into PageMaker using the Edit⇨Paste Special command. The information in this chart changes frequently, so a live link ensures that it is up to date.

Take a look at some variants of this layout in Figure 13-6. The pages have been resized to booklet form — 5.5 × by 8.5 inches rather than 8.5 × 11 inches — and so the large indents of the original layout didn't work. Figure 13-6 shows two possible solutions: running the text at the full column width and using a large indent for each paragraph to break up some of the boxiness (left) and reducing the indent amount but keeping the same basic style as the original layout (right).

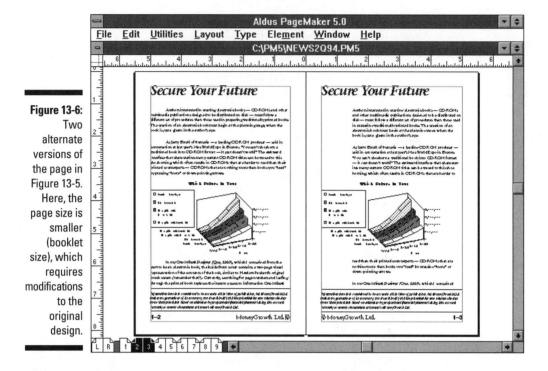

Figure 13-6:
Two alternate versions of the page in Figure 13-5. Here, the page size is smaller (booklet size), which requires modifications to the original design.

Manuals

Why bother worrying about making a manual look good? No one reads manuals anyway, right? Well, that attitude toward manual design has a lot to do with why no one reads them. It almost seems as if the manual is an afterthought. A good manual is a real treasure. You should consider a manual to be a book, and take the same care in writing, editing, and design you'd expect from a best-selling book.

You can develop straightforward manuals that don't take a lot of time to format but offer more than a mind-numbing sea of gray. Take a look at Figure 13-7 for an example. As you can see, it's not very adventurous, but it offers several visual niceties.

1. Notice the odd margins — the text takes only about three quarters of the width of the page. That setup does two things: First, it keeps the text from becoming too wide and off-putting. Second, it leaves some space for small graphics and *white space* (the designer term for empty page space used to provide visual relief).

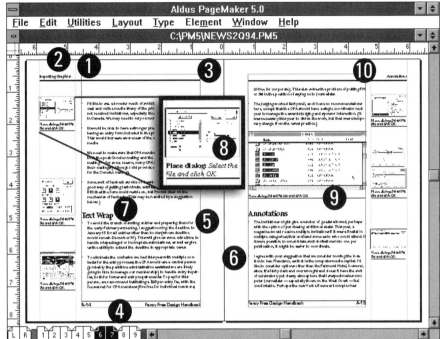

Figure 13-7:
A well-designed manual.

2. Guides pulled out from the rulers in the master pages automatically appear in all pages, and these guides help position the small graphics and their captions. (You can select Snap to Guides under Layout⇨Guides and Rulers or just use the keyboard shortcut Ctrl+U.)

3. The master pages also include a thick line that spans the full width of the page. Placed at the top of the page, this line ties in the text with the small graphics at the sides (without such a unifying element, the graphics could appear to be unrelated to the text).

4. The page numbering and manual name at the bottom of the page follow the text margins. They could have matched the margins of the ruling line at the top, but by being different yet aligned with a major element, the elements reinforce the text's margins while also adding some visual interest. It's hard not to notice the fact that the header and footer widths are different, which gives the reader an explicit clue that the designer was thinking about the design. Yet it's equally obvious that the margins were picked to reinforce the design. It doesn't look like the designer got bored but instead took time to do a thorough job.

5. With so many elements aligning against different margins, using justified text could make the manual appear too precise or machined. Left-aligned text creates a natural undulation along the right margin. To keep the text from getting too dense in a one-text-column format, new paragraphs are distinguished by extra <u>B</u>efore spacing instead of first-line indents. The text font is Cheltenham, which is a very solid-looking font. It's easy to read, even at small sizes, but it does tends to be a bit wide. Condensing the text to 95 percent in the Set <u>W</u>idth field in the Type Specifications dialog box is enough to turn the basic rectangular shape into a squarer shape. The effect is subtle enough that readers won't feel like the type is squished.

6. Another subtle effect (especially at this bird's-eye view) is the use of a bullet character to indicate a change in topic. The bullet lets readers know where a new point begins — if they don't want to read any more about the current point, they know where to go next. This technique works only when the various points are easily differentiated and are short enough to allow several bullets per page (on average). Otherwise, the text looks and reads as if you forgot to turn the bullets off.

7. The titles are simple, using a clean, simple font called Minion Semibold. Notice that the text is short — it helps the reader know immediately what the topics are.

8. Captions are a good place to use typographic effects. Here, the lead-in text is bold while the rest of the caption is italic. This treatment clearly separates the caption's "headline" from the caption's "text," while also providing some visual contrast. Another bonus: Readers can easily find captions cross-referenced from the main text. Notice, too, the ruling line below the caption (set in the Paragraph Rules dialog box, accessed from the Paragraph Specifications dialog box). The rule clearly delineates the end of a caption and picks up on the use of ruling lines in the header and footer. Having such mini-themes in your design has the same effect as repeating certain themes in music: It adds continuity, which is reassuring to readers.

9. Although space is set aside for small graphics, some require more space because they are complex. So in this design, the graphics can also fall in the main text's space. The caption is formatted the same as for the smaller graphics, which provides more of that ever-important continuity.

10. After the layout was done, PageMaker's Running Headers/Footers addition was used to add the name of the current topic for each page to the header.

You should take note of two other examples of well-designed manuals before moving on: this book, designed by the talented folks at IDG Books, and the PageMaker manual, designed by the talented folks at Aldus. Both manuals use a combination of margins, text formats, ruling lines, and small graphics to help you manage your way through the text. Both also use sidebars; the PageMaker multicolumn sidebar format is particularly interesting. The sidebars have the same number of columns as the main text — definitely not the norm — and they simultaneously look different from the rest of the manual while still looking like part of it. Notice, too, the two fonts that run throughout the PageMaker manual: A serif font is used for general explanations and a sans serif font is used for tips and technical details of the PageMaker dialog boxes and interface.

Common Threads

The examples presented in this chapter share some common techniques. That shouldn't surprise anyone — all the examples were created by the same designer, and designers tend to develop unique personal styles. That's good, because it fosters a sense of identity across a range of documents. But don't let yourself get straitjacketed into using the same techniques over and over. Experiment. Try different approaches. Yes, make related documents look related, but feel free to try out new ideas, whether they're your own or those from a colleague or from something that caught your eye.

With that in mind, you should keep the following few principles in the back of your mind — not too far back! They'll help make your business documents appealing yet completely appropriate for the audience that will read them.

- ✔ Stick to a smaller number of fonts per document. Use variations within them, such as boldface and italics, to provide further visual and editorial contrast.

- ✔ Use clean, easy-to-read, conservative fonts in business documents. Think of them as the typographic equivalent of suits and ties.

- ✔ Use devices such as lines to separate different elements. But don't go overboard and use lines everywhere. Moderation is key!

- ✔ Build enough white space into your design. The human eye needs a place to "park" when it's tired or figuring out what to look at next.

- ✔ Make sure that page numbers, headings, and other guideposts are easy to find and easy to read.

That's it for the business document. Now change into your cool party clothes. The artsy stuff is next!

Part V
Cool Designs They Never Knew You Could Do

The 5th Wave By Rich Tennant

"These kidnappers are clever, Lieutenant. Look at this ransom note, the use of 4-color graphics to highlight the victim's photograph. And the fonts! They must be creating their own— must be over 35 typefaces here...."

In this part...

Now that you've learned to satisfy your boss's utilitarian urges, let's have some fun and look at neat things, like cool graphics, color, and snazzy layout. Sure, using these features requires some sense of aesthetics, but you don't need an art degree to create good-looking documents that have a splash of originality. The basic secret is a willingness to try something different. After all, you can always go back to a safer option if you don't like the results of your experimentation.

Chapter 14
Even Prettier Pretty Pictures

- -

In This Chapter

▶ Working with lines, rectangles, and circles

▶ Filling rectangles with grays and patterns; creating special types of lines

▶ Creating special borders and backgrounds for text and graphics

▶ Using special effects such as rotation and skewing to distort graphics

▶ Combining various techniques to create simple drawings

▶ Making elements align along a row or grid

▶ Working with graphics inside text as if they were symbols

- -

*G*raphics really can add life to a publication. It's a cliché that a picture is worth a thousand words (although it's true in many cases). Well, a picture can also make you want to *read* a thousand words, and that's at least as important as conveying a message visually.

In Chapter 7, you learned how to import graphics and do text wrap. Here, you'll jump into PageMaker's graphics-creation tools and then revisit text wrap from a designer's point of view, take a peek at PageMaker's image controls, and finally, see how you can merge graphics into text. It'll be a fun ride. Hang on!

Creating Your Own Graphics

Most of the tools in PageMaker's toolbox work with graphics — only the *A*-shaped Text tool doesn't. You can use the middle four tools in the toolbox — the Line, Perpendicular Line, Rectangle, and Ellipse tools — to create graphics. (*Perpendicular* is techno-speak for lines that go only straight across or only straight up and down. In PageMaker-speak, it also means lines that go only at a 45-degree angle.)

When you create a graphic, PageMaker uses the default text-wrap settings (see Chapter 7). This can be a pain at times because your defaults for imported graphics may not be appropriate for lines and rectangles that you draw. For example, you might set a standoff margin of 0.2 inches around imported images so that text doesn't get too close. But you may want to put lines between columns that are closer than 0.2 inches to the text. There's really no way around this: You can have only one set of defaults for text wrap, so you should use the settings for the elements you use most often and just change the settings for the other types of graphics as needed.

When talking about graphics, people use the term *points* to refer to their thickness. Whether it's a straight line, the lines in a rectangle, or the line in a circle, you measure it in points. So what is a point? It's equal to $1/72$ inch or $1/12$ pica. (Imagine entering line sizes as inches: You'd have thicknesses like 0.175 and 0.050. No, thank you!)

Working with lines

Chances are, you'll draw lines more than any other type of graphic element in PageMaker. Lines — also called *rules* by publishing folks — are best used as separators. For example, you may put lines above your page numbers and newsletter name (traditionally placed at the bottom of the page) to make it clear where the text ends. Lines also make great separators between stories on a page. And thin rules can be used to separate columns of text — many newspapers use this effect, especially those like the *New York Times* that seek that old-fashioned look.

The reason people put lines between columns is that in the early days of print, typesetters tried to cram as many letters as possible on a page because paper and printing were so expensive. The font Times was developed for the *Times* of London to be readable at small sizes and with compact spacing, and it soon became a standard (although what is called Times on most printers is based on a version developed for the *New York Times* to improve readability). To crowd even more type on a page, newspaper layout artists pushed the columns very close together — to less than 1 pica, or 0.167 inches apart — making it necessary to add a thin line between the columns so that readers wouldn't get mixed up. These lines were so thin that they were called *hairlines*; today, the term refers to a line that's $1/4$ point wide.

Rules of thumb

When drawing lines, follow these rules of thumb (pun intended):

- ✔ Choose a thinner line over a thicker one. Thick lines can be overkill, and if you're not sure how thick something should be, tone it down. Generally,

use a hairline or $^1/_2$-point rule to separate small elemer
boundary between a shaded area and a nonshaded ar
1.5-point rule to separate larger elements, such as sto
box around a story. Use 2- or 3-point lines rarely; one
separate very different elements.

✔ Put at least 3 points of space between the rule and th
graphic — 6 to 9 points is best.

✔ Don't use too many different sizes of lines on the same page or too many
lines together.

✔ Consider putting a thin and thick line next to each other (perhaps 0.5-point
and 1.5-point, separated by 1 or 1.5 points of space). PageMaker has some
predefined line styles that do this automatically.

Selecting the right line tool

Because there are two line tools — regular and perpendicular — you have to
decide which one you want. For lines that go with text, such as separator lines,
use the Perpendicular Line tool. It makes life a lot easier because no matter
where you move the mouse, the line snaps to the nearest 45- or 90-degree angle.
No need for precision drawing (although you still have to start and end the line
at the right spots).

To draw a line, click on the tool that you want to use and begin dragging at the
point where you want the line to begin. Release the mouse button at the point
where you want the line to end.

What if you start drawing with the regular Line tool and then decide that
you want to make sure that the line is absolutely horizontal or vertical?
Eyeballing the line angle is tricky, even in a close-up view. The solution is to
hold down the Shift key while drawing. PageMaker ensures that your line is a
perpendicular line.

If you want to change a perpendicular line into a nonperpendicular line, just
change to the Arrow tool, select one end of the line and drag it to a new location. Because you can drag the end to any location, you can create a nonperpendicular line. (You could also rotate the line by using the Rotate tool in
the toolbox or the rotation settings in the Control palette.)

You can modify the size or position of lines by dragging their end points or by
selecting the line and using the Control palette's options (the palette is shown
in Figure 14-1). In either case, remember to use the Arrow tool to select the line
in question.

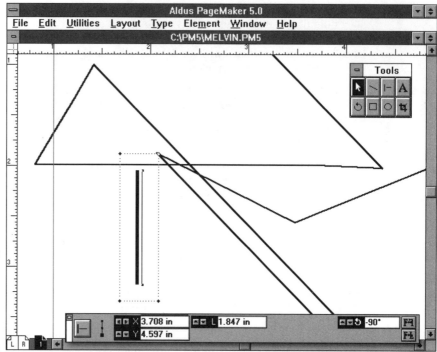

Figure 14-1:
The Control
palette
when a line
is selected.

Special lines

Not all lines are solid, and not all are 1-point thick. PageMaker offers several
types of lines, and it lets you create your own custom lines, too. Figure 14-2
shows the menu of line types (accessed via Element➪Line). As you can see,
PageMaker gives you a choice of dotted lines, double lines, even dashed lines,
all available in several predefined sizes. If you want something else, select the
Custom option to open the Custom Line dialog box, shown in Figure 14-3. Here,
you pick the thickness, style (such as dotted or dashed), and printing attributes.

You can also select the printing attributes — Transparent and Reverse — from
the Element➪Line menu; if the features are checked in the menu or in the dialog
box, they are active. The Transparent option, turned on by default, creates a
line that looks like it's printed directly on top of anything beneath it. If you
choose a dashed line, for example, anything between the dashes prints. But if
you uncheck the Transparent option, anything between the dashes appears in
the paper color (usually white). Figure 14-4 shows the difference between
having this option checked or not. The Reverse option inverts the color — a
black line becomes white, or vice versa. It's usually unchecked, which leaves
the line at its normal color (black, unless you apply a color via the Color
palette).

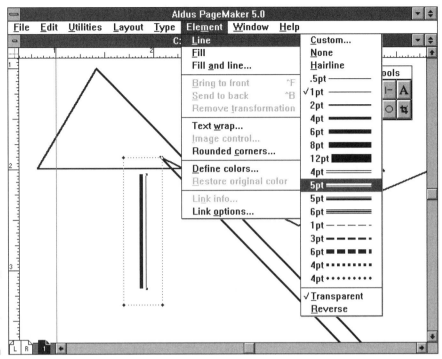

Figure 14-2:
The menu
options for
lines.

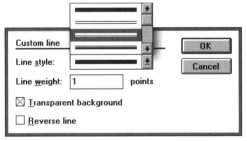

Figure 14-3:
The Custom
Line dialog
box lets you
create any
line weight
you want.

Fill is a techie-term for the color or shading you apply to the interior of an element; this book often uses the word *background* to mean the same thing.

When would you uncheck the Transparent option? Here's an example: Say that you're using one of the lines composed of two rules with a space between them. If this line rests on top of a gray box (or perhaps forms its border), it looks more dramatic if it has a paper-colored background. Figure 14-5 shows an example.

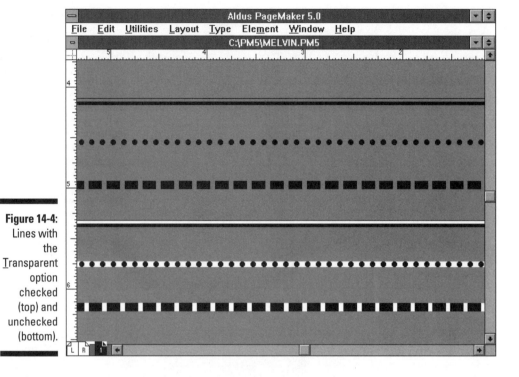

Figure 14-4:
Lines with the Transparent option checked (top) and unchecked (bottom).

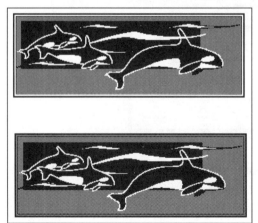

Figure 14-5:
Unchecking the Transparent option (top, in the border) can result in a more dynamic look for certain types of lines.

If you're working with several lines and you want them to be joined, change to a larger view so that you can ensure that they really do align. (Double-size is a good setting; choose Layout⇨View⇨200% or Ctrl+2). One way to help force the lines into alignment is to use PageMaker's snap-to feature. This feature is no panacea, mind you, but it can help. For example, if your lines will fall within the column boundaries, turning on Snap to Guides (Layout⇨Guides and Rulers⇨Snap to Guides or Ctrl+U) ensures that the lines end at the column boundaries (where the column guides are located).

Working with rectangles

Look again at Figure 14-5. Those four lines actually form a rectangle. For solid lines, it doesn't matter whether you draw a rectangle with the Rectangle tool or draw four lines with the Line tool — except, of course, for the extra work that it takes to draw and align four lines. But for other types of lines, it can make a big difference.

Look at Figure 14-6. The lines in the bottom example are the same lines drawn for Figure 14-5, except that this time the double-line option was used, making it obvious that these are four lines instead of a rectangle. See how the corners aren't beveled? You'd get similar mismatches if you chose dashed or dotted lines. Plus, when you use the Rectangle tool, you get the option of simultaneously filling in the rectangle with a shade or pattern.

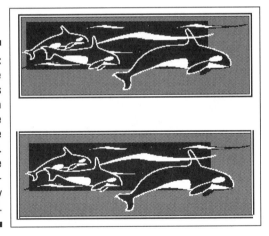

Figure 14-6: Using the line options with a rectangle (top, in the border) vs. drawing the four lines independently (bottom).

Rectangles often go hand in hand with lines. Whether you're putting a box around a piece of text (such as for a sidebar) or around a graphic, you'll likely want to combine a shade of gray with a line, as in Figure 14-5. That's why PageMaker gives you the Fill and Line dialog box (Element⇨Fill and Line). You can, of course, just use one or the other — it's a matter of personal taste and degree of emphasis. PageMaker also gives you separate submenus for line and fill (Element⇨Fill and Element⇨Line). Figure 14-7 shows the Fill and Line dialog box; Figure 14-8 shows the Fill submenu. (In case you forgot, Figure 14-2 showed the Line submenu.)

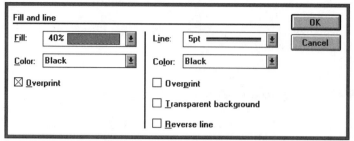

Figure 14-7:
The Fill and
Line dialog
box lets you
specify both
the fill and
line of an
element at
once.

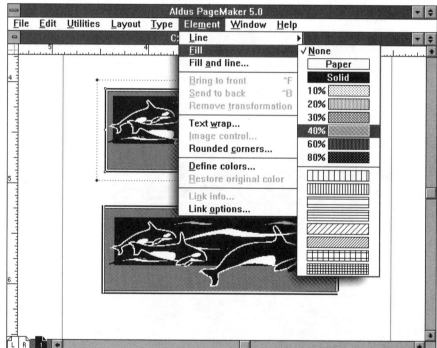

Figure 14-8:
The menu
options for
fills.

The Fill and Line dialog box brings together several options, which makes it a
real breeze to use. In addition to the lines and fills (you have a choice of any of
the shades of gray or any of the patterns — but not both), you can set the fill
color and decide whether the lines and/or fills overprint elements of a different
color beneath them.

To *overprint* means to print over anything behind the element instead of obscuring (or *knocking out*) whatever is behind. In most cases, you won't notice a difference. But if you overprint yellow on top of blue, for example, you get green where the two elements intersect. But if you don't overprint the yellow, you get yellow where the two elements intersect. Note that you may not see the color mixing on-screen.

You might think that you can create patterns by overlapping several rectangles, each filled with a different color, shade, or pattern, and then checking the Overprint option in the Fill and Line dialog box. Unfortunately, this works only if you are using color separations and overprint shades of different colors — it does not work for multiple overlapping elements of the same color, nor does it work for patterns (they all have white backgrounds and block anything under them).

Working with borders

Borders (lines) around rectangles deserve special attention because they are so common. Here are some tips to effective borders:

- Borders usually should be no thicker than 2 points. For multiline lines, such as the thick-and-thin line used in Figure 14-6, lines should usually be between 4 and 7 points thick. If they're much thicker, they probably will overwhelm the other elements.

- It's a good idea to put a hairline or 0.5-point rule around grayscale photographic or scanned images — the rule provides a clear demarcation of where the photo ends and the paper begins. This is not a requirement, but it often helps. However, such a rule is rarely needed for color images because the color stands out by itself from the rest of the black and gray elements on a page.

- Borders start at the edge of a rectangle and proceed inward. Thus, if you have a rectangle with a gray background and a thick-and-thin rule, the space between the two lines making up the rule will be white because that space is outside the rectangle's gray background. What if you want that space to be gray? Create a new rectangle that is as big as the outside of the first rectangle's border, fill it with the same background as the first rectangle, and then use Element⇨Send to Back (Ctrl+B) to position it behind the first rectangle. That puts your gray behind the space inside the rules (in fact, that's what happened in Figure 14-5).

- If you want a drop shadow effect for your rectangle (see Figure 14-9), create a new rectangle of the same size as the current one (you can just use copy and paste to do this). Then move it slightly to the left and down from the original rectangle and use Element⇨Send to Back (Ctrl+B) to position it behind the original rectangle. Make sure that the color or shade of the two rectangles is different enough so that the shadow is obvious. If you want the original rectangle to be white, you may have to set its fill to Paper so that the rectangle beneath does not show through it.

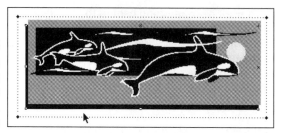

Figure 14-9:
Creating
a drop
shadow.

✔ A classy effect is to put rules on the top and bottom (sometimes of different thicknesses) of a background. You have to draw the two rules and make sure that they align with the top and bottom of the background — so that you don't get an awkward gap between the line and the background or see the background bleeding past the lines. And if you move the rectangle that serves as the background, be sure to select the two lines, too, so that the elements move together.

You may think that you can save a step by using the Line submenu to add a rule around a photograph or illustration. Sorry, it won't work. But what you can do is this: Select the object with the Arrow tool and choose Utilities⇨Aldus Additions⇨Create Keyline. Then click on the Attributes button to access the Fill and Line dialog box, select the line that you want to use, and press Enter. Enter a value into the Extends option box to specify the distance between the border and the object. For example, if you want to draw the border right on the object, enter 0. Then press Enter. You can also apply this command to text blocks, but if you do, use an Extends value of 2 to 6 points.

The gray shades available in PageMaker — 10, 20, 40, 60, and 80 percent — appear coarser on-screen than they do when printed. On-screen, type looks best over a 20 percent fill, but when printed, it looks best over a 10 percent fill, despite its hard-to-read appearance on-screen.

Working with backgrounds

When using rectangles as backgrounds for other elements, a few techniques can improve the look of your document.

✔ Don't use a gray level greater than 10 percent behind text. If you're using a light color such as yellow as a background, you can increase the value, depending on the richness of the color. A too-dark background can obscure text.

✔ You can use white or light-colored type on a dark background to highlight an element. Generally, the background should be at least 80 percent gray or a dark, rich color, and the type should be white or a very light color. Typically, the type should be in a bold face because it's harder for the human eye to read light on dark than it is to read dark on light.

✔ For really interesting backgrounds, create patterns or shapes in an illustration or photo-editing program and import the graphic into PageMaker. Crop the graphic to the size of a background rectangle, add rules around it if desired, and place your text or graphic on top. (The effect is sort of like wallpaper in the background of your Windows desktop.) Note that if you're using text, the background graphic should be muted (at least where the text appears) so that the text remains readable. For large text, such as in titles, using a bold typeface, perhaps with an outline or drop shadow, usually removes the need for a muted background.

Rotating, skewing, and flipping

The Control palette for a rectangle includes controls to flip, rotate, or skew (slant) the shape.

The flip controls are the ones at the far right that show the letter *F* being changed. The top one is flip vertically, or mirror; the bottom one is flip horizontally, or upside-down.

To rotate or skew a rectangle, just enter the angle of rotation: a positive number rotates or skews it counterclockwise (in the direction of the arrow in the rotation symbol), while a negative number rotates or skews it clockwise. You can also rotate an object by selecting the Rotate tool and holding the mouse button down while you move the mouse in the direction of the rotation you want. A line connects the Rotate cursor to the object being rotated; this line is the "lever" by which you are rotating the element.

When you rotate, pay attention to what handle is selected in the Control palette. This handle becomes the rotation point — the point around which the object is rotated. Figure 14-10 shows the effects. The three rotated rectangles at the bottom all used to line up when they were horizontal, but now that they're rotated, they don't. (The black box in each rectangle was added to show which handle was active; the box will *not* appear on your elements.) The figure also shows the Rotate tool in action. A last thing to notice: When you rotate an object, its icon in the Control palette changes to a diamond shape.

You can use multiple rotations, sometimes combined with skews, to create a sense of movement. Look at Figure 14-11 for an example. But be careful when you do something like this — the effect can be dizzying! The how-to's are simple: Select a rectangle, skew it slightly to make it look like it was drawn in perspective, and make a series of copies. Rotate each copy by a small amount — say 5 or 10 degrees. Enlarge each copy by about 10 percent, and reposition them so they seem to flow along a curve. You can enhance the flow by using different shades for each rectangle. Notice in the figure that the same rotation and skew were applied to the text as to the top rectangle (the settings are shown in the Control palette). By combining text and graphics and applying these effects to them, you can do some pretty amazing stuff.

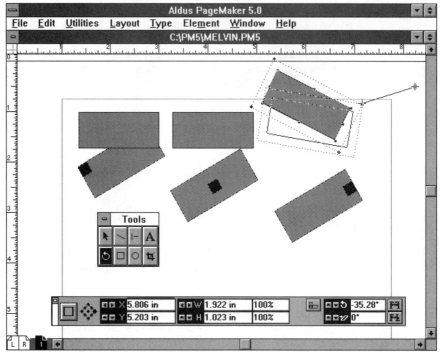

Figure 14-10:
The effects of the rotation point (shown as a black square) on an element.

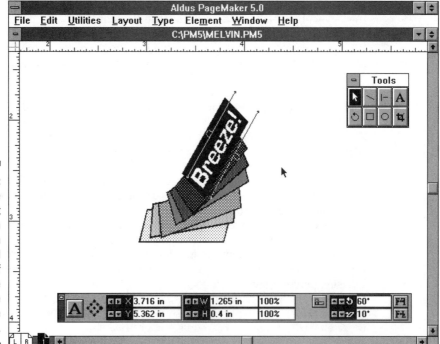

Figure 14-11:
One sample graphic that you can create with skewing and rotation of the same image multiple times.

Hate a rotation or skew that you created? You can get rid of it by changing the angle back to 0 degrees. Or, for a faster method if you have more than one effect applied, use the Element⇨Remove Transformation command. Presto! Everything's back to normal.

Working with ellipses

Ellipses work the same as rectangles except that you use the Ellipse tool to create them. So, either go back to the previous section and substitute the word *ellipse* for *rectangle* or go on to the next topic.

Creating other shapes

Lines, rectangles, and ellipses form the basic shapes in PageMaker. You can create variations of these shapes by using the flip, rotate, and skew features. For rectangles, you can add rounded corners with the Rounded Corners dialog box (Element⇨Rounded Corners). You can also create polygons by drawing several lines in succession, so that the end point of one is the start point of another. However, you cannot fill these shapes because they are, after all, just a series of lines, not a true polygon. Figure 14-12 shows examples of several shapes.

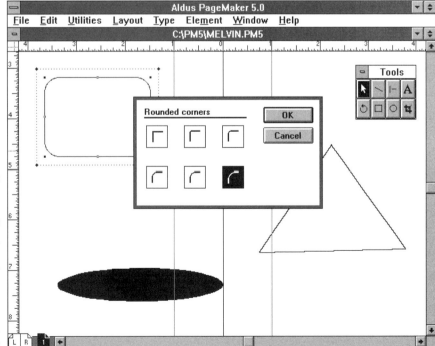

Figure 14-12: You can round off the corners of a rectangle by selecting options from this dialog box.

Simple drawings

You can create simple drawings by combining rectangles, ellipses, and lines. We're talking basic stuff here, like a yellow circle in a blue rectangle to represent the sun in the sky, a rounded-corner rectangle in a regular rectangle to represent a TV or computer monitor, or a pattern of lines to represent a mountain range. If you want to do more challenging graphics, use a drawing program or invest in some clip art (collections of simple illustrations and photos, available on disk and CD-ROM).

Figure 14-13 shows an example of do-it-yourself PageMaker art: a TV with a picture in it. The secret to creating this graphic is to place a transparent rectangle with a thick border line (5 points here) and rounded corners in front of the TV. The border line is a thick-and-thin combination, and <u>T</u>ransparent is unchecked so that the TV image does not appear between the two lines (instead, a white band appears). Using the rounded rectangle to hide the TV means that the TV image has to be larger than it would appear because there had to be enough to place that rounded-rectangle over.

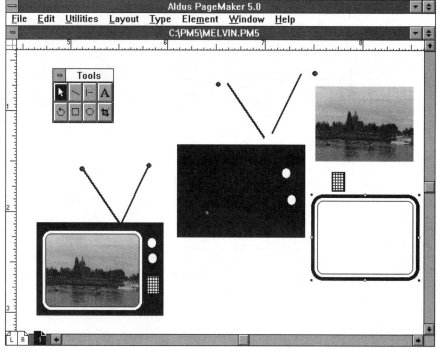

Figure 14-13:
Do-it-yourself PageMaker art: a TV with an image in its screen (left), plus the elements used to create it (right).

Techniques for Altering Graphics

You can use PageMaker's tools to customize imported graphics. In some cases, you can combine PageMaker graphics and text with the image. You can also use the rotation, flip, color, skew, and resizing features to modify the graphics.

Distorting a graphic

Take a look at Figure 14-14. The top image is a modified version of the bottom image. Resizing the graphic along the horizontal axis so that it is squeezed together to 53 percent (see the Control palette) changes the killer whales from sleek to fat. The new whales take a lot less room, leaving space for the logo type. Fat whales are friendly whales (nice and cuddly), and even if it wasn't essential to make room for the logo type, it might have been nice to squeeze the whales to make them look cuddlier.

Figure 14-14: Squeezing the illustration horizontally makes the killer whales cuddly and makes room for a logo.

Now take a look at Figure 14-15. Once again, the bottom image is the original. The top image is the same as the bottom image except for the 30-degree skew. The skew makes the killer whales look like they're swimming fast, giving them a sense of motion — don't get seasick! This slight change to an image produces noticeable results.

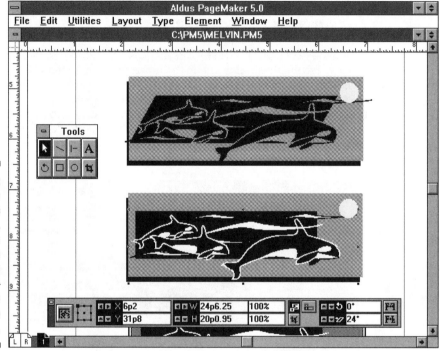

Figure 14-15:
When the killer whales are skewed, they seem to be swimming a lot faster — and they're no longer so cuddly.

The killer whales seem to have lost their white in the image at the top of Figure 14-15. They haven't, at least not in the printed version. The reason that the white is missing is that PageMaker sometimes incorrectly displays a skewed or rotated image's colors. But the printout is unaffected.

You'll rarely want to manipulate a photo or scanned image by skewing or distorting it. These effects work better on drawings because drawings don't look as real as photos — we're all used to seeing cartoons and sketches that are caricatures of the original. Photos tell us that something is real, so an altered photograph looks *un*real and can be distracting. Want proof? Look at Figure 14-16. Use your judgment in this matter, but be sure that you have good reason to stretch or skew a photo.

Figure 14-16:
Skewing or
otherwise
distorting a
photograph
makes
it look
unreal —
and often
unpleasant.

Embellishing a graphic

Sometimes, a very simple embellishment can alter a graphic considerably. Take a look at Figure 14-17. It's a picture of the government center in Victoria, British Columbia, a picturesque provincial capital in Canada. But by circling the parliament building (by using a circle with no fill, a thick line, and the Reverse option checked) and adding a line of text, the postcard-like photo now screams *political flier!* It could as easily be a photo shown in a spy movie, with the assassin's target circled. The point is, this technique calls the reader's attention to a detail, loud and clear.

Figure 14-17:
Adding a
circle
around part
of an image
tells the
reader to
focus on
that portion.

Other embellishments include adding a drawing to an image, like the TV graphic in Figure 14-13, or even adding text (such as a logo). Another option is to add a drop shadow by placing a rectangle or ellipse behind the graphic and having it slightly offset on two sides, as shown behind the whale graphics in Figure 14-14.

Positioning graphics

By now, you've probably noticed that the way in which you position graphics has an effect on how they look. For example, positioning graphics on top of each other lets you create simple artwork such as the TV in Figure 14-13.

Repetitive placement

You can also use positioning to achieve a tightly honed look. For example, look at Figure 14-18. Here, the document is an announcement trumpeting awards won by IDG Books and *Macworld* (these are real awards). What's so special? Well, notice how the award logos align, as do the text blocks below them. To do this, you could use the mouse and eyeball it — except that takes a lot of work and is usually not accurate. Or you could use the Control palette and calculate the positions for each element — except that takes a lot of work, and few of us are that great at math anyhow. So what's left? The Multiple Paste command, that's what, which you get via Edit⇨Multiple Paste.

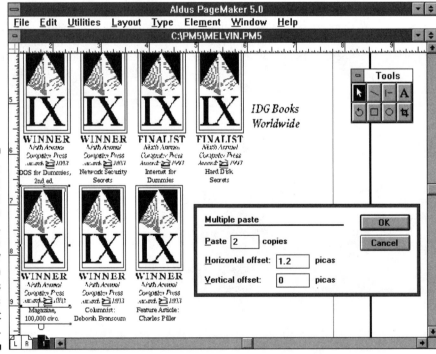

Figure 14-18:
By using
the Multiple
Paste
command,
you can
precisely
position
duplicates
of a graphic
or text
block.

1. **Select something (you can select multiple objects) and copy it.**

   Choose Edit⇨Copy or press Ctrl+C to transfer the element to the Windows Clipboard.

2. **Choose Edit⇨Multiple Paste and specify how many copies you want pasted as well as the horizontal and vertical offsets.**

   These offsets tell PageMaker how far apart to space each copy. In the figure, the spacing is 1.2 inches horizontally but 0 inches vertically, which places the copies from left to right in a straight row.

3. **Click on OK, and the copies appear.**

Notice that in the figure, not all the elements are the same. The text has been edited, of course, but the logos at the end are different than the original — they say *Finalist*, not *Winner*. How would you do that? Here's how. Copy the *Winner* logo via the Multiple Paste dialog box and then select one of the logos you want to replace with the *Finalist* logo. Use the Place Document dialog box (File⇨Place or Ctrl+D) to select the replacement graphic *and* turn on the Replacing Entire Graphic option. PageMaker places the new graphic precisely where the old one was. Cool, huh? You can use this technique any time you have a regular series of similar objects, even if they're different. One example is a stack of cards, where you might offset each card by, say, a quarter inch horizontally and vertically and then replace each of the copies with a different card — Queen, Jack, Ace, and so on.

Stacking order

You saw, in Figure 14-11, how to stack a series of graphics to create a layered picture. The Element⇨Send to Back (Ctrl+B) and Element⇨Bring to Front (Ctrl+F) commands let you arrange the elements. Note that you cannot choose the stacking order for an individual element: You must send elements to the back or to the front in turn, until you get the desired stacking order. Unlike some graphics programs, PageMaker doesn't offer commands to bring forward or send backward a graphic one layer at a time.

When you create elements, they are naturally stacked so that the first one created is at the back, the next one created is on top of that, and so on, until the most recently created element, which is at the front. But if you were to select an element and move it, it would be put at the front of the stack. (Resizing, rotating, or skewing don't do this.) You have no choice, unfortunately, but to select the elements that are supposed to be in front of it one at a time and bring them to the front, until they're all back in order.

Using Graphics in Text

The last thing you should know about graphics is how to work with them as if they were text. Although there are a lot of symbols available in various typefaces, there's no guarantee that you have the one you want — or that it even exists. A good example is if you have a corporate logo or icon that you'd like to use, say, as a bullet. (Or, if you're doing PageMaker books, you might want to include the various cursor icons in the text!) You could create your own font with this character using a program like Altsys Corp.'s Fontographer or Ares Software's FontMonger — these work best if you use the character a lot and you have several such characters. But for occasional or per-job use, why not just use PageMaker's embedded-graphics feature? (The PageMaker manual calls this an *in-line graphic*.) Figure 14-19 shows an example (the last bullet). Here's how it works.

1. **Place the text cursor where you want the graphic inserted.**

   Do *not* highlight a piece of text — embedding will not work if text is highlighted.

2. **Use the Place dialog box (File➪Place or Ctrl+D) to select the graphic you want to embed.**

3. **Turn on the As In-line Graphic option (it should be on if you've inserted the text cursor).**

4. **Click on OK.**

5. **The graphic is placed at the text cursor's location, and chances are that it will be too big.**

   You'll have to resize it. Switch to the Arrow tool and resize the graphic using the control handles — just like any other graphic. (Remember to hold the Shift key if you want to resize the graphic proportionally.)

You should know a few things about embedded graphics:

✔ The graphic is centered vertically on the line. So if the graphic is taller than the line it is placed in, space will be added above and below the line to make room for the graphic.

✔ If an embedded graphic is wider than the current column, it overprints text in any adjacent column.

✔ Text-wrap controls are grayed-out for embedded graphics — not that there's any reason you'd need them. (Well, you might want to insert a graphic in a line and have text wrap around it as it reflows with the text. Sorry, but no can do.).

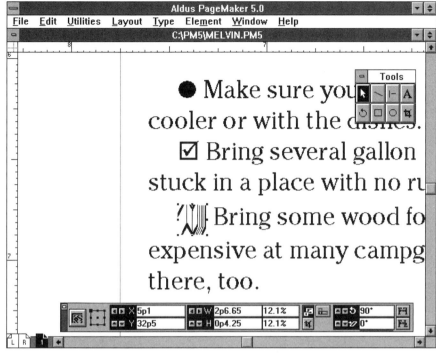

Figure 14-19:
An embedded graphic can be used as a bullet character.

✔ You can rotate, skew, or apply image controls (for supported image formats) to embedded graphics. And you can use fills, patterns, and colors — just like any other graphic.

✔ Graphics embedded in your word processor will be imported as embedded graphics into PageMaker. Note, however, that a graphic embedded in a word processor may not look as good as one embedded in PageMaker — Word, for example, sometimes substitutes a lower-resolution version, especially for formats like EPS.

✔ If you are editing text in the Story Editor, embedded graphics will be represented by a gray box. Don't worry — they look normal when you're back in layout view.

✔ You can embed graphics created in PageMaker. For example, say you want a box character. Draw it in PageMaker with the Rectangle tool. Then cut the graphic with Ctrl+X. Now switch to the text tool and place the text cursor where you want the box character to be. Paste the character via Ctrl+V. Instant embedded graphic!

Chapter 15
Better Than Crayons

● ●

In This Chapter

▶ An introduction to printing process and spot colors

▶ Applying colors from the Colors palette

▶ Defining your own custom process colors

▶ Accessing libraries of commercial spot colors

▶ Editing and deleting existing colors

● ●

*H*ave you ever commercially reproduced a document in color? If not, you may be in for a shock. Although it's better than using crayons, it's also more expensive and more complicated. You don't just present your printer with a color printout and say, "There you go, my good man. Let me know when you've printed 100 copies of that."

If you did, the printer might respond, "You want me to print this in color?" And he'd ask the question as if it were about the most unlikely fantasy he could imagine.

"Of course I want it in color!" you'd answer, showing him that you mean business. You're not to be toyed with.

"You realize," he'd say slowly, so as not to set you off, "That it'll cost you about nine million dollars to have this color-separated."

No doubt, you'd inspect this charlatan for a moment and come back with, "Did I miss a few days, or is the inflation in this city a little worse than I had imagined? I suppose that the next time I go to Burger King that a Whopper will set me back a cool billion plus change!"

If the printer happened to be a good-natured sort, he'd probably smile at your amusing joke, sit down with you in a quiet corner, and explain to you the realities of printing. On the other hand, if you happened across him on a particularly trying day, you might find yourself subjected to severe scorn and ridicule, if not actual physical threats. Just to be safe, this chapter gives you the lowdown on color printing so that you won't risk embarrassment or bodily harm when you take your PageMaker documents to the printer.

How Inks and Plates Work

There are all kinds of wacky printing techniques in the world, but the most common and least expensive commercial solution is *offset printing*. Copies are made by running paper against an inked *plate* that's wrapped around a cylinder. Each plate can handle only one color — called an *ink*. If you want to use more than one ink, you have to add plates, and each plate costs money.

In order to reproduce your color printout, the printer has to separate the colors into their *primary components*. Now, you may recall that in grade school, you learned that you can make any color by mixing blue, red, and yellow — the so-called *primary colors*. But for commercial printing, mixing blue, red, and yellow doesn't work very well. For one thing, blue and red are too dark. Instead of mixing to form a bright purple, like you heard they would, they make a blackish mud that isn't suitable for much of anything.

So, instead of using pure red, blue, and yellow, printers rely on the following primary inks:

- **Cyan**, a pale blue with a hint of green,
- **Magenta**, a deep pink with a hint of purple,
- **Yellow**, the only color your teacher got right, and
- **Black**, because all these light colors need some help when it comes to creating shadows and outlines.

The *color separation* process separates your artwork into its cyan, magenta, yellow, and black components. The good news about this process is that you can print a rainbow of colors using only four inks. The bad news is that traditional color separations cost a lot of money — not nine million dollars, but easily a few hundred.

A less expensive solution is to print color separations directly from PageMaker. As described in more detail in Chapter 17, PageMaker separates colors when you select the Separations option in the Color portion of the Print Document dialog box.

You can print two kinds of separations in PageMaker:

- ✔ **Process colors:** Process colors are the cyan, magenta, yellow, and black separations discussed a moment ago. Process inks are also known by the acronym CMYK. Why not CMY*B*? In the print world, *B* stands for blue, so *K* was adopted for black. Process colors offer the advantage of producing lots of colors using few inks.

  Another reason that *K* designates black is that as the darkest color, black serves as what printing experts call the *key* registration color in process-color printing. Isn't that interesting? Now you have something you can throw out at bridge parties and chess club meetings.

- ✔ **Spot colors:** Spot colors are separations created using inks *other than* cyan, magenta, and yellow. For example, maybe you want to print a two-color newsletter made up of black and brick red. Rather than using four inks to emulate the brick red, you can just pick a premixed brick red ink and use that instead. You don't have a wide range of colors this way, but you only have to pay for two inks.

Professionals with money coming out their ears sometimes mix process and spot colors together. Suppose that you're creating a very colorful piece that requires process colors. But the client's logo — which normally appears in a vibrant orange — looks a little lackluster when printed using CMYK separations. To make sure that the logo looks as vibrant as possible (there's absolutely nothing more sacred to a company than its logo), you throw in a spot color orange. It means five inks, but the client is willing to pay.

What you see isn't what you'll get

Pantone is probably the best known and most prolific vendor of premixed spot colors. PageMaker provides access to the enormous Pantone color library. If you decide to use Pantone colors, you should invest in one of the company's swatch books, which show a printed sample of every single color. Why not just rely on the appearance of the color on-screen? Because the screen isn't particularly well suited to displaying spot colors. A particular shade of blue, for example, may appear purple on-screen. But regardless of how it appears on screen, it will print as it appears in the swatch book.

The screen can be equally bad at representing process colors. A color that looks orange on-screen may turn red when printed. What's the solution? Purchase a process color swatch book from a company called Trumatch. This excellent book shows just about every color you can create by mixing cyan, magenta, yellow, and black inks. Better yet, it's the only swatch book created using a personal computer, ensuring the highest degree of accuracy possible.

You should be able to purchase both Pantone and Trumatch swatch books from your commercial printer.

Using Color in PageMaker

PageMaker provides access to a few colors right of the bat. If you choose Window⇨Color Palette (or press Ctrl+K), you display the Color palette, shown in Figure 15-1.

Fill icon

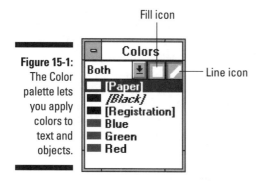

Figure 15-1:
The Color palette lets you apply colors to text and objects.

Line icon

The palette offers six color options, which work as follows:

- ✔ **Paper:** The first color represents the color of the paper. If you'll be printing to a colored paper stock, change this color as described in the upcoming "Changing a named color" section.

- ✔ **Black:** Black is the default ink. Use this color when creating black-and-white documents, spot-color documents, and process-color documents. In other words, you always need black. The fact that Black is italicized shows that it's a process color.

- ✔ **Registration:** Text and graphics colored with Registration appear on all separations printed from PageMaker. For example, suppose you are creating a process-color document. If you type your name and assign the Registration color to it, your name appears on the cyan separation, the magenta separation, the yellow separation, and the black separation. You wouldn't want to actually print this information; it's just a label that tells the printer who the separations belong to.

- ✔ **Blue, Green, and Red:** These colors are just hanging out. They don't have any real significance in PageMaker; they're just provided as samples of the kinds of colors you can create.

Incidentally, you may have noticed that some colors — Paper, Black and Registration — appear in brackets and others don't. The brackets indicate that the color is permanent and cannot be removed from the document. You can remove nonbracketed colors at whim.

Applying colors

To assign a color to a selected object, follow these simple steps:

1. Select the element that you want to color.

You can select text with the type tool or entire text blocks and objects with the arrow tool.

2. Specify whether you want to assign color to the fill and/or line.

The fill affects the interior of a character or graphic; the line affects the outline. Click on the fill icon in the Colors palette to apply a color to the fill; click on the line icon to color the outline (see Figure 15-1). Select Both from the pop-up menu to the left of the fill icon to change both fill and line.

You cannot change the line of a character of text, only the fill.

3. Select the desired color.

Click on a color in the scrolling portion of the Colors palette.

If you want to see more colors at a time, drag down on the size box in the bottom right corner of the palette. Of course, you won't have many colors to choose from until you add them as described in the next section.

Adding process colors to the palette

Black, Red, Green, and Blue do not a pretty picture make. To add variety to your palette, choose Element⬄Define Colors, which displays the dialog box shown in Figure 15-2. To create a new color, click on the New button.

Figure 15-2:
The Define
Colors
dialog box
lets you
create, edit,
copy, and
remove
colors.

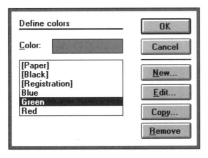

PageMaker next displays the Edit Color dialog box, shown in Figure 15-3. To define a color, you have to select a color model from the Model line and then manipulate the color by adding and subtracting primary colors. The *color model* determines what the primary colors are. You can select from three options:

✔ **RGB:** In the world of printed pigments, cyan, magenta, yellow, and black rule the day. But in the world of light, the primary colors are red, green, and blue. All colors mix to form lighter colors. Red and green, for example, mix to form yellow. Believe it or not! But who cares? You're printing to paper, not lighting a stage. So don't worry about the RGB model.

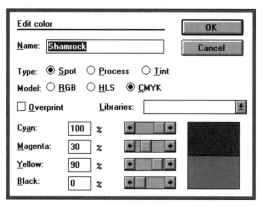

Figure 15-3:
Use the options in this dialog box to define and edit colors.

✔ **HLS:** Here's another model you don't have to worry about. You might call this the television color model. You know those knobs on a TV that control tint, brightness, and color? Well, they work just like this model. HLS stands for hue, lightness, and saturation. Hue changes the color, just like the tint knob on a TV. Lightness makes the color lighter or darker, just like the brightness knob. And saturation controls whether a color is vibrant or a little diffused, just like the color knob. If you want to get to know these options, experiment with your TV set. But don't use HLS in PageMaker.

✔ **CMYK:** Ah, finally, the color model of choice! CMYK stands for our old friends cyan, magenta, yellow, and black, the process colors. To make life simpler, leave the CMYK option selected at all times.

When CMYK is selected, the Edit Color dialog box displays four option boxes, one each for cyan, magenta, yellow, and black. To the right of each option box is a scroll bar. Move the scroll box to the right to add a primary color; move it to the left to delete it. You can also enter values between 0 and 100 percent in the option boxes. As you might expect, 100 percent is full intensity color, 0 percent is no intensity, other percentages are somewhere in between.

After you mix the desired amounts of primary colors together, enter a name for your color in the Name option box. Make sure that the Process radio button is selected below the option box. (Spot colors must correspond to standardized printer's inks; you can't just make them up. The next section shows you how to create spot colors.) Then click on the OK button or press Enter.

PageMaker returns you to the Define Colors dialog box from Figure 15-2. You can now create more colors, edit them, and so on. Or you can press Enter to exit the dialog box. Your new colors appear in the Colors palette. Provided they are all process colors, their names appear italicized.

Adding spot colors

Adding a spot color to the Colors palette is very much like adding a process color. You choose Element⇨Define Colors. Then you click on the New button to display the Edit Color dialog box. But instead of mucking about with the CMYK option boxes, you select an option from the Libraries pop-up menu, as shown in Figure 15-4.

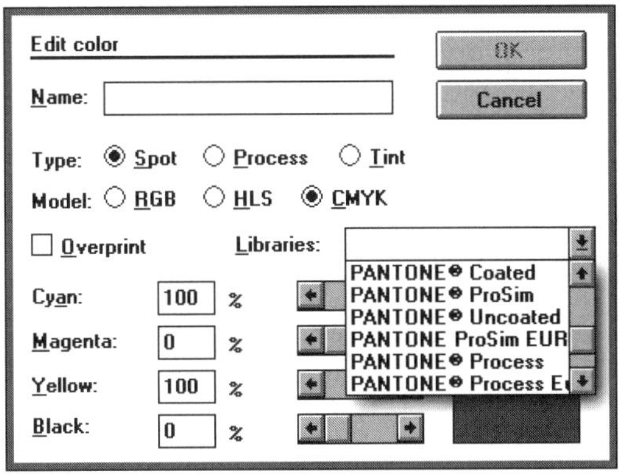

Figure 15-4: You can select predefined colors from the Libraries pop-up menu.

Now, it would be natural if you got a little overwhelmed at this point. If your pop-up menu is like most, it contains enough options to give you the cold sweats. Luckily, it's not nearly as difficult as it looks. Assuming that you're working in the United States or with a Pantone-supplied printer, you can stick to *Pantone Coated* or *Pantone Uncoated.*

> ✔ **PANTONE® Coated:** Select this option if you'll be printing your final piece to coated paper like the stuff you see in magazines.

> ✔ **PANTONE, Uncoated:** Select this option when printing to newsprint, bond paper, or other uncoated stock. If you're in doubt, you're probably using uncoated stock, so go ahead and select this option. It really doesn't matter, though. Your printer is probably smart enough to use the correct ink when the actual time comes to reproduce the pages.

You can also use the color libraries to import process colors. Although it's not necessary, it's frequently easier to import several colors *en masse* than to create them one at a time. Our personal favorite among the process color libraries is the Trumatch 4-Color Selector. Use it in good health!

After you select a color library, the Library dialog box appears, as shown in Figure 15-5. Most libraries contain hundreds of colors, so don't expect to see all of the colors at the same time. To locate a color, use the scroll bar at the bottom of the palette or enter a number into the option box. For example, if you enter 3 when viewing the Pantone collection, the color list scrolls to show the first of the 300-series colors; enter 4 to display colors 340 and up; and so on.

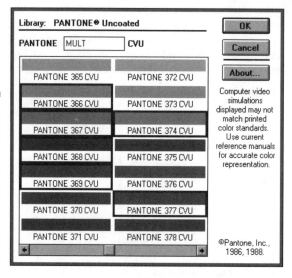

Figure 15-5: Importing colors from a predefined library is as simple as clicking and Shift-clicking on a few colors.

To select a color that you want to add to the Colors palette, just click on it. To add two or more colors at once, Ctrl+click on each color you want to select, or Shift+click to select a range of colors. To select the colors shown in Figure 15-5, for example, you would click on color 366 and then Shift+click on color 369, which also selects colors 367 and 368. Then you would Ctrl+click on colors 374 and 377, which selects each of those colors separately from the neighbors. After you select the colors you want to import, click on the OK button to return to the Edit Color dialog box. Or better yet, Shift+click on OK to exit all the dialog boxes and return to the layout window.

All your selected colors now appear in the Colors palette. Assuming that you used one of the Pantone libraries, the color names are upright — not italic — to show that they're spot colors.

Changing a named color

After you create a color, it's by no means set in stone. You can edit a color long after you create it and, in doing so, change the color of all text and graphics to which the color has been applied. In this sense, colors are a lot like style sheets, enabling you to edit elements globally.

Suppose that you created a two-color document using black and Pantone 3385 Teal. After you've hassled with the document for several days, your boss takes a look at it and says, "Gee whiz, this is great. But I don't like this — what did you say this color is? — this pasty green. I want something brighter, you know, something you might find in Oz. Yeah, that's it, I want Oz Green!"

In the old days, you would have had to hire a hit man to knock off your boss and just hope that the next one was more open to teal. Nowadays, you can change the color of your teal items with almost no effort. Just choose Element⇨Define Colors, select the color, and click on the Edit button. Or better yet, save time and effort by Ctrl+clicking on the color you want to edit in the Colors palette. Ctrl+clicking bypasses the Define Colors dialog box and opens the Edit Color dialog box directly.

If you want to change a process color, just muck about with the CMYK option boxes and press the Enter key when you're finished. If you want to edit a spot color, select the appropriate collection from the Libraries pop-up menu, select one — and only one — color from the scrolling list, and then Shift+click on the OK button. PageMaker changes your color and all elements colored with that color in less time than it took to read this sentence.

Changing the paper color

Before moving on, you need to know a little bit about one technical color-editing issue related to paper color. Generally speaking, white paper is the best solution when you're printing full-color artwork from PageMaker, because white paper doesn't adversely affect the colors of the inks and permits a wider color range. However, if you're working on a black-and-white document, or one with only one or two spot colors, you may want to reproduce the document on colored paper stock. To get a general feeling for how your elements will look on paper, edit the Paper color in the Colors palette to match the paper stock. Ctrl+click on the word Paper in the palette. Then manipulate the CMYK values until the color matches the paper stock as closely as possible and press Enter. PageMaker changes the on-screen page to match the color you specified. All transparent and paper-colored shapes, as well as any reversed text, also update to the new color. Note that this doesn't show how the color of the paper will mix with the colors of the inks applied to the objects on the page. You just have to imagine the colors as best you can.

Other stuff you should know

You now have been introduced to most of what you need to know about color in PageMaker. But you may want to file away the following additional tidbits for future recall. Some of these items you probably could have figured out on your own, and others are incredibly useful tips. Here goes:

- To add a new color to the Colors palette, you don't have to go through all the rigmarole of entering the Define Colors dialog box. You can enter the Edit Color dialog box directly by Ctrl+clicking on either the Black or Registration color in the Colors palette. Because these colors aren't editable, PageMaker lets you add a new color instead.

- To delete a color from the Colors palette, choose Element⇨Define Colors, select the color from the scrolling list, and then click on the Remove button. If the color is applied to some text or a graphic, PageMaker warns you that these elements will be changed to black. If that's okay with you, press Enter.

- All colors that you create are saved with the current document. This means that colors created in one document are not necessarily available to another. To transfer colors from Document A to Document B, begin by opening Document B. Then choose Element⇨Define Colors and click on the Copy button. Locate Document A on disk and double-click on it. Then click on OK to return to the layout view. The colors from Document A are now available in the Colors palette.

- In addition to editing the appearance of a color, you can change it from process to spot or vice versa. To convert a color on the fly — without bothering with the Edit Color dialog box — just Ctrl+Shift+Alt+click on it. If the color is a process color, it changes to spot; if it's a spot color, it changes to process. But you really shouldn't convert a process color to a spot color unless you're going from a Pantone process color to a Pantone spot color. Otherwise, your spot color won't correspond to any ink available at your printer.

Chapter 16

Tips for Making a Good Impression on Everyone

● ●

In This Chapter

▶ Tips for good ad design

▶ Tips for good newsletter design

▶ Tips for good report design

▶ A collection of cool design tips

● ●

*B*eauty is in the eye of the beholder, and by combining PageMaker's strengths and some basic design know-how, you can put a lot of beauty in the eyes of lots of beholders. Chapter 13 showed you how to make good-looking but effective business documents. This chapter explores some more creative endeavors: newsletters, ads, and annual reports.

As with any good design ideas, the ones here are based on years of experience and, of course, honest-to-goodness pilfering of other people's good work. Imitation is the sincerest form of flattery, and as long you as don't cross the line into blatant copying, go ahead and flatter as many people as you can. Go to the newsstand and thumb through a bunch of magazines. (But buy just the ones you really like.) Get a couple of colleagues — or just pull in some passersby — and look through those magazines together. Talk about what you like, what you don't like, and — most important — *why* you react the way you do. You can call this flower-power consciousness-raising or being a copycat, but it's the best way to learn good design. A couple more clichés to drive home the point: Good writers read good writers. (Someone surely has also said, "Good designers look at good designers," but that statement hasn't gotten enough buzz to become a cliché yet.) Good artists imitate, great artists steal. (There — an explicit art connection. What else do you need?)

One last point: Don't confuse the following examples with recipes. We don't pretend to be Picassos or even Harings. Even if we were Big Artists, our designs might not make sense for your documents. After all, the designs you produce must meet several needs: your sense of aesthetics, the requirements of the content being presented, the image you and your organization want to convey, and the financial limitations you are working under (we'd all love to do everything in full, glorious color, but until money comes out of laser printers without resulting in jail terms, we do have some teensy weentsy concerns about the costs).

Look at the following examples as starting points, and don't confuse the techniques and fundamental principles they show with the implementation we happened to choose for the particular example. You could use those same techniques and fundamental principles and come up with completely different designs for your projects. So don't worry if you come up with designs for your work that look nothing like these. Great artists may steal, but they also improvise.

Ads and Circulars

The design of ads, circulars (fliers), and other such sales- and marketing-oriented materials is critical because such publications must work the first time. Readers may be willing to put up with a newsletter design they don't like if the newsletter contains information they find valuable. But an ad has the burden of needing to attract attention, to hold the reader long enough to deliver its message, and leave that reader with a favorable impression. Let's look at three ads to see the techniques they use to accomplish these goals. Remember, whether you're working on an ad, a report cover, a prospectus, a pamphlet, or other such publication, these techniques apply.

Figure 16-1 shows an ad for a fictitious airline. (Of course, with the way that airlines seem to come and go, it may be a real one when you read this. Remember: You saw the name here first.) Notice the following about its design:

1. The large type is kerned so that the spacing between each pair of characters is the same — the letters are just at the point of touching. You can use the Control palette or press Ctrl+Backspace and Ctrl+Shift+Backspace to kern.

2. The small type forces the eye to take a look because of the contrast with the big type above and all the space on either side. This use of contrast is a good way to get attention. Never underestimate the power of type — it is as important as graphics in garnering attention and conveying both the substance and the nuances of the message.

3. The airline logo uses reverse-video and shadow effects on a fairly common font (Bauhaus). Notice the sun symbol to the left of the logo: that's a symbol in the Zapf Dingbats font. The use of symbols really helps establish a logo as a logo, rather than just a bunch of letters. Also notice the use of a

catch phrase in the same font as the logo. You would do this for a catch phrase that you plan on using in several places — it becomes an extension of the logo. (The desert tableau is a color image, and in color, the text is very striking against the colors; in black-and-white, it loses a little of that zing.)

4. Notice the use of blank areas — what designers call *white space*. It provides a visually calm port in a storm of images and text. Be sure to provide these resting spots in all your work.

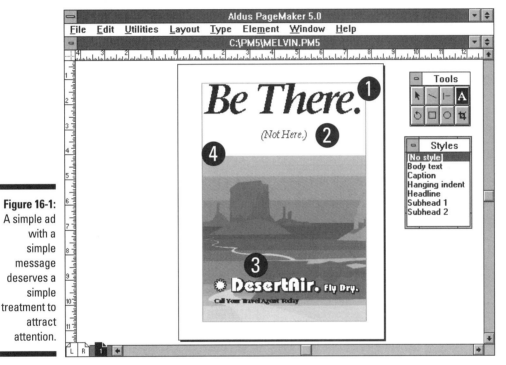

Figure 16-1:
A simple ad with a simple message deserves a simple treatment to attract attention.

The ad in Figure 16-2, for a seafood restaurant, shows a tighter interplay of text and graphics. It also shows, although not at first glance, the power of PageMaker's graphics manipulation tools.

1. Look at the schools of fish (they're in glorious color, although you can't see that in black-and-white). Three fish were then copied and pasted to create the schools. To make sure that your copies don't look like copies, you might use the rotate and skew tools to make each fish slightly different from the others. A very slight skew — less than 5 percent — was used in Figure 16-2. The rotation accounts for most of the difference in the fishes' appearance. The lesson: Don't forget to use basic tools such as rotation and copying.

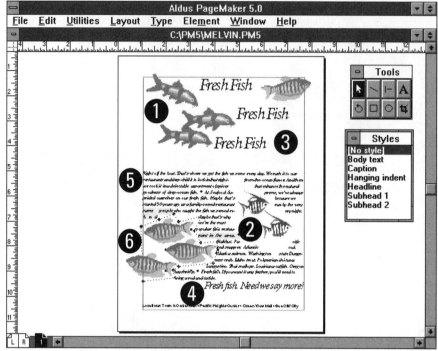

Figure 16-2:
An ad that has interplay between the text and graphics.

2. The text describing all the sumptuous seafood options is wrapped around the pictures of fish, using PageMaker's text wrap feature. Even though the schools of fish are actually multiple copies, just one text-wrap border is used for each school. Look at the left school to see one wrap border. It's actually for the middle fish in that school, but because you can make the wrap area anything you want, it's easier to turn text wrap on for just one graphic and make its wrap border cover any other nearby graphics, too. Of course, if you were to move the other fish, the text wrap would "think" they were still there.

3. Can you tell what this ad is selling? Why, fresh fish, of course! The repetitive use of the text reinforces the message. Placing the repeating text in different positions among the fish makes sure that it doesn't look repetitive. (Predictability is a major reason that repetition is boring, and this design finds a way to repeat without being boring.)

4. More repetition. Again different. A tag line like this reinforces the primary message. In the case of this ad, there's no large text identifying the restaurant (it is in the body text), but this tag line is one the restaurant uses a lot, so the ad can get away with the low-key play of the restaurant's name — for example, if an ad just said, "Have it your way," you'd probably think of Burger King, while "Just do it" would probably evoke images of Nike shoes.

5. All the text here, except the list of locations at the bottom, is in italics, which is unusual. But the fluidity of italics works well with the fish theme (under water — get it?), and because the text is large enough and the layout uncluttered, it works.

6. The fish swim past the margins on the page, which makes the page feel less boxed-in. It's often a good idea to break the strict margins to provide a feeling of flexibility and give the eye something unusual to flag on.

Let's take a look at one more ad. This one, shown in Figure 16-3, is not a full page. It's the kind of ad you'd probably run in an in-house publication: what the big magazines call a PSA (public service announcement). It's the kind of thing that you can easily put together using clip art and basic typefaces when you have a hole to fill or need to make an announcement or advertisement for your organization.

1. This simple graphic works well in black-and-white. Photos can be very effective attention-getters because they scream "real!" The simple composition is also pleasing. You'll find many such images in clip art libraries.

Figure 16-3:
A public service announcement designed for black-and-white reproduction.

2. Simple text with a simple message that ties into the image — that's the ticket. A loud, bold title would have competed with the photo. This one's easy to read but it doesn't fight for attention. If you see the photo and stop, you'll see the headline, and that's all that's required. The centering makes sure that it's clear that the headline goes with the text below. It also follows the centered shape of the chair — the more different ways things line up, the more distracting a layout can be, so try to use only one or two alignments. A left alignment might have worked here, but then the symmetry of the chair would not have been picked up in the rest of the ad — and such reuse of basic visual themes is a hallmark of pleasing design. People just get all warm and fuzzy with such continuity.

3. The text is short, readable, and justified. Although having justified text may seem to violate the minimal-alignment rule above, the fact is that centered text is rarely easy to read if there's more than a few lines of it. Having the text justified keeps the symmetry of the centered text because the right and left margins in justified text are symmetrical.

4. We all know what a dashed line means — the page fairly yells, "Cut me out!" To create a dashed box, use PageMaker's rectangle tool and change the line to a dashed one. (Here, it is a 1.5-point rule, defined via Element⇨Line⇨Custom.) To reinforce the "cut me!" message, you could add a pair of scissors (from a symbols font or from clip art) along a top corner of the dashed box.

5. The box contains the coupon the advertiser wants people to fill out. The font here is different (a condensed sans serif, compared to the text's normal serif). This reinforces the idea that the coupon is a separate element. You want the reader to think of the coupon as separate so that they know it's okay to remove it from the rest of the ad. (You're trying to make people unlearn all those elementary school years of Miss Snodgrass threatening to slap them with a ruler if they mutilated books.) The use of a condensed font also leaves more room for people to fill in the information you want. The underlines are right-aligned tabs using an underline leader — that's the simplest way to create fill-in-the-blank lines.

Newsletters

Several chapters of this book use a newsletter as an example. The newsletter is the source of identity for the nonprofit group that publishes it, so even though it's done very inexpensively, it has to look professional, not cheap.

Well, that newsletter has changed several times in the six years it's been produced. Figure 16-4 shows the first three pages from three different issues, one from 1990, one from 1991, and one from 1994.

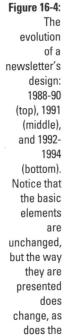

Figure 16-4:
The evolution of a newsletter's design: 1988-90 (top), 1991 (middle), and 1992-1994 (bottom). Notice that the basic elements are unchanged, but the way they are presented does change, as does the overall feel.

Newsletters generally are redesigned every few years. The redesign may be subtle, it may be extreme. But it happens. Why? Because the new art director or publisher wants to put an imprint on the publication? Well, that's partially true, but the real reason is more basic: If you don't revisit your look every once in a while, you look stale, and people think you're lazy or don't care about them. People do the same redesigning of their personal appearance, too. (Take a look at a snapshot of yourself from five years ago. 'Nuff said!)

Changing needs

The different versions of the newsletter use different fonts and embellishments, yet they all share a basic design:

- ✔ All are based on a three-column format, although the 1991 version uses a staggered three-column grid (notice how the pull-quotes and other elements hang out from the sides).

- ✔ All use the same basic elements on each page: pull-quotes, a short table of contents on the cover, a large masthead on page 2, kickers over the headlines, and bylines.

Yet they differ significantly in other areas:

- ✔ The 1988-90 design is the most basic: sans serif headlines and serif body copy. Both fonts (Helvetica Bold and New Century Schoolbook) are clean and easy-to-read. The use of condensed, underlined type for the kickers adds the only visual counterpoint to the open, solid look of the type, and even the kickers are clean-looking. The look is solid and respectable because the organization was making an effort at the time to look clean and fresh.

- ✔ The 1991 design was a radical departure. It's bolder, busier. There's a lot of contrast: bold headlines (Helvetica Black and Helvetica Black Condensed) with clean, light text (News Gothic). Both fonts are sans serif fonts — highly unusual because there's an unspoken rule that you should never put headlines and text in the same type of font (serif or sans serif) and particularly that you should never use a sans serif font for both. Nonsense! Also, more symbols are used, and the layout is staggered. Things can line up to the three columns, or to the halfway points between columns (or past the first and last column). The look is animated and energetic, suggesting an organization on the move. It was more work to do this layout, and it relied on having sidebars and photos to break out (as on pages 2 and 3) from the body text. Unfortunately, it was difficult to pull off every issue, so it was abandoned a year later. It was adventurous, but maybe too much for its subject.

> ✔ The current look (1992-94) is hyper-traditional — the "cardigan sweater and fireplace" look. It uses two serif fonts — Century Oldstyle for the heads and ITC Cheltenham Book for the body text. Cheltenham is very easy to read because it's a wide font, and it contrasts nicely with the Century Oldstyle, which is bold and angular. Some symbols are used, but they're more subdued than in the previous design. The new design also incorporates drop caps, which add more contrast to the page, and grays, which mellow out the page. This design was meant to reinforce solid traditionalism (it was designed for the organization's 10th anniversary in 1993, although it came out a year earlier). But it's actually a mix of the two previous designs, borrowing the simple structure of the first with the high contrast of the second, the conservatism of the first with some of the flair of the second. The use of nonrectangular text wrap adds interest to the graphic — an extension of the flair in the second generation without the hard edge.

As you can see, the newsletter was designed with a set of goals in mind. The goals changed over time, even though the basic content did not. The opposite can also happen: the content may change over time while the design and "image" goals do not. That scenario presents a trickier design problem, because you need to update the design to accommodate the new content (such as increased use of profiles, short stories, gossip and rumors, question-and-answer interviews, and so on) while reflecting the feel of the old. For examples, take a look at current issues of *The New York Times, Wall Street Journal, Business Week, Time,* or *Newsweek.* Then compare their issues from five years ago. Different look and mix of content, but the same feel.

Newsletter basics

A newsletter's main goal is to provide information. So the focus should be on text: how to make it readable, how to call attention to it, how to make sure that the reader can locate all relevant content. Take a look at the newsletter in Figure 16-5. It's the same newsletter as in Figure 16-4 (and elsewhere in this book), but the pages chosen are typical interior pages. They show the basic components of the newsletter, around which you add embellishments such as graphics.

1. Most newsletters are two or three columns wide. A three-column format gives you more flexibility because you can make graphics, sidebars, and separate stories three different sizes (one, two, and three columns wide), making it fairly easy to add such elements to a page. A two-column format is more straightforward but gives you fewer options. It's best for newsletters that are essentially sequential — without multiple stories and sidebars on a page or spread.

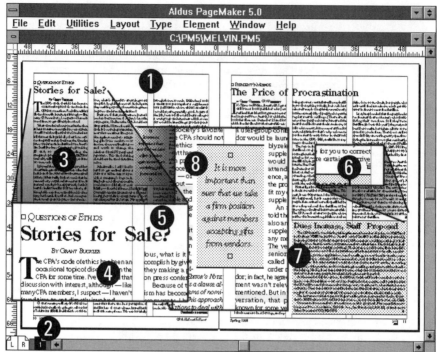

Figure 16-5:
The basic
elements
in a
newsletter.

2. As always, make sure that you include page numbers and an identifier of the publication (called a *folio* in magazine-speak). Here, a corporate symbol is placed after the page number to add visual interest and reinforce the identity.

3. The body text uses a very readable, straightforward font: ITC Cheltenham Book. It's a typical size for newsletters and magazines: 9 points with 11 points of leading. Generally speaking, point size should range from 9 to 10 points (you can use half-point sizes), and leading from 10.5 to 13 points, with the most typical leading being 2 points more than the text size. The text is justified here simply because that makes it look typeset and thus more authoritative. But a flush-left style would have been fine, too. The paragraph indents are fairly small (0.15 inches) because in justified text, a small indent is enough to give the reader's eye the visual clue it needs to see the new paragraph.

4. The use of a drop cap is an effective way to alert the reader to the beginning of a new story (you can also use it for the beginning of the story's conclusion). A drop cap also adds visual contrast to the page. Note in this example that the drop cap is a different font than the body text: Century Oldstyle Bold, which is the same font as the headline. Generally, you should boldface the drop cap because that makes it more readable — and otherwise, the drop cap looks wimpy, which is not how you want such a big element to look.

5. The headline, the kicker (the type above it, also called a *slug line* for reasons that have nothing to do with gardening), and the byline are all related. Both the kicker and the byline use small caps (a classy look when done in moderation) and italics. They're also in a different font (Goudy Oldstyle) than the headline (Century Oldstyle Bold) and the body text (ITC Cheltenham Book). That gives them continuity with each other while providing a subtle difference from the rest of the text. But be careful when combining multiple fonts like this: If they don't work together, it can be a disaster. A rule of thumb is to restrict the number of fonts (not including variants like boldface and small caps) to two per page. You can break this rule occasionally by using a font that has similarities to one of the other two. In this case, Goudy Oldstyle has the feel of a cross between the other two fonts, so it works well.

6. Ending a story with a *dingbat* — publishing-speak for a symbol — is a nice touch. Here, the dingbat is the corporate logo, which adds another identity reinforcement. It's easy to make a dingbat: just add the symbol after the last paragraph, either by putting a tab before it (and defining the tab in your text style to be flush right against the right margin) or an em space (Shift+Ctrl+M). Either way is fine for justified text — pick one based on your preferences. But use only the em space if your text is not justified.

7. You can make a sidebar or separate, minor story distinct by putting a shaded background behind it (draw a rectangle, change its fill pattern, and send it behind the text). Make sure that you have a margin between the edge of the background and the text. You can also box a sidebar, with or without the background. Or you can just put a line above and below the background, as done here. Notice, too, that the text is two columns wide, so it really looks different from the surrounding text.

8. A pull-quote attracts readers' attention by calling out some interesting material in a story. In this example, the style follows that of the sidebar: a shaded background and lines above and below. There's also a square character above and below (it's an embedded graphic in the text, so if the text grows or shrinks, the squares move with it). The characters are just an embellishment — something that adds that little extra touch. The font is the same as that in the byline and kicker (again, to create continuity with other elements on the page but difference from the text immediately around it).

Annual Reports

An annual report is a weird combination of a magazine and a report. It's where you showcase the company to its investors or stockholders, and you want to impress them with your financial performance — or hide the dismal truth, if your earnings were less than stellar. You want to look good in an annual report; it's like having dinner with the boss the week before your annual review. You also have to include a lot of information. A good annual report does all of this.

Figure 16-6 shows an example of an interior spread for a bicycle manufacturer's annual report, which manages to combine information and an inviting graphical look. Whatever image you want to convey — hip, traditional, solid, adventurous, irreverent, slick — make sure that your design and graphics reinforce the point throughout.

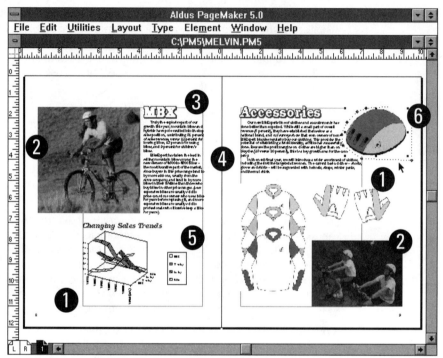

Figure 16-6: Interior pages from an annual report.

1. The margins are a bit lopsided, with plenty of room on the outside to let graphics hang off from the text. Because this annual report is for a sports company, it makes sense to give it an active, dynamic look. One way to do that is to create a lot of visual motion, which is what you get when elements break outside the basic margins. Note that the text always stays in the margins, but the graphics do only if they show financial information (as on the left page). This reinforces the fact that the basic content is within the margins, while the illustrations can be anywhere. By ensuring that information is treated consistently, the rushed reader who just wants the facts knows where to look — and where not to look.

2. Color photos are a great way to enhance an annual report, especially if they show something active. A picture of the assembly plant workers would probably be boring, but a picture of, say, a group of workers from the same shift racing in a velodrome adds excitement and action while

at the same time reinforcing the image that the workers trust the products they build. Look for pictures that convey a basic message — "fun," "trust," "hip attitude," "young," "distinguished," "creative" — and you'll make a real impression on your readers.

3. The headlines are in shadow and a color. This makes them hard to miss and visually distinct.

4. The text is basic, with only left alignment so that there is no hard-and-fast boundary. Because this annual report is supposed to be active and fluid, using justified text would look too precise.

5. The financial chart, first produced in Excel, uses a headline entered in PageMaker to match the font of the main headlines. The 3-D chart follows the theme of dynamism and motion.

6. Text wraps around the helmet, which introduces more movement in the page and connects the graphic to the text more closely. Because this page has so many graphics, something was needed to connect at least one of them to the text so that the page didn't have a choppy, disjointed look.

Cool Stuff

By combining various techniques, you can create some cool-looking stuff for any of a variety of documents. Figure 16-7 shows some examples:

- You can create various embossed-text effects by duplicating a text box and making one slightly overlap the other. Then make the one on top white (or the paper color).

- By duplicating a text box several times, rotating each copy at a different angle, and then applying different shades of gray to each, you can create a textual graphic. Here, each subsequent copy is rotated 10 degrees more and is 10 percent darker than the preceding copy.

- Each letter in the word *STRETCH!* is 10 percent wider than the previous letter, which gives the text the effect of being stretched.

- Increasing the space between letters is a popular design effect. You could put spaces (regular spaces, en spaces, or em spaces) between the letters, but using the tracking control ensures that the text is treated as one word. This method also makes it easy to change your spacing settings (it's easier to adjust the tracking than to, say, replace em spaces with en spaces between every character).

- By combining the skew feature with the shadow feature for text, you can alter how a font looks. You might want such an effect when creating a logo, for example. In this logo, the designer went a step further and mirrored the text block and changed its color to a shade of gray (by defining a tint of 40 percent black).

Figure 16-7:
Combining
techniques
can produce
cool-looking
stuff.

- ✔ For grayscale images, you can apply a color or tint to make them ghostly or subtle. It's a great way to mute a photo enough so that you can place text over it.

- ✔ By placing a white rectangle or oval (with a very thick line) with no fill over a photo, you can create a cameo effect — it's a way to create a different type of shape or frame.

- ✔ In some publications, the text on the opening page has a radically different style from the rest of the pages. Often, there is little text on the opening page because the title and graphics usually take up much of the space. The text that is on the page is also treated graphically. One method is to have no paragraph breaks but to use a symbol instead to indicate paragraph breaks, as in the top right example in Figure 16-7.

✔ While drop caps are popular, you can also use an embedded graphic to accomplish the same purpose. If you want the graphic to be dropped down into the text, you can place the graphic at the appropriate location and turn text wrap on.

✔ The bottom right example in Figure 16-7 was created by making a copy of the original dolphin image, flipping it horizontally, copying the two resulting images, and flipping them vertically.

Common Threads

Creative design means taking risks, trying out new ideas. Because it's easy to use PageMaker to try out ideas — and to abandon those that don't work — set aside some time in every project to play around with your design. Save a copy of your original and then see if you can discover some new approach that adds that special edge. While you're doing that, keep some basic principles in mind:

✔ Use enough white space. People need a visual resting place as they thumb through a publication. Give it to them. If you don't, they'll stop reading.

✔ Remember that the basic point of publishing is to convey information. Make sure that text is readable, that captions and headlines are informative and interesting, and that people can tell where a story continues.

✔ Invest in several fonts and use them creatively by applying effects such as small caps, colors, banner backgrounds, rotation, and skewing.

✔ Graphics should be fairly large — lots of small images are hard to look at — and should complement the rest of the layout.

✔ Create visual themes. Use a core set of fonts. If you use lines in one place, they may be effective in another. If you use boxes to separate some elements, don't use colored backgrounds to separate others — instead, pick one approach and stick with it.

✔ Use color judiciously. It's expensive and can overwhelm the content. Used well, grays can provide as much visual interest as color. In fact, in something laden with color, a gray image stands out and gains more attention than the surrounding color ones.

Part VI
You Mean There's More?

The 5th Wave   By Rich Tennant

Bob, the laser printer repairman, finds an idle moment that costs him his sideburns.

In this part . . .

*L*ayout is cool. Layout is fun. But layout is not everything. You also need to know a few other pesky details,
including how to print, how to send files to a service bureau,
and how to exchange files with colleagues, some of whom
may work on Macintosh computers. This part covers all
these issues — in inimitable style, of course.

Chapter 17

The Journey to Paper

*T*he wonderful thing about PCs is that they offer you so many choices. The terrible thing about PCs is that they offer you so many choices. Menus full of commands, dialog boxes brimming with options — figuring out which choices will work best for you can be daunting, to say the least.

Printing your documents from PageMaker, unfortunately, requires you to make many choices, some simple, some more complicated. But never fear. This chapter helps you sort out the various decisions you need to make to get your PageMaker masterpieces from screen onto paper.

PostScript or LaserJet PCL?

One of the first decisions you have to make is whether to print your document on a PostScript or LaserJet PCL printer. PostScript and PCL (which stands for *printer command language*) are formats that tell a printer how to print a page. The printer does its work based on the instructions in these print formats. Of course, the printer needs to understand the format before it can follow the instructions.

Each format offers different capabilities. PCL is the language designed for Hewlett-Packard LaserJet printers, although many printers from other companies understand PCL. PostScript is a language designed independently of a particular brand of printer, and it's favored by professional publishers. In a nutshell, PostScript lets a printer do more with text and graphics than PCL does. But PCL is most common on PCs and PC networks because in the early days of PCs, PCL's low cost and crisp text output was perfect for the PC programs of the times. Artsy folks used Macintoshes, which used PostScript.

Today, you can get printers that understand both formats and even switch automatically from one to the other. Apple, Hewlett-Packard, NEC Technologies, and Dataproducts are some companies that offer bilingual printers.

If you have a PostScript or bilingual printer, you're all set. Use PostScript as your default printer driver in Windows, and you'll be able to print anything at its best quality. And if you work with a service bureau, you'll have no unhappy surprises; service bureaus all use PostScript, too, and what you print on your proofing printer will be what they print on their imagesetter.

If you have a PCL-only LaserJet or other printer, consider buying a PostScript cartridge or trading the printer in for a bilingual model. You can print from PageMaker using PCL, but you'll find that text may not be as sharp and some types of graphics simply won't print. The EPS file format generated by all high-end illustration programs requires a PostScript printer. If you print an EPS graphic on a PCL printer, the best you'll get is a coarse representation of the graphic, as Figure 17-1 shows. What prints is actually the on-screen preview of the graphic, not the EPS graphic itself, which is why it appears coarse.

Make sure that you use Adobe Type Manager software so that you can print PostScript fonts on a PCL printer. That way, if you're going to eventually send your work to a PostScript-based service bureau for final output and you're using PostScript fonts, you'll be able to print your document with the correct fonts on your PCL printer. (Most service bureaus cannot print TrueType or PCL fonts.) ATM is free with many programs, although not with PageMaker. You can also buy it from Adobe Systems. Note that you cannot print EPS files at true quality to a PCL printer even with ATM installed.

Figure 17-1:
A PostScript printer (left) provides better graphics output for some types of images than a PCL printer (right).

Windows Printer Setup

Because PCs give you millions and millions of options, you have to work through lots of dialog boxes to set up those options. Your system may already be set up, but before you start printing in PageMaker in earnest, at least double-check the settings to make sure that you get the best, fastest output you can.

No matter what kind of printer you use, you go to the same place to set it up: The Printers dialog box in the Windows Control Panel. Find the Control Panel icon in the Main group and double-click on it. Then find the Printers icon and double-click on it to get the Printers dialog box, shown in Figure 17-2. Select the printer you will be using with PageMaker and click on the Setup button to open the Setup dialog box. Figure 17-3 shows the dialog box for a PCL printer. If you're using more than one printer, you need to set up each one.

Figure 17-2:
Set up your printers in the Printers dialog box in the Windows Control Panel.

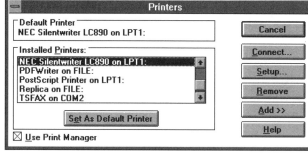

Figure 17-3:
The Setup dialog box for a PCL printer.

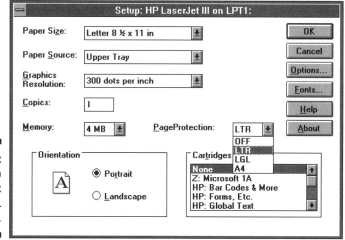

PCL printers

The Setup dialog box contains most of the options you need to worry about for PCL printers. The ones that affect print quality and output speed are the following:

- ✔ **Graphics Resolution:** Set this value to 300 dots per inch (dpi). Any other setting (they're all lower) results in coarse, unattractive graphics. Today, 300 dpi is the printing standard. If you have a higher-resolution printer, pick the highest value it supports (probably 600 dpi). The higher the resolution, the truer the output.

- ✔ **Memory:** This value tells Windows how much printer memory you have installed. No, Windows has no clue what's in your printer, and it's not smart enough to check on its own. While we're on the subject, this is as good a time as any to tell you to get several megabytes of printer memory if you're using lots of fonts or graphics. The extra memory speeds up printing considerably because it gives the printer the headroom to process all the font and graphics information. If you have insufficient memory, printing will either be slow or will stall out and end the print job without completing the current page. How much memory do you want? At least 4MB.

- ✔ **PageProtection:** Set this value to the size of paper you're using. (Again, Windows isn't smart enough to choose the setting automatically.) What this setting does is complex, but in a nutshell, it squeezes more memory out of the printer. Leave it turned on to help the printer process the page most efficiently and quickly. To use this option, you need at least 1MB of printer memory.

- ✔ **Gray Scale:** This important option resides in the Options dialog box, shown in Figure 17-4. To open the dialog box, just click on the Options button in the Setup dialog box. The Gray Scale option lets you tell a PCL printer how to handle shades of gray. Most of the time, you should select the Photographic Images option because it does the best job of preserving variations in shades, thus making scanned images and the like look their best.

  Select Line Art Images for printing scans of black-and-white drawings; this setting removes subtle variations in shades, making an image appear sharper, which is fine if it's black and white. For photos and the like, Line Art Images causes a loss of some of the shades. Use the third option, HP ScanJet Images, with documents that have many images scanned in from — you guessed it — a Hewlett-Packard ScanJet scanner.

Never check the Print TrueType as Graphics option. This converts all TrueType fonts to graphics, which makes printing much, much slower. This option exists for older laser printers that weren't designed to handle TrueType fonts, and using it if you have just one or two TrueType fonts in a document won't cause noticeable slowdown. But frankly, there's very little need for this option today because Windows 3.1 and most modern printers are designed to deal with TrueType.

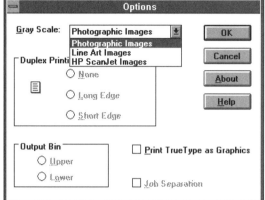

Figure 17-4:
The Options
dialog box
for a PCL
printer.

PostScript printers

To get to options that affect print quality and speed on a PostScript printer, first click on the Setup button for the printer you want to set up, as explained earlier. Then choose Options⇨Advanced to open the dialog box shown in Figure 17-5.

TrueType font options

Unless your printer has a built-in TrueType interpreter in addition to its PostScript rasterizer, you'll have just two options in the Send to Printer As pop-up menu: Adobe Type 1 and Bitmap (Type 3). If your printer has special circuitry to process TrueType fonts directly, you should also have an option for Native TrueType. Pick Adobe Type 1 unless you have the option for Native TrueType. The Bitmap (Type 3) option converts TrueType fonts to bitmaps before sending them to the printer, which slows down your computer *and* the printer, so don't use it.

✔ Make sure that you select the Use Substitution Table checkbox rather than Use Printer Fonts for All TrueType Fonts. The substitution table gives you more control over printing by letting you decide which TrueType fonts can be replaced by PostScript fonts stored inside the PostScript printer and which TrueType fonts must be translated into PostScript format.

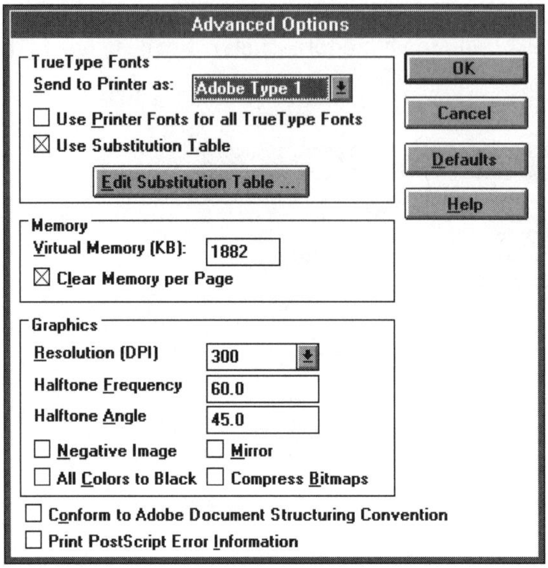

Figure 17-5:
The Advanced Options dialog box for a PostScript printer.

For example, the TrueType font Garamond Condensed is different enough from its PostScript equivalent that, even if your PostScript printer had the PostScript version in its memory or hard disk, you'd want to use the actual TrueType font. But the TrueType font Arial is just a knock-off of the PostScript font Helvetica, which is in every PostScript printer's memory. There's no need to send Arial to the printer when using the built-in Helvetica results in virtually identical output and fast printing speeds.

If you select Use Substitution Table, you decide which fonts are substituted. If you select Use Printer Fonts for All TrueType Fonts, Windows substitutes a PostScript font for each and every TrueType font, no matter how appropriate the substitution is.

✔ You can edit the substitution table by clicking on the Edit Substitution Table button, which displays the dialog box shown in Figure 17-6. The list on the left shows the fonts in the system. The list on the right shows the fonts in your printer memory or hard disk. If you want to substitute a font, first select from the TrueType list at left and then select the PostScript font you want substituted for the TrueType font from the list at right. If you don't want any substitution for a particular TrueType font, select the Download as Soft Font option from the list at right. Windows then sends the TrueType font to the printer as either a Type 1 or Type 3 PostScript font, depending on the option you picked earlier.

Figure 17-6:
Tell
Windows
which
TrueType
fonts you
want to
substitute
with
PostScript
printer fonts
in this dialog
box.

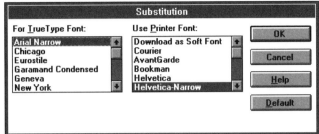

Memory options

The more memory in your printer, the faster your printing will be. PostScript printers use a lot of memory because they have to translate the PostScript language into the dots that make up the printed page. Basically, a big chunk of the printer memory is used to run the PostScript program. So having, say, 4MB in a PostScript printer leaves only about 2MB for holding fonts and for doing the translation. You need to tell Windows to use as much of the free memory as possible.

You tell Windows how much memory is free by changing the Virtual Memory (KB) value. How do you know how much is free? Windows won't find out for you, but it does provide a tool for you to use. First, turn on your printer. Then, from the DOS prompt (yes, really!), type the following command:

```
copy c:\windows\system\testps.txt lpt1:
```

Note that the drive may be D: or something other than C:, depending on how your system is set up. And instead of lpt1:, you may need to use lpt2: or some other port, depending on how you've connected your PostScript printer. (Ask a computer guru for help if this all seems too confusing.)

After you type the command, press enter, and a page will print that tells how much VM (virtual memory) is available. Put that value in the Virtual Memory (KB) option box in the Advanced Options dialog box.

If you check the Clear Memory Per Page box, the printer's memory is cleared after each page is printed. Generally, you should check this box because doing so gives the printer the most flexibility when handling font- and graphics-intensive documents. But if you have few graphics and you use the same fonts on most pages, unchecking this box speeds printing up slightly because the printer can save the calculations that are common to each page (such as the font translation) and reuse them. If the memory is cleared for each page, the printer must recalculate such things on a page-by-page basis. When you have lots of fonts (more than six) or graphics, being able to clear the memory lets the printer more efficiently manage its workspace for each page.

Graphics options

✔ Generally, you don't have to set the Resolution to match that of your current printer; it's set automatically. And PageMaker has its own controls for devices such as imagesetters that support multiple resolutions.

✔ Ditto for the Halftone Frequency and Halftone Angle settings. Adjust these in the PageMaker Page Setup and Print dialog boxes for each specific job.

✔ If you're having trouble with inconsistent printing — sometimes pages print, sometimes fonts don't print correctly — check the Print PostScript Error Information checkbox. Doing so tells the printer to print an error message after something goes awry. Sometimes, the error messages are even understandable enough that you can figure out how to solve the problem. If not, you can show the message to a printer guru and beg for help.

Before You Print in PageMaker

With that printer setup business out of the way, you can now focus on printing, which of course is the ultimate aim of publishing anything.

You're all done with a page, and you want to print it. You just use File⇨Print or Ctrl+P, right? Well, not quite.

First, make sure your print setup is correct for the target printer. Notice the word *target* — that means the ultimate printer for the publication you're working on. That may not be the printer you're printing to at the moment.

Suppose that you're doing the company newsletter, which will be output by a service bureau at high resolution (1270 or 2540 dots per inch). Or maybe you're producing a project status report, and the target printer is a 600-dpi printer that will output pages for later photocopying. In either case, your proofing printer — the one at your desk or in your part of the building — is a humble 300-dpi laser printer. So you should set PageMaker for a 300-dpi printer, right? Wrong.

Normally, you use File⇨Printer Setup in a Windows program to set the output for the printer you'll be printing to. But things are different in the publishing world. In PageMaker, you set the Page Setup dialog box's settings for the target printer. That lets PageMaker output the truest rendering possible of your document's bitmap images when you print to another printer, such as that 300-dpi printer used to proof the pages. Basically, it treats your proofing printer like it's a preview device, not the ultimate image.

Figure 17-7 shows the Page Setup dialog box set for publishing a standard-size magazine. The target printer resolution was set at 2540 dpi because that's standard for a graphics-intensive publication. If your document will be produced by a Linotronic or other imagesetter, but you won't be including images, 1270 dpi is enough. (See Chapter 18 for more details on sending your document to high-end printers.

Note that the Page option is set to *Magazine narrow* — that happens to be a typical size for magazines. PageMaker includes a whole bunch of preconfigured page sizes in the Page pop-up menu. Again, pick the size based on the ultimate printer. If your proofing printer uses standard letter-size paper ($8 \frac{1}{2} \times 11$ inches), *don't* change the paper size to Letter unless that's the ultimate size of your document.

Figure 17-7:
The Page Setup dialog box should be set for the resolution of the printer that will produce the final output for your publication.

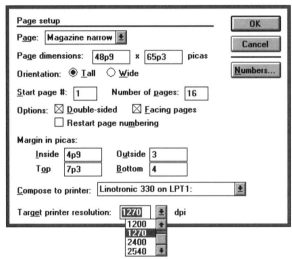

Sending Stuff to the Printer

To open the Print dialog box and take a step closer to an actual printed page, choose File➪Print or just press Ctrl+P. PageMaker responds by showing you a dialog box that offers a lot of printing options. Fortunately, they're arranged in a series of dialog boxes that actually make sense. And you don't have to worry about most options most of the time, anyhow.

When you enter the Print dialog box, you actually are in a series of four linked dialog boxes. You can switch from dialog box to dialog box by clicking on the buttons on the far right of the dialog box — if you're using a PostScript printer, the buttons are labeled Document, Paper, Options, and Color. If you're using a PCL printer, the Paper button in the Print Document dialog box is Setup. The Setup dialog box includes the specific configurations for your printer, such as paper size, font cartridges, and paper-bin source.

When you first choose File⇨Print or press Ctrl+P, PageMaker puts you into the dialog box associated with the Document button, the Print Document dialog box. This dialog box is shown in Figure 17-8.

Choosing which pages print and in what order

In the Print Document dialog box, look for a boxed area labeled *Pages*. In this section of the dialog box, you can specify exactly which pages you want to print. You can mix ranges and individual pages; if you want to print pages 1, 3, 8, 9, and 10, for example, you can type **1,3,8,9,10** into the option box or **1,3, 8-10**. This option is great if you only want to print pages that have been corrected since the last draft or pages that need your boss's sign-off, for example.

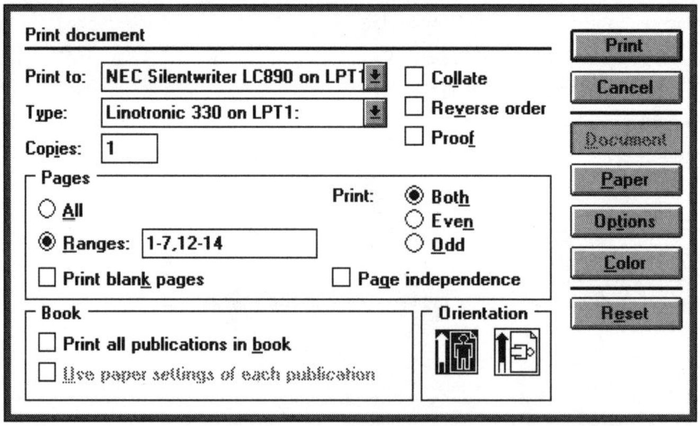

Figure 17-8:
The Print Document dialog box lets you print any set of pages in your document, among other things.

Print document	
Print to: NEC Silentwriter LC890 on LPT1	☐ Collate	Print
Type: Linotronic 330 on LPT1:	☐ Reverse order	Cancel
Copies: 1	☐ Proof	Document

Pages
○ All
◉ Ranges: 1-7,12-14
☐ Print blank pages

Print: ◉ Both ○ Even ○ Odd
☐ Page independence

Paper
Options
Color
Reset

Book
☐ Print all publications in book
☐ Use paper settings of each publication

Orientation

The other options, also shown in Figure 17-8, are the same as you find on most photocopiers:

✔ Check the Collate box if you are printing more than one copy of your document and you want to print each set of pages in order. If you don't check this box, PageMaker prints all copies of one page and then moves on to print all copies of the next page. It may take longer to print your document if this option is checked.

✔ Checking Reverse Order makes the last page print first, followed by the preceding page, and so on, until the first page.

✔ Select Reverse Order or Collate based on convenience. It may be worth the longer print time for the printer to collate the copies. Or maybe your printer stacks pages in reverse order, and you'd like that stacking order changed to the sequential order.

✔ If you have a duplex (two-sided printer), make sure you move to the Paper dialog box and select from the Duplex options.

If you're printing a book, you have two additional options in the Book area of the Print Document dialog box. Check the first, Print All Publications in Book if you want to, well, print all the publications in a book. The other option — Use Paper Settings of Each Publication — should generally be checked. It assumes that each publication may have different page sizes, orientations, or margins and that the printer can handle this. If the printer can't, you shouldn't print all the publications in the book at once anyhow.

Printing thumbnails

There's another neat little option that should come in handy for you: the Thumbnails option in the Paper dialog box. By selecting this option and specifying how many thumbnails are to print on each sheet of paper, you can output small previews of each page. These are great for showing your layout to others for comments or approval. Because the pages are miniaturized, people quickly get a feel for the document as a whole. And if you print enough thumbnails on a page,they can't read the text, so they're forced to keep focused on the overall appearance — which is what you want their comments on at this point, anyhow.

Determining output quality

Notice in Figure 17-8 that the Type field lists a printer that is not the same as the Print To printer above it. That's because the Silentwriter 95 is being used as a proofing printer for a document that will ultimately be printed on a Linotronic 300 imagesetter — here's an example of where the target printer, set in Page Setup as described earlier, is different from the current printer. Note that the Type field doesn't appear if you're working with PCL printers.

There's a slight effect on quality when the target printer doesn't match the current printer. For example, spacing is finer on a high-resolution printer, and fonts are more delicate. In this situation, the proof copy may appear to have awkward spacing and lighter fonts than expected. Why? Because the printer is trying to simulate a higher-resolution printer, and in so doing, it comes up against some of its own limitations. Still, overall, the spacing and look will be more accurate than if you change the target printer setting to match the proofing printer.

Note, however, that it's possible that having the printer type set to something other than the printer currently being used could result in error messages while printing. If this happens, change the printer type to match that of the current printer.

You can save time when printing by checking the Proof checkbox. It replaces graphics in a publication with solid rectangles, which take less time to print. Of course, when you want to see what the images look like, or when you print your final version, you'll want to uncheck this option.

A related option for PostScript printers is in the Options dialog box, in the area labeled Graphics (the PostScript version of this dialog box is shown in Figure 17-9). Here, you set the resolution for graphics. The reason that there are options for low-resolution TIFFs and omitted TIFFs is that these bitmapped files often take a lot of time to print, and so lowering their quality or masking them out while making proof copies makes sense. When you print your final copy, make sure that you select the Normal option.

The Optimized option is the default setting, but because it reduces the resolution of some images, it's better to use the Normal option.

Figure 17-9:
The Options
dialog box
for a
PostScript
printer.

Options

Graphics
○ Normal
● Optimized
○ Low TIFF resolution
○ Omit TIFF files

Markings
☐ Printer's marks
☐ Page information

PostScript
☐ Include PostScript error handler
☐ Write PostScript to file: [   ] Browse...
● Normal   ☒ Include downloadable fonts
○ EPS   ☐ Extra image bleed
○ For separations

Print
Cancel
Document
Paper
Options
Color
Reset

Dealing with fonts

Although most of the options in the Print Document dialog box are self-explana-tory, one is definitely not: Page Independence. This option — available only for PostScript printers — should normally be left unchecked. What does it do? It loads the fonts for each page into printer memory separately instead of loading all the document's fonts all at once. If you have the same fonts on every page, checking this option slows down printing because fonts keep getting reloaded. But if each page has mostly a unique set of fonts, checking this option means that only the fonts for each page are downloaded with that page, rather than all the document fonts. This uses less printer memory per page, making output time faster. We suggest you leave it unchecked until you know you need it.

Another key option for font control — again, just for PostScript printers — resides in the Options dialog box: Include Downloadable Fonts. This option should almost always be checked, even though that's not the default. If this option is checked, the fonts used in the document are loaded into your printer's memory when you print. (Figure 17-9 shows the dialog box.)

Why wouldn't that be the default? Who knows. But there is a good reason that you'd uncheck this option: The fonts already reside in the printer. If you're a service bureau, you load a document's fonts directly into printer memory or onto a hard disk attached to the printer and uncheck this option because that speeds up printing for such high-end printers. If everyone in your department uses the same fonts, and they reside on the printer disk or in printer memory, then fine, uncheck the box. But most users don't work in such situations, which is why it's best to have the fonts loaded to the printer each time you print.

Printing to file

If you're working with PostScript printers, you can *print to file* by choosing Write PostScript to File in the Options dialog box. Printing to file just means that instead of sending your document to the printer, PageMaker saves the docu-ment and all the encoded printing instructions to a file on your hard disk, a floppy disk, or other storage device (like a SyQuest cartridge). Why would you do this instead of just saving your document to disk as you normally would? Perhaps because you want to take the file to a service bureau, but you don't want to give them a chance to alter your print, font, or color settings.

If you don't want to print color separations, choose Normal under Write PostScript to File. If you do want color separations, choose For Separations. If you intend to import your pages into another layout or program, such as to reproduce the cover in miniature on the contents page, choose EPS. Check Extra Image Bleed if your document uses bleeds (images or text that go beyond the page boundaries).

You can print to file in PCL format, but you have to set up Windows to do so — PageMaker doesn't give you any options to print to file in this format. Go to the Windows Control Panel (it's usually in the Main program group) and double-click on the Printers icon. Select your PCL printer and select the Connect button. Choose DISK: as the port, as Figure 17-10 shows. You may want to keep two PCL printers set up in your Printers dialog box: one connected to the printer port and one connect to DISK:. That'll save you the effort of having to switch back and forth each time — just choose the appropriate printer/port combination in the PageMaker Print dialog box.

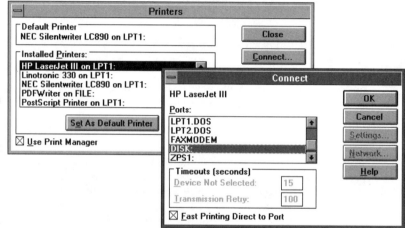

Figure 17-10:
Use the
Connect
dialog box to
set up print-
to-file for
PCL printing.

Printing odd page sizes

If you're outputting unusual page sizes — whether half sheets, magazine sheets, CD labels, whatever — to an imagesetter, PageMaker's got an option for you. In the Paper dialog box (for PostScript) or Setup dialog box (for PCL), you choose the paper size. Typically, you'll leave it at Letter and forget it. But if you need to print other sizes, this is the place to change them. Figure 17-11 shows the Paper dialog box with the paper-size choices available. Note that you won't see the same options as in the figure for many desktop printers because they support a different selection of sizes in their paper trays.

The pop-up menu of page sizes offers some options that have *.Extra* in their names. These options add margins around the standard size for each page so that elements that bleed will really bleed. You'll recall that a bleed is an image or text that intentionally runs off the page. (No, it's not something from a horror movie.) Well, if you pick a standard page size, the image or text gets cut off right at the border of the page. So what happens if the paper slips while being printed or copied or cut — the bled image or text moves, too, and all of a sudden it may not bleed any more. By having extra margin, PageMaker can print enough of the bleed image to account for any such variations. You can use one of the .Extra pages options in the pop-up menu if you're outputting a corresponding page size (such as Legal.Extra for printing a legal-sized document), or you can use the Custom option to create your own size with sufficient margins (give yourself at least 0.375 inches on each side).

The extra margin also gives PageMaker room to print crop marks and page information (which you set in the Options dialog box). This information is typically used by service bureaus, although some in-house artists use crop marks to ensure that pages are cut correctly, especially if the final product is being cut down to a smaller size than the paper it's printed on. If the paper size you selected is not big enough to accommodate this information, you get a warning message as you print.

Figure 17-11:
You set
the paper
size for
PostScript
printers in
the Paper
dialog box.
For PCL
printers, the
Options
dialog box
offers a
similar
feature.

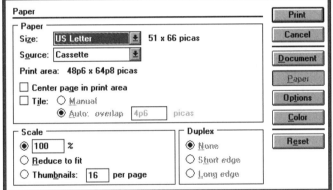

Inglorious color

PageMaker offers controls over how color negatives print through its Color dialog box (see Figure 17-12). Select Composite if you're printing to a color printer and Grayscale if you're printing to a black-and-white laser or inkjet printer. Select Print Colors in Black only if you want fast printing and don't care if images appear as big blotches. For PostScript printing, select Preserve EPS Colors if your document contains a color EPS image that has its own color definitions and you want those colors to be used rather than colors defined in PageMaker that happen to have the same names.

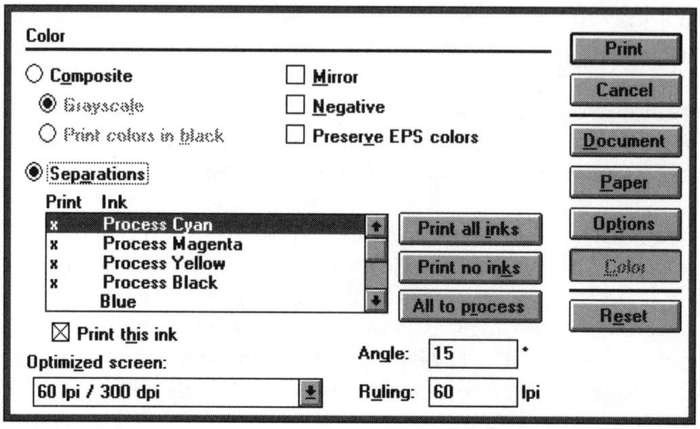

Figure 17-12:
The Color
dialog box
for printing.

If you are printing to an imagesetter and want a separate negative for each color plate, select Separations and select each ink for which you want a color plate. Typically, you'll want just the four process colors (select the All to Process button). For PostScript printing, select the Optimized Screen setting that matches your publication's standards. If you're not sure what this means, you shouldn't be printing the page — get help from someone experienced with commercial color printing.

For PCL printing — whether to a high-resolution laser printer or to a color inkjet printer for color transparencies — select the Allow PCL Halftoning to get the best color or grayscale output.

Chapter 18
Dealing with the Outside World

· ·

In This Chapter

▶ Exchanging files with colleagues

▶ Working with Macintosh PageMaker users

▶ Preparing files for output by a service bureau

· ·

*I*t's good to share — really. By working with others, you can use your combined strengths to better effect and help each other out in your weaker areas. Desktop publishing is a collaborative enterprise — the folks who do the writing are usually not the folks who do the artwork, and neither of these folks usually does the layout. Even if you work in a small business and you're the one who does most or all of the work, you still have to exchange the PageMaker document with a client or a service bureau.

PageMaker is designed for collaboration, so your efforts to share are strongly supported by the program's design. And for those areas in which PageMaker isn't quite strong enough, this chapter shows you how to get around its limitations.

Chapters 4 and 5 tell you how to collaborate with people who provide the text for your documents. (Style sheets and text formatting — remember?) In this chapter, you learn about sharing entire PageMaker documents, whether you're working with several people on the same document, passing on your work to someone else for approval or final touches, or sending your file to a service bureau for output on a high-resolution typesetting device.

Exchanging Documents with Colleagues

If several people are working on a document — whether they work collaboratively during the layout process or move the file from one person to another for specific tasks — they need to have access to all the components of the PageMaker document. However, those components can differ from document to document, depending on how you set up each document.

Sharing options

What do you do when you're ready to share PageMaker files with colleagues? First, determine the level of access people should have to your layout's elements. Here are some common file-sharing scenarios and how to handle them:

- ✔ Scenario 1: You want a colleague to go through the layout to make sure that elements align, everything is placed correctly, no text is overset, and handle other such touch-up details. Use the Links dialog box (File⇨Links or Shift+Ctrl+D) to unlink each element from its source (by using the Unlink button for each element). Your colleague can still edit text but can't inadvertently update it with a linked text file; graphics won't be updated either. Unlinking also tends to make the file smaller — sometimes as small as two-thirds the original size.

- ✔ Scenario 2: You want a colleague to go through the layout to add elements but not to update any elements already in the layout. You may want to modify your own work when you get the document back. Use the Links dialog box (File⇨Links or Ctrl+Shift+D) to disable automatic updating of links for text and graphics (for each element, use the Options button to get the Link options dialog box and uncheck the Update Automatically option).

  Have your colleague do the same when returning the file to you. Note that either of you can use this option to override these settings if needed or use Element⇨Link Options to re-establish a link between a selected text block or graphic and an external file.

- ✔ Scenario 3: You've done a rough or conceptual layout, and you want a colleague to do the final layout. Graphics files may change, but you finalized the text in PageMaker's Story Editor. Unlink the text as described in Scenario 1. Set the Link Options dialog box so that Update Automatically is checked and, if the files may change while the other person is working on the layout, disable the Alert Before Updating checkbox.

- ✔ Scenario 4: You simply want the other person to go through your file and proofread it. Send a printout, fax it, or use a program like No Hands Software's Common Ground portable-document software to e-mail an electronic version. Or open the file, unlink everything, save the file under a new name, and then send it. When you get the file back, you can compare it (probably from printouts) to your original to see what has changed.

If you're sharing PageMaker files with others on your office computer network, ask your network administrator for help in setting up your directories and establishing file-sharing guidelines.

Fonts, libraries, and support files

When sharing files with other users, you may find that your setups differ, which can lead to unexpected results, such as bad tracking or incorrect font usage.

Fonts

Everyone working on a project should have the same fonts. Many companies put directories of fonts on a network server or set of disks so that users can install them when working on the same project. If colleagues don't have a certain font used in your PageMaker document, PageMaker displays an alert box when they try to use the document. They can still work with the file, because PageMaker lets them substitute a different font temporarily. But this substitution can affect the line spacing because substituted fonts usually have different character sizes and tracking values. For more details about PageMaker's font-substitution options, skip to the next section in this chapter. Font substitution is more valuable for cross-platform document exchange and is thus covered in detail there.

Libraries

A PageMaker document keeps a link to any libraries opened in it. If someone copies the PageMaker file, that link is retained, and the next person to open the file may get a dialog box requesting the location of the library file. If you don't need the library contents, just click on the Cancel button. If you do need to use the library, you have to relink it. If that library is available on your office network, great. Otherwise, you have to cancel the library relinking and get the library from your colleague by e-mail, on disk, or by some other method.

Tracking

If you save a PageMaker file with the Files Required for Remote Printing option selected in the Save Publication dialog box, the tracking values (stored in a file named TRAKVALS.BIN) for that file are copied with it. If you select any other option, the next user's copy of PageMaker uses the tracking file located in the PageMaker file's new location (if there is a tracking file there) or in the ALDUS\USENGLSH directory. It's a good idea to use the Files Required for Remote Printing option to ensure that the tracking files are up to date. This option also copies linked graphics not wholly loaded into the PageMaker file. If everyone needs to use a standard set of tracking values, make sure that a master file is kept somewhere (on a disk or on a directory in the network, for example) and installed in everyone's ALDUS\USENGLSH directory.

Working with Macintosh Users

In most cases, PageMaker files created on the PC can be read on the Mac, and vice versa — the file formats are the same, and most differences relate to external components.

But when dealing with Mac colleagues, be prepared for some snobbery. The Mac (with the help of PageMaker) gave birth to desktop publishing, and Mac aficionados won't let you forget it. Plus, Mac users really like the Mac — it's often more than just a tool to do the job. They can't imagine why anyone would ever choose to use a PC, even with Windows, which they regard as a poor imitation of the real thing. Let them enjoy their computer of choice while you enjoy yours. And lead them gently through the issues of cross-platform transfer, because they tend to get all bug-eyed when they hear terms like *extensions*.

For PageMaker, working across platforms is a way of life — Aldus says that a fifth of its PageMaker customers use both the Windows and Mac versions. That number reflects individual people who use both forms themselves, not just companies that have both systems in use. So some of the snobbishness (on both sides) is starting to go away.

Here's what you need to know technically.

Filenames

Macs and PCs use different types of *filenames*. Mac filenames can be phrases of up to 31 characters. PC filenames comprise up to eight characters followed by a period and an extension of up to three characters (for example, MASTERPG.DOC). This difference in naming conventions can easily become a source of great confusion.

When you transfer PageMaker document files across platforms and then open them, you get a dialog box asking you whether you want to translate the filenames (Figure 18-1 shows the dialog boxes in Mac and Windows PageMaker). You should answer in the affirmative by checking the Translate File Names in Links option. If you don't, the Links dialog box simply says PC Text or PC Graphic (or Mac Text or Mac Graphic), which doesn't help when you later try to relink to the original files). This is PageMaker's way of dealing with the differences in filenames across platforms.

Going from the PC to the Mac is easy, because PC filenames are also legal Mac filenames. If you check the Links dialog box after transferring from Windows PageMaker to Mac PageMaker, you see that all the files remain linked with their PC names.

Figure 18-1:
The dialog
box to
translate
linked
filenames
and PICT
and to
translate
Windows
Metafile
files. The
Windows
dialog box is
on the top;
Mac is on
the bottom.

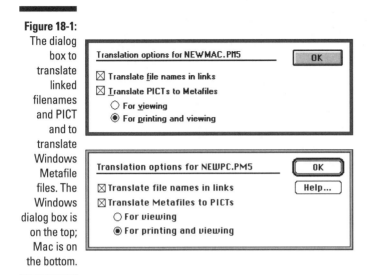

But going from a Mac to a PC is trickier: PageMaker translates the names it uses internally to refer to the linked files, but it can't always do so correctly when going from the Mac to the PC. It's best to use DOS-style filenames (up to eight characters followed by a period and a three-character extension that identifies the file type) if you'll be moving PageMaker files and linked files across platforms. If you don't change the Mac-style 31-character names to DOS names when moving files from Mac PageMaker to Windows PageMaker, you have to relink the files in Windows PageMaker.

Note that some characters don't transfer well across platforms. For example, spaces on the Mac often go away or become underscores (_) in Windows. And filenames that contain an ampersand (&) often display with an underline in a Windows dialog box (for example, CAT&DOG.TIF appears as CAT_DOG.TIF in a Windows dialog box).Why? The & character tells Windows programs when to put an underline in their menu items and dialog box labels.

You'll find that your Mac colleagues are clueless about PC filenames, especially file extensions. After all, the Mac doesn't require them because it uses icons to identify file types. So be prepared to tell your Mac colleagues which extensions to use. Typical extensions are PM5 for PageMaker files, PT5 for PageMaker templates, DOC for Word files, TXT for ASCII (text-only) files, WPD for Word-Perfect files, TIF for TIFF files, PIC for PICT files, WMF for Windows Metafiles, EPS for Encapsulated PostScript files, and PCX for PC Paintbrush files.

Graphics format translation

When you transfer PICT files to Windows (PICT is the Macintosh graphics format), PageMaker gives you the option of translating them to Windows Metafile format. Going the other direction, you have the option of translating from Windows Metafile to PICT. Use this option; you can't view or print the files otherwise. You have a choice of translating for viewing only or for both viewing and printing. If you plan to print the file on the other platform, make sure to choose the option for both viewing and printing.

You may lose some quality in the translation. That quality loss may become even worse when you move the file back to the Mac, because PageMaker translates the graphic from Windows Metafile to PICT again. Sometimes PageMaker also can produce a lower-quality version of TIFF, PCX, or other bitmap formats when it moves them across platforms. This usually occurs for bitmap images stored within PageMaker (whether they are linked or not). Figure 18-2 shows how PageMaker identifies such files for Macs (the solid diamond symbol in front of the filename) and PCs (the ¿ symbol after the filename) in the Links dialog box. (The hollow diamond in the Mac dialog box indicates that a file that has been modified since it was placed into PageMaker.)

In either case — to avoid quality loss in PICT/Windows Metafile translation or to avoid quality loss for bitmap files stored internally in your PageMaker document — you can always relink the original graphic. If you're moving the document just one way, you may want to use a format such as TIFF or EPS that requires no translation across platforms instead of using a PICT or Windows Metafile.

Fonts

Fonts cannot be moved across platforms. If you use custom fonts, use a font-translation program such as Ares Software's FontMonger or Altsys's Fontographer to translate the fonts. These programs are often used to create fonts, and they can create both Mac and Windows fonts from the original font. Both programs are available in Windows and Mac versions.

Some fonts with the same names — and from the same developer — may not print exactly the same on Windows and the Mac due to minute differences in spacing. This difference can lead to reflowed text, so print your document on a laser printer after transferring it across platforms to ensure that nothing bad happened.

Some fonts have different names on different platforms. For example, Windows fonts tend not to have spaces in their names, while Mac fonts often do — thus the font Century Old Style on the Mac is known as CenturyOldStyle on the PC.

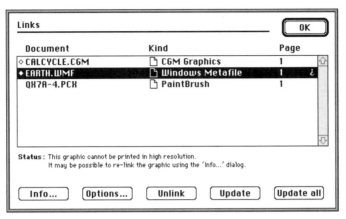

Figure 18-2:
The Links
dialog box
showing the
translated
file names
for linked
files. The
Mac version
of the dialog
box is on
top; the
Windows
version is on
the bottom.

PageMaker lets you tell it which fonts have mismatched names so that it knows to rename the fonts in a transferred document in the future. The first time a mismatch occurs, PageMaker uses a tool called the *Panose Matching System,* essentially a table of fonts that indicates which are the same as others with different names and which are similar, in case you need to substitute another font. The Panose tool displays the dialog box shown in Figure 18-3. Panose recommends substitutions for you, but you can select a new name from the list at the bottom.

If the font really doesn't exist on the new platform, substitute a similar font and click on <u>T</u>emporary. When the file is transferred to a system that has the missing font, the original font is substituted for the temporary font.

But if you want to make a particular substitution permanent — whether based on Panose's recommendations or your own selection — click on the <u>P</u>ermanent radio button. Doing so saves the substitution in Panose's database so that it knows what to do the next time it encounters the situation. You can also change or add to this substitution table in the Font Matching dialog box (File⇨ Preferences⇨Map Fonts), shown in Figure 18-4.

The dialog box also lets you decide the degree of substitution tolerance via a slider. There's no reason to change it from normal unless you have many similar fonts and want Panose to be more discerning in its recommendations.

Figure 18-3: When PageMaker can't find a font used by a PageMaker file on your system, it gives you a chance to substitute another font for the missing font.

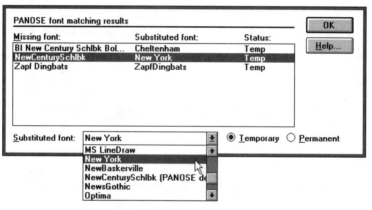

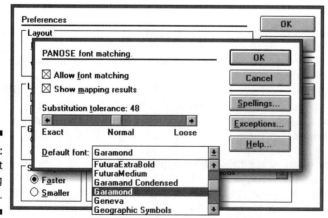

Figure 18-4: The Font Matching dialog box.

Use the <u>S</u>pellings button to get a list of Windows font names and their Mac equivalents. You can add to, modify, or remove names from this list. Notice that the names differ essentially in spacing and capitalization. You use the <u>E</u>xceptions list for wholesale substitutions of fonts, such as when you always want to replace Times with the Times Ten font — not a clone but a distinct font with its own look and feel. (Panose uses the Exceptions list for matching.) Figure 18-5 shows the dialog boxes for the <u>S</u>pellings and <u>E</u>xceptions buttons.

Figure 18-5:
The two lists available in the Font Matching dialog box: a list of Windows and Mac names for the same fonts (top) and the user-defined changes or additions to the Panose database (bottom).

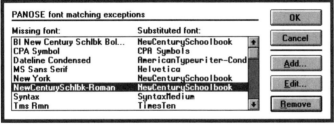

You can use font substitution when moving files from one Windows system to another where their fonts differ, not just when moving between Macs and Windows systems.

Incompatible elements

Some PageMaker support files cannot be moved across platforms. One such file type is the tracking file (Tracking Values on Macs and TRAKVALS.BIN on PCs). The two platforms' font formats are different, and tracking files are font related.

Library files also cannot be moved across platforms — the formats are not compatible. If you use a library in a PageMaker file moved across platforms, PageMaker prompts you to locate the library, and you either have to select a similar library on the new platform or click on Cancel.

Sending Documents to Service Bureaus

In Chapter 17, you learned how to prepare a file for output, including some of the settings of interest to a service bureau. Here, you learn what to send to a service bureau — and how to send it.

Service bureau in this case refers to anyone to whom you send your PageMaker layout for final output. It may be a separate company, a division of your company, or someone down the hall. Typically, a service bureau produces negatives used by a commercial printer to actually print your document; the service bureau usually uses a typesetter or imagesetter to produce these files. But a service bureau may also produce *positives* — black ink on white paper — at high resolution, or even on a laser printer (if you don't have one yourself). Some copy centers are, in essence, low-end service bureaus.

Before you begin, note the following:

- Remember that by copying graphics wholly into the document (see Chapter 8 for details), you can minimize file size. A good rule of thumb is to copy any graphic that is 64K or smaller into your PageMaker document.

- Make sure that all grayscale bitmap images have the correct line screens and other image settings applied via Element⇨Image Control.

- If you are doing four-color printing, make sure to check All to Process in the Color section of the Print dialog box.

- Make sure that the printer and resolution selected in the Print dialog box (File⇨Print) match those of the target printer. Check that other print settings are appropriate for the document, as described in Chapter 17.

Now you are ready to give the service bureau what it needs: everything related to printing the document.

- Use PageMaker's Save Publication dialog box (File⇨Save As) with the Files Required for Remote Printing option selected. This ensures that any linked graphics not wholly imported into PageMaker are included (usually, these linked files are TIFF and EPS files). Also copied is the TRAKVALS.BIN file, which ensures that the service bureau has all spacing and kerning values that you've set for your document.

✔ Depending on the size of the file and its images, save the document onto a high-density (1.4MB) floppy disk or cartridge (SyQuest and Bernoulli are the most popular — check with your service bureau to see which type it uses).

✔ Enclose a list of all the fonts your document uses. Also, copy all the fonts to a separate disk. Your service bureau may have your fonts, but by enclosing the fonts on disk, you save the service bureau the time of tracking them down. At the very least, make sure that you include any custom fonts.

You can get the fonts from the fonts directory in your system — remember that there are two types of files for every PostScript font; the PostScript printer font, which has the extension .PFB; and the font metric file, which has the extension .PFM. PostScript fonts are usually stored in directories called PSFONTS and PSFONTS\PFM. Service bureaus rarely use TrueType fonts, but if yours does, look for TrueType files in the WINDOWS\SYSTEM directory; the printer files have the extension .TTF and the screen-display files have the extension .FOT. You don't need to give the service bureau the .FOT files, and not all TrueType fonts have .FOT files. The directory names for these files may be different on your system, depending on how you installed the fonts.

✔ Enclose a printout of the document so that the service bureau can check the output versus your expectations.

Most service bureaus don't have a clue about PC files. Many tell you that they can't process Windows PageMaker files, even though they can if they follow the advice in this chapter for moving files across platforms. Others take your Windows files and then transfer them to a Mac for output, but they aren't aware of the subtleties of cross-platform transfer, which can result in errors. The most typical error is a font mismatch.

PC users are the minority in commercial publishing, and most service bureaus are Mac-based. Even if they can get your PageMaker and graphics files into their Macs, which isn't hard, they'll be stymied about what to do about a typeface that you have in PC format but they don't have (or can't get) in Mac format. This is particularly true for fonts that you create yourself and for TrueType fonts with no PostScript equivalents. You may be stuck translating the fonts for the service bureau by using a program like FontMonger or Fontographer. But don't despair — more and more service bureaus are becoming PC-savvy, and if you demand that they support you (and give them enough work to justify it), they'll invest the $5,000 or so in a basic Windows publishing setup.

You're Done!

Believe it or not, you now know the basics of creating and printing PageMaker documents. Up next is the Part of Tens, which is both an amusing and informative collection of wisdom, observations, and useful information about PageMaker. Think of it as the icing on your PageMaker cake — enjoy!

The 5th Wave   **By Rich Tennant**

"SOFTWARE SUPPORT SAYS WHATEVER WE DO, DON'T ANYONE START TO RUN."

Part VII
The Part of Tens

In this part...

You know the problem with most computer books? (*Besides* the fact that their turgid prose violates all known measurements for tedium and unoriginality.) They don't offer enough sound bites. When you set the book down, you should be humming the tunes, as it were, conjuring up images of pages gone by, psyched to the gills to put a few techniques to the test. In other words, you should be raring to use PageMaker.

That's what this section is about. Now that we've discussed a few thousand issues pertinent to PageMaker in context, the rest of the book hurls factoids at you completely out of context. The idea is that if we hurl enough of them and hurl them hard enough, a few will get stuck in your brain. It is our supreme wish that on your deathbed, you say something completely meaningless to your surviving relatives like, "To create a line break, press Shift+Enter." If you do, try to get someone to videotape it, will you? We may be able to use it in a marketing campaign; you never know.

Chapter 19

The Top Ten Custom Styles Everyone Should Have

· ·

In This Chapter

▶ Body text

▶ The first paragraph of body text

▶ Captions

▶ In-line graphics

▶ Bulleted and numbered lists

▶ Big headlines

▶ A couple of subheads

▶ Table entries

▶ Table headlines

· ·

Styles are the great equalizers. By maintaining a consistent set of styles on every computer in your company, you ensure that one person's work resembles another's, even though both people have unique working habits and approaches. The idea isn't to stifle creativity, but rather to make everyone's uniqueness compatible.

This chapter suggests 10 custom styles that every user should add to the Type⇨Style submenu. You'll want to customize these styles to fit your specific design requirements — for example, you might change a typeface here, tweak the size a little bit there — so think of these styles merely as jumping off points.

To make your styles available to all future PageMaker documents, close all open documents so that only the PageMaker menu bar is available. Then choose Type⇨Define Styles (or press Ctrl+3) to display the Define Styles dialog box and create and edit styles as described back in Chapter 4. These styles will become PageMaker's new defaults.

To be safe, quit PageMaker after you finish defining your default styles. PageMaker saves the default settings to disk when you quit the program. This way, if your machine crashes or you encounter a system error, you don't lose all your work.

Body Text

Body Text is one of the default styles provided with PageMaker. By default, it's set to give you 12-point Times and automatic leading. Change the font to whatever you use throughout your publications, and definitely lower that type size to 10 or 11 points; anything larger will make your stuff look like storybook time. (Of course, if your publications are geared toward children or older adults who have problems reading small text, you should leave the type size unmolested or even raise it to 14 points.)

This style also comes equipped with a 2-pica first-line indent to help distinguish the paragraphs. If you like a roomier look, you may want to throw in a few points of paragraph spacing. Use the After option in the Paragraph Specifications dialog box so that the spacing follows each paragraph. (For example, to add 6 points of spacing, enter *0p6* into the After option box.)

Body Lead

PageMaker includes one default Body Text style, but you really need two. No matter what kind of document you're creating, a paragraph that immediately follows a headline — known as a *body lead* — should *not* be indented. The headline already sets off the paragraph; it doesn't need further distinguishing.

Create a style named Body Lead, as shown in Figure 19-1, and apply it to any paragraph that follows a head. Set the Based On and Next Style options in the Edit Style dialog box to Body Text and then change the first-line indent to 0. Assign the standard Body Text style to the paragraph following the body lead paragraph and any other paragraph that does not follow a headline.

Caption

Like Body Text, the Caption style is one of the defaults. It calls for 10-point Times Italic with automatic leading. You can go two ways with this one. You can change the typeface to the same face you used in the Body Text style. If you do, leave the caption text italic to set it apart.

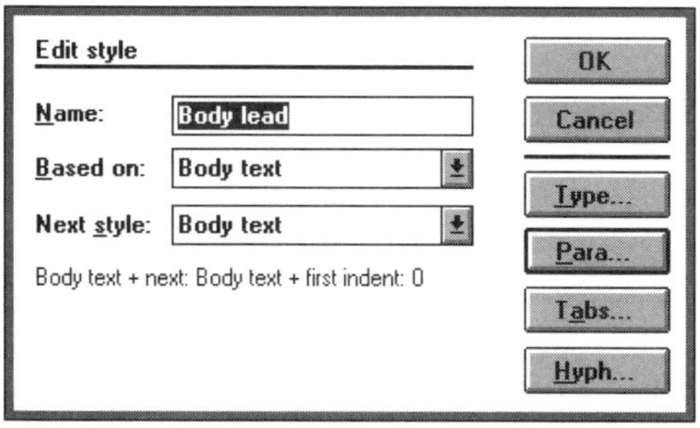

Figure 19-1:
How to set
up the Body
Lead style.

> **Edit style**
>
> **Name:** Body lead
> **Based on:** Body text
> **Next style:** Body text
>
> Body text + next: Body text + first indent: 0
>
> OK
> Cancel
> Type...
> Para...
> Tabs...
> Hyph...

But not all designers like this approach. Some prefer to balance a serif Body Text style, such as Palatino, with a sans serif Caption style, such as Helvetica. If you choose this approach, don't italicize the Caption style, and reduce the type size to around 9 points. Sans serif fonts are typically legible at smaller sizes than serif fonts.

For some reason, PageMaker's default Caption style doesn't include any paragraph spacing, which is nuts. Be sure to add 9 to 15 points of After spacing. Also, the Next Style option is set to Same Style; change it to Body Text.

Figure

Okay, so now you have a style for the caption, but what about the graphic itself? A style can be very useful for establishing spacing before and after an in-line graphic. Create a new style named Figure and base it on the Caption style. Set Caption to be the next style, and change the Before spacing for the paragraph to a pica (12 points) or so. You can leave the After spacing the same as the Caption style. Figure 19-2 shows the result.

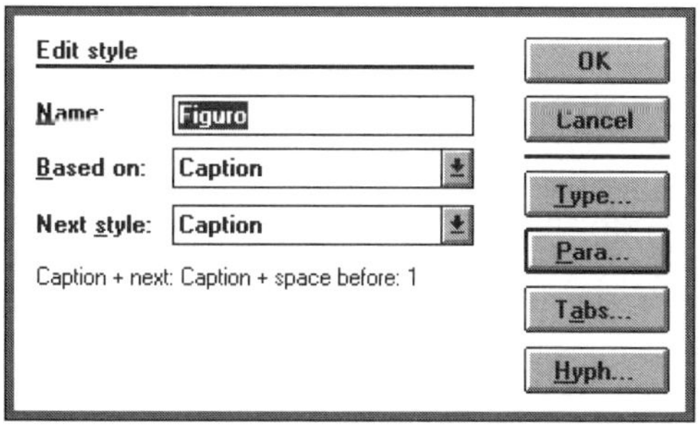

Figure 19-2:
A Figure
style helps
to evenly
space out
in-line
graphics.

> **Edit style**
>
> **Name:** Figure
> **Based on:** Caption
> **Next style:** Caption
>
> Caption + next: Caption + space before: 1
>
> OK
> Cancel
> Type...
> Para...
> Tabs...
> Hyph...

To use this style, actually apply it to the in-line graphic itself. After applying the style, press Enter and enter the caption text below the graphic.

Hanging Indent

This default style might be better named *List Entries,* because that's what it's really used for. You can use it to indent bulleted and numbered lists in your document.

To make the style your own, change the font and type size to exactly match the font and size used in the Body Text style. You can even select Body Text as the Based On style to make sure that you get it right.

The problem with this style is that it doesn't accommodate numbered lists. By default, the indents are only one pica, which is hardly the width of a single numeral. Change the indent to two picas to match the first-line indent of the Body Text style. To do this, click on the Para button in the Edit Style dialog box, change the Left value to 2p and the First value to –2p, and then press Enter. Next, click on the Tabs button. You'll see a tab marker between the first-line and left indent markers. Click on the tab marker, enter 2p in the Position option box, and then select Move Tab from the Position pop-up menu. Press Enter twice to finish off the style.

Headline

This default style is set to 30-point Times Bold with automatic leading. Change the typeface and size as desired; pick a font that goes well with your body text. You can either make it a bold version of the same typeface, or experiment with a different font.

Want to know the weird things about this style? It doesn't include any paragraph spacing, and the next style is set to Same Style. Really, when's the last time you saw one headline directly following another? Never, that's when. Maybe a subhead following a head, but never two heads in a row, not even in the *National Enquirer.* So, add about a pica of Before spacing and then change the Next Style option to Body Lead. This way, the lead paragraph with no first-line indent will follow the Headline style.

Subhead 1 and Subhead 2

PageMaker includes two Subhead styles, one smaller than the other. The Subhead 1 style calls for 18-point type; the Subhead 2 style calls for 12-point type. Both styles are based on the Headline style, so the typeface and Before spacing automatically correspond to whatever you used for the Headline style.

You may want to experiment with the typeface, type style, size, and Before spacing on the styles to get them just right. But if you do nothing else, at least change the Next Style option to Body Lead.

Table Entries

Tables are common elements in all sorts of documents, including newsletters, reports, catalogs, and more. Formatting these tables always takes some work. You can't create a style that will address every table, because you have no idea how long each table entry will be. But you can at least establish a rough style to serve as a starting point.

Make a new style and base it on the Body Lead style. Then click on the Tabs button and position tab stops every inch or inch and a half. Press the Enter key to return to the Edit Style dialog box and name your style *Table Entries.* That's all there is to it. Later on, when you apply the style to your table entries inside an actual document, adjust the tab stops to fit your specific text using Type⇨Indents/Tabs (Ctrl+I).

Table Head

Just as every graphic needs a caption, every table needs a headline. In fact, the two should match. To establish a table headline style, create a new style, base it on the Caption style, and select Table Entries as the next style. The only difference between a caption and a table headline is that the paragraph spacing occurs after a caption, while it should precede a headline. So click on the Para button and change the Before value to match the After value. Then change the After value to 0, press Enter, and name the style Table Head. Figure 19-3 shows the result.

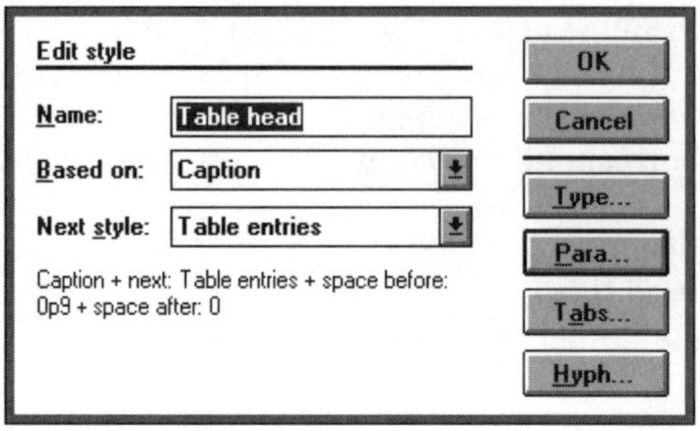

Figure 19-3:
The Table
Head style is
an upside-
down
version of
the Caption
style, with
paragraph
space at the
beginning
instead of
the end.

Edit style

OK

Cancel

Name: Table head

Based on: Caption

Type...

Next **s**tyle: Table entries

Para...

Caption + next: Table entries + space before:
0p9 + space after: 0

Tabs...

Hyph...

Other Styles

It is possible that you'll want to create even more default styles to use throughout future PageMaker documents. In fact, it's more than possible; it's very
likely.

For example, what if a caption immediately precedes a headline? Won't the
After spacing from the Caption style and the Before spacing from the Headline
style conspire to create a massive gap? Yes, of course it will. To combat this
problem, you may want to create yet another style called Caption Pre-Head.
You might base this new style on the Caption style — with Headline set as the
next style — and include the same amount of after spacing as the Body Text
style.

Get the idea? If any common formatting scenario pops up time and time again,
make it into a default style. You'll have to create a few documents before you
discover all the style permutations.

Chapter 20

Ten Special Characters
to Assign to Memory

- -

In This Chapter

▶ Curly quotes and the apostrophe

▶ The bullet

▶ The em space

▶ The em dash

▶ The discretionary hyphen

▶ The nonbreaking space, hyphen, and slash

▶ The line break

▶ Copyright and trademark symbols

▶ Common fractions

▶ The automatic page number

- -

*W*hen we say *characters*, we don't mean the guys down at the local bar. We're talking about the most elemental building blocks available to you in PageMaker: text characters. Some characters — a, e, i, o, u, sometimes y — are readily available to the most casual PageMaker user. But others lie hidden beneath PageMaker's murky surface. These special characters make it possible to space text more elegantly, prevent text from breaking onto different lines at weird places, and just plain make your words look more beautiful. Who'd have thought something so small could be so powerful?

The Curly Quotes and Apostrophe

Wouldn't that make a great title for a children's book? "The curly quotes and apostrophe all went out to tea. They sat down on a page that was as spiffy as could be." Boy, given half a chance, we could come up with something guaranteed to nauseate the most desensitized parent.

Ctrl+Shift+[and Ctrl+Shift+]

Well, children's book or no children's book, curly quotes are the number one symbol on our hit parade. If you walk away knowing nothing else, learn how to create a curly quote. Press Ctrl+Shift+left bracket to get the open quote ("), Ctrl+Shift+right bracket to get the close quote (").

Ctrl+]

Meanwhile, press Ctrl+right bracket to get the apostrophe ('). Practice it, memorize it.

Alt+key equivalents

When you roam out of PageMaker, you don't have to leave your curly quotes behind. Just use the Alt+key equivalents. Hold down the Alt key and type **0147** (sequentially, not all at the same time) on the keypad to create the open curly quote. Alt+0148 produces the close quote; Alt+0146 creates an apostrophe. These key equivalents also work inside PageMaker.

The Bullet

Ctrl+Shift+8

Guns and lists have two things in common: They're favorites of the NRA — "Senator, you're on our blacklist!" — and they don't deliver without bullets. Luckily, your PC provides an inexhaustible arsenal of bullets at the touch of three keys, Ctrl+Shift+8. Inside other applications, press Alt+0149.

Zapf Dingbats

If you're interested in something more lively, check out the Zapf Dingbats font. You'll find special stars, shapes, numbers, and arrows that you can use to jazz up your text. You can even access check marks similar to the ones used as bullets in this book.

The Em Space

Ctrl+Shift+M

The em space is an alternative to the tab. But rather than creating even columns of numbers, prices, and so on, the em space results in a fixed gap between a word and the word that follows it. The gap is exactly as wide as the type size is tall. If you want to see an example of this amazing space in action, refer back to Figure 6-11. To access the em space, press Ctrl+Shift+M.

The Em Dash

Ctrl+Shift+equal

It's good to know where all your punctuation is. Unlike the em space, which appears only in the most highfalutin of publications — it's okay, you should be highfalutin — the em dash is as common as mud. This paragraph uses two of them, in fact. To insert an em dash into your next sentence, press Ctrl+Shift+equal.

The Discretionary Hyphen

Ctrl+hyphen

PageMaker is supremely talented at hyphenating text, but doesn't always get it right. If PageMaker misses an opportunity to hyphenate a word, you can help it by clicking at the desired point and pressing Ctrl+hyphen. If PageMaker can use the hyphen, it breaks the word according to your specifications. If it can't quite manage to squeeze even the hyphenated syllable onto the preceding line of text, no hyphen appears. That's the beauty of discretionary hyphens; they only appear when they're needed. That way, you don't have to worry that when you edit your text, you'll be left with a bunch of hyphens that are no longer needed.

Nonbreaking Characters

Ctrl+Shift+H, Ctrl+Shift+hyphen, Ctrl+Shift+slash

PageMaker breaks words separated by a space, a hyphen, or a slash. If you don't want PageMaker to break two words separated by one of these characters, you have to use special nonbreaking characters. The nonbreaking space is Ctrl+Shift+H (for *hard* space); the nonbreaking hyphen is Ctrl+Shift+hyphen; and the nonbreaking slash is Ctrl+Shift+slash. Remember, these characters bond like Krazy Glue. (So be sure not to get any on your fingers.)

The Line Break

Shift+Enter

If you don't want to deal with nonbreaking characters, you can break a line at any point without creating a new paragraph by pressing Shift+Enter. Lines divided by a line break character are all part of the same happy paragraph; PageMaker doesn't insert new paragraph spacing and indents as it would if your had inserted a standard carriage return by pressing the Enter key without Shift.

The Copyright and Trademark Symbols

Ctrl+Shift+O, Alt+0153, Ctrl+Shift+G

Don't like folks stealing your precious ideas? You can protect those ideas with a few commonplace symbols. The copyright symbol (©), produced by pressing Ctrl+Shift+O or Alt+0169, tells folks that what they're looking at is your original work. The trademark symbol (™), which you can create by pressing Alt+0153, says that this name is indicative of your product, that it's unique, and that you're in the process of filing it with the proper authorities. The registered trademark (®), produced by pressing Ctrl+Shift+G or Alt+0174, says that the name is now registered — government authorities have accepted the name as absolutely unique — so everything's official. Together, these symbols are the *No Trespassing*, *Beware of Dog*, and *Protected by Neighborhood Watch* signs of typography.

Common Fractions

Decimals are formal and exact; fractions have a more informal and approximate feeling. For example, you might say, "I drank about $^1/_4$ of my glass of milk before I realized it was blinky," but only a pencil-necked geek would say, "0.25 glass of milk." On the other hand, both pencil-necked geeks and beefy-necked geeks like us can say "blinky."

Alt+188, Alt+189, Alt+190

Anyway, you can access three common fractions using Alt+key equivalents. Alt+0188 produces the $^1/_4$ fraction, Alt+0189 produces $^1/_2$, and Alt+0190 produces $^3/_4$.

The Automatic Page Number

Ctrl+Shift+3

You don't have to be on the master page to use page numbers; you can enter them anywhere you like. To tag any page with its page number automatically, press Ctrl+Shift+3. Even if you later renumber your pages, the page number character will update automatically.

Chapter 21

The Ten Shortcuts You'll Always Use

In This Chapter

- ▶ Choosing commands in the file menu
- ▶ Zooming in and out of the page
- ▶ Scrolling and changing pages
- ▶ Displaying PageMaker's palettes
- ▶ Activating tools from the keyboard
- ▶ Choosing the Undo command
- ▶ Choosing Clipboard commands
- ▶ Using PageMaker's word processor
- ▶ Applying formatting attributes
- ▶ Creating and editing styles and colors

*I*t's amazing how much money we spend on computers and other hardware that operate faster than our previous hardware. For a mere thousand dollars, you can shave seconds off your working day. But while your computer pushes new frontiers in speed, you're working at the same pace you always were. Imagine it from your computer's perspective: Here it is stuck with this same old-model user with no chance to update, *ever*.

The point is that you'll get a lot more work done a lot more quickly without spending a single penny if you learn to work more efficiently. And the best way to save time is to learn the essential shortcuts, which are laid at your feet in this one-of-a-kind, efficiency-building chapter. No seminars, no weight-lifting, no pyramid schemes. Just a few moments of your time, and you'll witness the most amazing transformation your computer has ever seen.

Opening, Saving, and Quitting

Ctrl+N, Enter

To create a new one-page, letter-sized document (assuming default settings), press Ctrl+N and then press Enter. Don't even bother to look at the dialog box. If you want to customize the document a little, press Ctrl+N and change the settings in the dialog box as desired.

Ctrl+O

To open a document that you created previously and saved to disk, press Ctrl+O.

Ctrl+S

To save your document to disk, press Ctrl+S. Do this early and do it often.

Ctrl+Q

To escape the generous clutches of PageMaker and return to the Windows Program Manager, press Ctrl+Q. If you haven't saved your most recent changes, press Enter to do so.

Zooming with Keyboard and Clicks

Right-click

When you first enter a new document, you view it at the fit-in-window size, the equivalent of viewing your page on the ground from the vantage point of a satellite in space. To get a little closer — the 100 percent view size, to be exact — right-click on the page with any tool. To return to the fit-in-window view, right-click again.

Shift+right-click

To magnify the page to 200 percent of its actual size, Shift+right-click on the page. Shift+right-clicking a second time takes you to the 100 percent view size.

Ctrl+1, Ctrl+2, Ctrl+4

The advantage of the preceding mouse shortcuts is that you specify the exact center of the magnification with your click. However, if you prefer to zoom in or out on a selected bit of text or a selected graphic, you don't need the mouse. Press Ctrl+1 to access the 100 percent view size; Ctrl+2 for 200 percent; and Control 4 for 400 percent.

Ctrl+spacebar+drag

To magnify the screen beyond 400 percent, press and hold Ctrl+spacebar to access the magnifying glass cursor, and then drag around the portion of the page you want to magnify. The surrounded area grows to fill the window.

Ctrl+spacebar+click, Ctrl+Alt+spacebar+click

You can also Ctrl+spacebar+click to magnify the view incrementally. Ctrl+Alt+spacebar+click to reduce the view incrementally.

Ctrl+5, Ctrl+7, Ctrl+W

Anyone for the 50 percent or 75 percent view size? Just press Ctrl+5 or Ctrl+7, respectively. The itsy bitsy, 25 percent view size is the weird one; you have to press Ctrl+0, which should tip you off that you won't be able to see squat from this vantage point. And to fit the page in the window, press Ctrl+W.

Navigating Inside Your Document

Alt+drag

To move the page inside the window, Alt+drag with any tool. Your cursor changes to the cute little grabber hand for the duration of your drag.

F11, F12

Press F11 to move to the previous page or set of facing pages. To move forward a page, press F12.

Ctrl+G, p#, Enter

If you want to go to a specific page, press Ctrl+G, enter the page number, and press the Enter key. To go to a master page, press Ctrl+G, select the desired radio button, and press Enter.

Shift+choose Layout⇨Go to Page

To peruse every page of your document, press the Shift key while choosing Layout⇨Go to Page. PageMaker shows the next page spread, waits a few seconds, and then shows the page spread after that. PageMaker continues cycling, displaying the first page after the last page, until you click your mouse button. Give it a try!

Displaying Palettes

Ctrl+6, Ctrl+quote, Ctrl+Y, Ctrl+K

Including the toolbox, PageMaker provides four palettes that you can display and hide by pressing key combinations. Press Ctrl+6 to hide and show the toolbox; press Ctrl+quote to hide and show the Control palette. To access the Styles and Colors palettes, press Ctrl+Y and Ctrl+K, respectively.

Selecting Tools

If you work on a 13-inch screen, here's a tip you're going to love. Hide the toolbox by pressing Ctrl+6 and leave it hidden. Never bring it up again for the rest of your life. The screen real estate is too precious! Besides, you can access all of PageMaker's tools from the keyboard by pressing Shift plus a function key. Except for the Arrow tool, the function keys correspond to the tools in the order that they appear in the toolbox. The Line tool is Shift+F2, the Perpendicular Line tool is Shift+F3, and so on, down to the Crop tool, which is Shift+F8.

Shift+F4

The main tool to remember is the Text tool, Shift+F4. Along with the Arrow tool, the Text tool is far and away the most commonly used tool in PageMaker.

Shift+F2, Shift+F6

Of secondary interest are the Line tool, Shift+F2, and the Rectangle tool, Shift+F6. These tools are useful for drawing rules and borders.

Shift+F5, Shift+F8

Every once in a while, you may need the Rotate tool, Shift+F5, and the Crop tool, Shift+F8. You'll never need the Perpendicular Line tool — just Shift+drag with the regular Line tool — or the Oval tool, so don't bother memorizing their shortcuts.

F9

To switch between the Arrow tool and the tool that is currently selected, press F9 (or, if you prefer, Ctrl+spacebar). For example, if the Text tool is selected, pressing F9 selects the Arrow tool. Pressing F9 again takes you back to the Arrow tool. Go ahead, give it a try. You'll fall in love all over again.

Undoing Mistakes

Ctrl+Z

If you want to eliminate the last action you performed, press Ctrl+Z (or Alt+Backspace). Unfortunately, PageMaker can't undo as many operations as it should — it can't undo text formatting, for example — but sometimes the Undo feature comes in handy. For example, if you go and delete an entire text block, Ctrl+Z brings it back to life.

Making Copies

Ctrl+X, Ctrl+C, Ctrl+V

To cut some selected text or a selected graphic and transfer it to the Clipboard, press Ctrl+X. If you use your imagination, the X looks like a pair of scissors, hence *cut.* To copy a selection, press Ctrl+C. And to paste the contents of the Clipboard into your PageMaker document, press Ctrl+V.

Shift+Delete, Ctrl+Insert, Shift+Insert

The X, C, V keys are three keys in a row, so associating them with three commands in a row — Cut, Copy, and Paste — makes a certain amount of sense. But, like many things engineered by Microsoft, the *original* Windows keyboard equivalents made very little sense. These shortcuts — Shift+Delete, Ctrl+Insert, Shift+Insert — access Cut, Copy, and Paste respectively. Unless you just like to be flexible for flexibility's sake, don't worry about these keystrokes.

Editing Text in the Story Editor

Ctrl+E

To enter the Story Editor, select some text with either the Arrow or Text tool and press Ctrl+E. Pressing Ctrl+E again takes you back to the layout view.

Ctrl+L, Enter

Inside the Story Editor, you can press Ctrl+L and then Enter to check the spelling of your text. (The Enter key activates the Start button inside the Spelling dialog box.)

Ctrl+9, text, Enter

To search for some text, press Ctrl+9, enter the text, and press Enter. To search for one bit of text and replace it with another, press Ctrl+9, enter the text your want to search for, press Tab, enter the text you want PageMaker to substitute, and press Enter.

Formatting Text

PageMaker provides lots of ways to change the formatting of text from the keyboard. Here are just a few of the most popular shortcuts.

Ctrl+period, Ctrl+comma

To increase the type size to the next menu size — 10, 11, 12, 14, 18, and so on — press Ctrl+period. Press Ctrl+comma to reduce the type size. Both shortcuts are applicable only to characters selected with the Text tool.

Ctrl+Backspace, Ctrl+Shift+Backspace

To kern two letters closer together, click between them with the Text tool and then press Ctrl+Backspace. Press Ctrl+Shift+Backspace to kern the letters apart. Both shortcuts are also applicable to multiple selected characters, enabling you to kern several letters at a time.

Ctrl+Shift+L, Ctrl+Shift+C, Ctrl+Shift+R, Ctrl+Shift+J, Ctrl+Shift+F

To change the alignment of a paragraph selected with the Text tool, press Ctrl and Shift plus the first letter of the alignment. Left is Ctrl+Shift+L, for example. Centered is Ctrl+Shift+C. Right is Ctrl+Shift+R, and justified is Ctrl+Shift+J. To make fully justified text — in which the last line of the paragraph is also justified — press Ctrl+Shift+F.

Ctrl+T, Ctrl+M, Ctrl+I, Ctrl+H

These shortcuts access PageMaker's tried-and-true dialog boxes of formatting options. To display the Type Specifications dialog box — which controls the formatting of selected characters — press Ctrl+T. To format entire paragraphs, press Ctrl+M to display the Paragraph Specifications dialog box. (PageMaker adopted this keyboard equivalent from Microsoft Word, but where Microsoft got it is anyone's guess.) To set tabs, press Ctrl+I to display the Indents/Tabs dialog box. And for hyphenation, press Ctrl+H.

Making Styles and Colors

Ctrl+click

With the Styles palette on-screen, you can edit styles and create new ones by Ctrl+clicking. Ctrl+click on any style name to edit it. Ctrl+click on No Style at the top of the palette to create a new style sheet.

This same technique allows you to edit colors in the Colors palette. Ctrl+click on any color name to edit it. To create a new color, Ctrl+click on the Black or Registration color.

Chapter 22

The Ten Typefaces
Everyone Should Have

. . . .

. . . .

*1*f you're a new PageMaker user, one of your first questions probably will be, "What typefaces should I use?"

The answer, of course, is, "Why, whatever you think looks good."

"But," you say, "I have no taste."

"Yes, you do," we respond, "You just need to have more faith in yourself. Try experimenting with a few fonts to see how they look together, and build your library based on that."

"No, you don't understand," you protest. "I still wear leisure suits and I drive a Gremlin."

"Uh oh, this is worse than we thought."

For those of you who need a little help — taste or no taste — we offer this chapter. Keep in mind, however, that selecting typefaces is an incredibly subjective task. So rather than throwing out a hit parade of favorites, we'll steer you toward a few tried and true solutions that have been around long enough to find mainstream acceptance.

These fonts were selected from the Adobe Typeface Library because it is probably the most established. Adobe also licenses its fonts from the source, meaning that you get the font as it was originally designed. See, you can't copyright typefaces, only their names. So if other font manufacturers see a typeface they like, they can feel free to copy it as long as they name it something different, like Missive instead of Mistral. As your grandpappy told you, life ain't always fair.

The upshot of all this is that Adobe's fonts are of the absolute highest quality. They are also readily available at your local service bureau or commercial printer. But they're expensive — roughly $100 to $200 per family of four type styles. For that same price, you can get 100 fonts from a knockoff vendor. Either way, you'll get basically the same font.

Whether you decide to ante up for authentic Adobe fonts or opt for knockoffs, here are ten choices you'll want to keep in your collection.

Helvetica

If you were to conduct a scientific survey to determine the most legible font at all type sizes, Helvetica would probably come out the winner. Sure, it's kind of boring and it appears in just about every desktop-published document in the Western world, but it absolutely epitomizes stability and flexibility.

Its no-nonsense approach seems to provide type designers with constant inspiration. It's sort of the Meryl Streep of fonts, a blank canvas that lends itself well to one makeover after another. Since its debut in 1957, Helvetica has been the subject of countless stylistic variations, just a few of which are shown in Figure 22-1. The Adobe Type Library alone contains nearly 100 different styles of the font, including outline, condensed, expanded, and rounded. Our recommendation: Buy all the Helveticas you can get your hands on.

Helvetica

Helvetica Light

Helvetica Black Oblique

Helvetica Condensed

Helvetica Condensed Bold Oblique

Helvetica Compressed Extra

Helvetica Inserat

Figure 22-1: These are but a few of the half-billion variations on Helvetica.

Antique Olive

If you're looking for a sans serif face with a little more flair than Helvetica, you can't go wrong with Antique Olive. Although its name may conjure up images of Popeye's girlfriend in a retirement home, it's actually a highly distinctive font, sporting angular terminals (the ends of the characters) and variable-weight strokes, as demonstrated by the variations shown in Figure 22-2.

Don't you just love this font talk? Well, the practical upshot is, if you want to add a little attitude to your sans serif text, use Antique Olive. And if Antique Olive isn't quite your cup of tea, try out Optima, Kabel, or Eras, each of which is equally distinctive and offers its own unique flair. They all prove that sans serif fonts don't have to be as boring or dated as the PostScript standard, Avant Garde Gothic.

Antique Olive

Antique Olive Italic

Antique Olive Light

Antique Olive Black

Antique Olive Nord

Antique Olive Compact

Antique Olive Condensed Bold

Figure 22-2:
Antique Olive shows that sans serif fonts can be as individual and as stylish as their serifed cousins.

New Baskerville

Ultimately a conservative and symmetrical face, New Baskerville is at the same time stylish and versatile, as shown in Figure 22-3. Though named after 18th-century book designer John Baskerville, New Baskerville bears only passing resemblance to Baskerville's specimens. If you want to get a little closer to his roots, look to Berthold Baskerville Book from the venerable Berlin-based foundry.

New Baskerville

New Baskerville Italic

New Baskerville Bold

New Baskerville
Bold Italic

Figure 22-3:
The four
basic styles
of New
Baskerville.

Garamond

Claude Garamond designed type back in the 16th century and is considered by many to be the father of modern typography. His primary legacy is a font that's named for him but is actually based on a recutting made by contemporary Jean Jannon and wrongly ascribed to Garamond around the turn of our century. Meanwhile, the italics came from Robert Granjon, a friend of Garamond's who helped to divide the labor. Still, the modern font looks a lot like the stuff Claude used to carve, so the name stuck.

After that introduction, you'd expect Garamond to be a dusty relic, of interest only to type historians and wholly illegible by modern standards. But as Figure 22-4 shows, this is anything but the case. Garamond is perhaps the most widely available, modified and remodified typeface short of Helvetica. At last count, the Adobe Typeface Library contained 12 complete families of Garamond. And unlike Helvetica, the font is the absolute picture of grace and elegance, almost soft in appearance and full of little flourishes that keep it interesting after many years of use.

For other typefaces with historic appeal, try out Bembo (based on the first roman typeface designed by Aldus Manutius), Granjon, Galliard, and Caslon. The last of these is based on the 18th-century designs of William Caslon and was, according to type historian Douglas C. McMurtrie, "as good a book type as has ever been produced." He wrote that in 1938, before most of the fonts in this chapter had been produced, but it's still one heck of a recommendation.

Garamond Light

Garamond Book Italic

Garamond Bold

Garamond Ultra

Garamond Three Regular

Garamond Three Bold Italic

Berthold Garamond

Berthold Garamond Medium Italic

Berthold Garamond Condensed

Figure 22-4: Garamond and its many variations are based on some of the oldest roman type designs in existence.

Palatino

All this history making you thirsty for something a little more modern? Well, then, look no farther than Palatino. Created by modern type wiz Hermann Zapf, Palatino is a modernization of the age-old designs of Garamond and gang. The font features chiseled terminals, sculpted transitional strokes, and calligraphic italics, all of which appear in Figure 22-5.

Figure 22-5:
The four
styles of
Palatino
built into
most
PostScript
printers.

Palatino

Palatino Italic

Palatino Bold

*Palatino
Bold Italic*

The best news about Palatino is that it's built into virtually all PostScript printers. If you want to add to your Palatino collection, more styles are available. Ironically, Zapf created Palatino exclusively for headlines and logos, but it caught on for body text as well. To complement Palatino, Zapf created a lighter font called Aldus — yes, just like the company that created PageMaker — that looks better at very small type sizes, such as 9 points and smaller.

Bodoni

The Didots were an illustrious family of French printers from the late 18th century. It is said that François Ambroise Didot tutored Benjamin Franklin's grandson in the art of typography. Ironically, however, the most famous creator of so-called Didone fonts was an Italian named Giambattista Bodoni. Some say he got in cheap by lifting Didot's style. Some say he *perfected* it. Either way, he ended up creating something along the lines of the styles shown in Figure 22-6.

Like all Didone styles, Bodoni features very thick vertical strokes and hairline horizontal strokes. This radical contrast between neighboring stems makes for a highly stylized font that works well at larger sizes, say, 12 points and up. Other Didone styles include New Caledonia and, to a lesser extent, New Century Schoolbook, the font built into most PostScript laser printers.

Figure 22-6: The Bodoni family includes dozens of variations, including the ultra-heavy Bodoni Poster.

Bodoni

Bodoni Italic

Bodoni Book

Bodoni Bold Italic

Bodoni Poster

Bodoni Condensed Bold

Bodoni Compressed Poster

American Typewriter

If you want to impart a typewriter look to your pages, avoid Courier and instead try out American Typewriter, shown in Figure 22-7. It's just the thing for that "Extra, extra, read all about it!" look.

American Typewriter falls into a category of type called *slab serifs,* which gained momentum during the Industrial Revolution of the 1800s. (They're called slab serifs because the serifs are so big and slabby.) The difference between Typewriter and other slab serifs — such as Clarendon and Melior — is that the stroke weight of Typewriter characters is uniform throughout. In other words, the serifs are just as thick as the stems, perfect for hearty text that reproduces well even at small sizes.

American
Typewriter Light

American
Typewriter
Medium

**American
Typewriter Bold**

American Typewriter
Condensed

Script Faces

Having the gang over for a few hands of pinochle? Thinking of getting hitched, and you want to create your own invites? Well, then, you'll need some script faces. As shown in Figure 22-8, characters set in script faces typically join together, just like they do in cursive handwriting. This means that you can't kern them or change the letter spacing, as in a justified paragraph. If you do, you'll change the amount of space between neighboring characters and the letters will no longer join correctly.

Mistral

Brush Script

Shelley Allegro

Shelley Volante

Snell Roundhand

Snell Roundhand Black

Figure 22-8:
Text set in script faces generally looks like it was written in one continuous stroke.

Display Faces

One thing you may have noticed about the fonts discussed so far is that they're not very wacky. That's because wacky fonts — like the ones shown in Figure 22-9 — aren't particularly legible at small sizes. For example, can you imagine reading a whole paragraph set in Arnold Böcklin? Only a unicorn could put up with that font for more than a few words. But although they aren't suitable for body text, these so-called display fonts are great for headlines, logos, and other large type (18 points or larger).

It's good to have an arsenal of these fonts at your fingertips. Why? Because you can't use them very often. They're so unique that your readers will notice if you use them over and over. For example, you might set the headline for a monthly column about World War I paraphernalia in the font Wilhelm Klingspor Gotisch. But if you did, you wouldn't want to use that font anywhere else in your newsletter. It's just too obvious.

Zapf Dingbats

The last font on the hit parade, illustrated in Figure 22-10, is Zapf Dingbats, another font built into most laser printers. Rather than being composed of letters, Dingbats comprises more than 250 symbols. You'll find check marks, crosses, stars, flowers, arrows, and a bunch of other do-hickeys. Some of them are a little dated — Hermann Zapf created the font in the '70s — but you can find all sorts of useful stuff if you search around.

Other useful symbol fonts include Symbol (built into all PostScript printers), Carta, Bundesbahn Pi, and Lucida Math.

Figure 22-9: There are literally thousands of display faces on the market, and most look much goofier than these.

HERCULANEUM

Aachen Bold

BANCO

Arnold Böcklin

Wilhelm Klingspor Gotisch

MACHINE

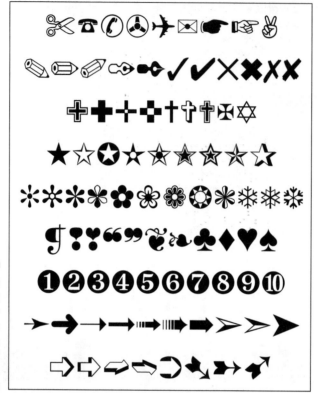

Figure 22-10:
A smattering
of the many
symbols
available in
Zapf
Dingbats.

More Fonts!

By limiting this list to ten (or so) fonts, we can't even begin to scrape the surface of what's out there. If you're feeling ambitious, here are some other faces that we suggest you look into:

- ✔ **Melior:** Our favorite font, bar none. Its squarish forms make it highly readable at very small sizes. The screen font is especially nice when you're working on long blocks of text.

- ✔ **Berkeley Oldstyle:** Armed with unusual diagonal crossbars, angled vowels, and calligraphic italics, this face hearkens back to the first roman typefaces. Based on a design for the University of California Press created by the father of American typography, Frederic W. Goudy, this font is another favorite.

✔ **Souvenir:** Okay, it's been called the "happy face of type," but the sloping letterforms and plastic transitions of Souvenir are hard not to like. The designer of this font is Ed Benguiat, who also created Korinna, Tiffany, and, of course, Benguiat.

✔ **Tekton:** Invented by Adobe's type staff, this face is based on the meticulous hand lettering of architect Francis Ching, complete with little balls at the terminals of the letters.

✔ **Lithos:** Available only in capital letters, these chiseled letterforms are available in a variety of weights. Also check out Trajan and Charlemagne.

There's still tons more, but if we continue like this, you'll think that we're total type dweebs (a label that we wear proudly, thank you very much). So, to finish things off, how about if we stop telling you which fonts we like and focus a moment's attention on the ones we *don't* like?

✔ **Wood Type:** These display faces hearken back to the woodcut letters of the Old West. They're kind of fun, but honestly, how many "Wanted!" posters are you going to typeset?

✔ **Zapf Chancery:** This font has become synonymous with cheesy restaurant menus. Thanks to the fact that it's installed in nearly all PostScript laser printers, Zapf Chancery is absolutely the most over-used script in existence. And — with all due respect to Mr. Zapf — it's ugly to boot.

✔ **Courier:** Your PC is not a typewriter.

✔ **Futura:** Perhaps the least interesting sans serif font on the planet, Futura features miserable little lowercase letters and overly geometric letterforms. Futura Condensed is a marked improvement; at large sizes, it can even look stylish.

Of course, these are just personal peeves. You may love all these fonts. But if you use them, keep in mind that at least two snooty typeface aficionados out there are looking at your document and saying, "Yuck." And it's likely that we're not alone. So if you're tempted to use one of these rather cliché fonts, try experimenting with something more sophisticated instead. It's a pretty sure bet that you'll get a better response from readers. At the least, you'll make us very proud.

How to (Re)Install PageMaker

Before You Install

Before installing PageMaker, make copies of your original program disks. It's rare, but floppy disks can lose data over time, and if that happens, you'll need a backup copy. If you don't copy your disks, you'll have to send in your defective disk to Aldus for a new one, a time-consuming process. (Call Aldus technical support at 206/628-4501 if you get stuck with a defective disk and no usable backup.)

You can use the Windows File Manager, in the Main program group, to copy your disks. Use the Copy Disk command under the Disk menu. Be sure to lock your original PageMaker disks so that you can't accidentally overwrite them during the copy process. To lock a 3 $^1/_2$-inch disk (the kind with a hard casing), turn the back of the disk toward you and slide the black tab in the left corner upward, so that you have two holes at the top of the disk. To lock a 5 $^1/_4$-inch disk (the bendable kind), put a piece of tape (usually included with the disks) over the tab.

Label your copied disks, giving them the same names as the originals. Also copy the serial number onto the label for Disk 2. You'll find the serial number (which begins with 03) on the original Disk 2 and in the "Register Today" flier inside the disk envelope.

Installing PageMaker

After you make duplicates of all your disks, take the copied disks — no sense in risking damage to the precious originals — and insert Disk 1 in the disk drive. Then follow these steps:

1. **In the Program Manager, choose File⇨Run.**

   Windows asks you which file you want to run.

2. **Enter A:\ALDSETUP.EXE and press Enter.**

   This assumes that your disk is in drive A. If it's in drive B, enter B:\ALDSETUP.EXE instead. Windows then launches the installer program. After a few moments, the Aldus Setup Main Window appears.

3. Select an option from the left-hand list.

If you have disk space to burn, select Install Everything. Otherwise, select all the options at the bottom *except* Tutorial. You do this by clicking on one option, such as PageMaker 5.0, and then Ctrl+clicking on the others (except Tutorial).

4. Press the Enter key to get things going.

A dialog box tells you that the Setup program wants to create a new directory called PM5. If that's okay with you, press Enter. If not, change the disk or directory name and press Enter.

5. Select the import and export filters you want to use.

Filters are needed to import text and graphics into PageMaker, as well as to export text. Base your selections on what types of files you expect to use. At a minimum, select the options EPS Import, PM5 Story Importer, RTF Import, Text-Only Import, ASCII Text Export, and Rich Text Format (RTF) Export, as well as the import and export filters for the word processor you use. Ctrl+click on the options to select multiple filters. If you want to play it safe, click on the Select All button. Finally, press Enter. Note that if you selected the Install Everything option in Step 3, you won't get this dialog box, and instead every single filter is installed.

6. Select the additions you want to install.

Additions are independent modules that PageMaker uses to perform certain special tasks. To be safe, click on the Select All button and press Enter. (Again, if you selected Install Everything earlier, you won't get this dialog box.)

7. Select some PPD files.

Whether you selected Install Everything or everything but Tutorial in Step 3, an alert box appears, explaining in ridiculous detail how PPDs are PostScript printer description files and that they only apply to PostScript printers. If you'll be using a PostScript printer, go through the list and select the items that match your printers. Don't forget to include any printers, such as a Linotronic imagesetter, that your service bureau will use to output your documents. Then press Enter.

8. Enter your name, company name, and serial number.

You'll find the serial number on Disk 2. Remember to type it exactly as it is printed, including hyphens.

9. Insert disks as requested.

Just do as you're told.

Reinstalling PageMaker

After using PageMaker for a few days or months or years or whatever, you can add a filter, addition, or PPD file by repeating the installation process. Follow Steps 1 through 3 above, but rather than selecting Install Everything or every other option besides Tutorial in Step 3, just select the option that you want to install. For example, to install some more PPD files, select the Printer Files option. Then press the enter key and select the options you want to install.

Index

• L •

• *M* •

Notes

Notes

Notes

Notes

Notes

Notes

Notes

Notes

Notes

Notes

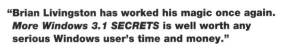

Order Form

Order Center: (800) 762-2974 (8 a.m.-5 p.m., PST, weekdays) or (415) 312-0650

For Fastest Service: Photocopy This Order Form and FAX it to: (415) 358-1260

Quantity	ISBN	Title	Price	Total

Shipping & Handling Charges

Subtotal	U.S.	Canada & International	International Air Mail
Up to $20.00	Add $3.00	Add $4.00	Add $10.00
$20.01-40.00	$4.00	$5.00	$20.00
$40.01-60.00	$5.00	$6.00	$25.00
$60.01-80.00	$6.00	$8.00	$35.00
Over $80.00	$7.00	$10.00	$50.00

In U.S. and Canada, shipping is UPS ground or equivalent.
For Rush shipping call (800) 762-2974.

Subtotal _____

CA residents add
applicable sales tax _____

IN and MA residents add
5% sales tax _____

IL residents add
6.25% sales tax _____

RI residents add
7% sales tax _____

Shipping _____

Total _____

Ship to:

Name _____

Company _____

Address _____

City/State/Zip_____

Daytime Phone _____

Payment: ❑ Check to IDG Books (US Funds Only) ❑ Visa ❑ Mastercard ❑ American Express

Card# _____ Exp._____ Signature_____

Please send this order form to: IDG Books, 155 Bovet Road, Suite 310, San Mateo, CA 94402.

Allow up to 3 weeks for delivery. Thank you!

IDG BOOKS WORLDWIDE REGISTRATION CARD

RETURN THIS REGISTRATION CARD FOR FREE CATALOG

Title of this book: **PageMaker 5 For Windows For Dummies**

My overall rating of this book: ❏ Very good [1] ❏ Good [2] ❏ Satisfactory [3] ❏ Fair [4] ❏ Poor [5]

How I first heard about this book:

❏ Found in bookstore; name: [6] _____

❏ Advertisement: [8] _____

❏ Word of mouth; heard about book from friend, co-worker, etc.: [10]

❏ Book review: [7] _____

❏ Catalog: [9] _____

❏ Other: [11]

What I liked most about this book:

_____

_____

What I would change, add, delete, etc., in future editions of this book:

_____

_____

Other comments:

_____

_____

Number of computer books I purchase in a year: ❏ 1 [12] ❏ 2-5 [13] ❏ 6-10 [14] ❏ More than 10 [15]

I would characterize my computer skills as: ❏ Beginner [16] ❏ Intermediate [17] ❏ Advanced [18] ❏ Professional [19]

I use ❏ DOS [20] ❏ Windows [21] ❏ OS/2 [22] ❏ Unix [23] ❏ Macintosh [24] ❏ Other: [25] _____
(please specify)

I would be interested in new books on the following subjects:
(please check all that apply, and use the spaces provided to identify specific software)

❏ Word processing: [26] _____

❏ Data bases: [28] _____

❏ File Utilities: [30] _____

❏ Networking: [32] _____

❏ Other: [34]

❏ Spreadsheets: [27] _____

❏ Desktop publishing: [29] _____

❏ Money management: [31] _____

❏ Programming languages: [33] _____

I use a PC at (please check all that apply): ❏ home [35] ❏ work [36] ❏ school [37] ❏ other: [38] _____

The disks I prefer to use are ❏ 5.25 [39] ❏ 3.5 [40] ❏ other: [41] _____

I have a CD ROM: ❏ yes [42] ❏ no [43]

I plan to buy or upgrade computer hardware this year: ❏ yes [44] ❏ no [45]

I plan to buy or upgrade computer software this year: ❏ yes [46] ❏ no [47]

Name: _____ Business title: [48] _____ Type of Business: [49] _____

Address (❏ home [50] ❏ work [51]/Company name: _____)

Street/Suite# _____

City [52]/State [53]/Zipcode [54]: _____ Country [55] _____

❏ **I liked this book!** You may quote me by name in future
IDG Books Worldwide promotional materials.

My daytime phone number is _____

IDG BOOKS

THE WORLD OF
COMPUTER
KNOWLEDGE